NEW GCSE SCIENCE

Separate Sciences A
For Specification Modules B7, C7 and P7

OCR
**Twenty First
Century Science**

Series Editor: Ed Walsh

**Authors: Peter Ellis,
Dave Kelly, Gareth Price**

Student Book

William Collins' dream of knowledge for all began with the publication of his first book in 1819. A self-educated mill worker, he not only enriched millions of lives, but also founded a flourishing publishing house. Today, staying true to this spirit, Collins books are packed with inspiration, innovation and practical expertise. They place you at the centre of a world of possibility and give you exactly what you need to explore it.

Collins. Freedom to teach

Published by Collins
An imprint of HarperCollinsPublishers
77–85 Fulham Palace Road
Hammersmith
London
W6 8JB

Browse the complete Collins catalogue at:
www.collinseducation.com

10 9 8 7 6 5 4 3 2 1

ISBN-13 978 0 00 741525 0

British Library Cataloguing in Publication Data
A Catalogue record for this publication is available from the British Library

Commissioned by Letitia Luff
Project managed by Jane Roth
Contributing authors: Ed Walsh and John Beeby
Typesetting, design, layout and illustrations by Ken Vail Graphic Design
Design manager: Emily Hooton
Edited by Joan Miller and Karen Williams
Proofread by Anne Trevillion
Photos researched by Caroline Green
Production by Kerry Howie
Cover design by Julie Martin

Printed and bound by L.E.G.O. S.p.A. Italy

Acknowledgements can be found at the back of the book

Contents

C7 Further chemistry 64

P7 Further physics – studying the Universe 126

How to use this book

Welcome to Collins New GCSE Separate Sciences for OCR 21st Century

The main content

Each two-page lesson has three sections.

◯ The first section outlines a basic scientific idea.

◯ The second section builds on the basics and develops the concept.

◯ The third section extends the concept or challenges you to apply it in a new way.

The third section can also provide extra information that is only relevant to the Higher tier (indicated with 'Higher tier only').

Each section contains a set of questions that allow you to check and apply your knowledge.

Look for:

> 'Did you know?' boxes

> internet search terms (at the bottom of every page)

> 'Watch out!' hints on avoiding common errors.

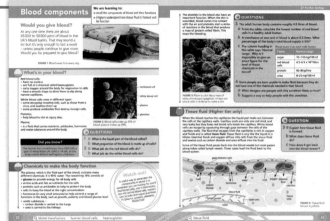

Watch out!

ALL the content of the book, except that marked 'Higher tier only', will be assessed at both Foundation and Higher tier.

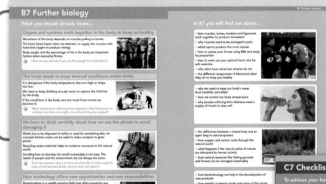

Module Introduction

Each Module has a two-page introduction.

This helps you to link the science you will learn in the coming Module with your existing scientific knowledge.

Module Checklists

At the end of each Module is a graded Checklist.

Summarise the key ideas that you have learnt so far and check your progress. If there are any topics you find tricky, you can always recap them!

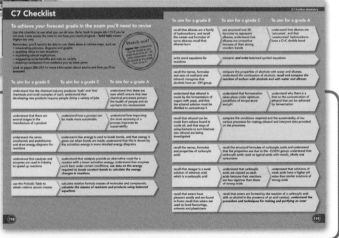

Exam-style questions

Each Module contains practice exam-style questions for Foundation and Higher tier. There is a range of types of question and each is labelled with the Assessment Objective that it addresses.

Familiarise yourself with all the types of question that you might be asked.

Worked examples

Detailed worked examples with examiner comments show you how you can raise your grade. Here you will find tips on how to use accurate scientific vocabulary, avoid common exam errors and improve your Quality of Written Communication (QWC), and more.

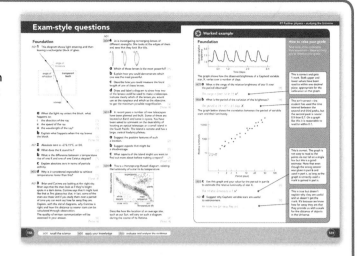

Preparing for assessment

Each Module contains two Preparing for Assessment activities. These will give you practice in tackling the essential skills that you will need to succeed in your Controlled Assessment tasks, as well as in your exam.

There are two types of Preparing for Assessment activity.

> Planning and collecting: build skills in formulating a hypothesis, designing techniques and choosing equipment.

> Analysing, evaluating and reviewing: build skills in analysing data, evaluating procedures and reviewing your confidence in the hypothesis.

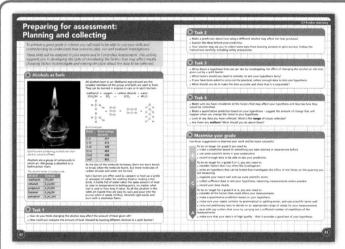

Practical work and exam skills

A section at the end of the book guides you through your practical work, your Controlled Assessment tasks and your exam, with advice on: planning, carrying out and evaluating an experiment; using maths to analyse data; what to expect in your Controlled Assessment; the language used in exam questions; and how best to approach your written exam.

Glossary

Check on the meaning of scientific vocabulary that you come across.

B7 Further biology

What you should already know...

Organs and systems work together in the body to keep us healthy

Movement of the body depends on muscles pulling on bones.

The heart beats faster when we exercise, to supply the muscles with food and oxygen to produce energy.

Body weight and the percentage of fat in the body are important factors when assessing fitness.

 How can you decide if you are fit enough for a marathon?

The body needs to keep internal conditions within limits

It is dangerous if the body temperature rises too high or drops too low.

We need to keep drinking enough water to replace the fluid lost by the body.

If the conditions in the body vary too much from normal we become ill.

 When someone is suffering from exposure after being lost on a snowy mountain overnight, how should they be treated?

We have to think carefully about how we use the planet to avoid damaging it

Waste has to be disposed of safely or used for something else, for example kitchen waste can be used to make compost to grow plants.

Recycling waste materials helps to conserve resources in the natural world.

Deciding how to develop the world sustainably is not easy. The needs of people and the environment are not always the same.

 Give two reasons why is it more eco-friendly to make a pencil case out of recycled drinks cartons than new plastic.

New technology offers new opportunities and new responsibilities

Biotechnology is a rapidly growing field that offers powerful new products and processes, for example powerful anti-cancer drugs and screening for genetic illnesses. Many of these developments require us to think carefully about how scientific work should be controlled and directed to benefit people.

 What are the advantages and disadvantages of knowing in advance if you are likely to suffer from a disease in later life?

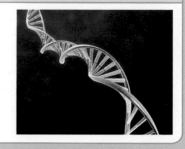

In B7 you will find out about...

> how muscles, bones, tendons and ligaments work together to produce movement

> why muscles need to be arranged in pairs

> which sports produce the most injuries

> how to assess your fitness using BMI and body fat proportion

> how to work out your optimal heart rate for safe exercise

> why veins have valves but arteries do not

> the different components of blood and what they do to keep you healthy

> why we need to keep our body's water level carefully controlled

> how we control our body temperature

> why people suffering from diabetes need a supply of insulin to stay well

> the difference between a closed loop and an open loop in natural systems

> how oxygen and carbon cycle through the natural world

> what happens if the natural cycles of nature are disrupted by human activity

> how natural resources like fishing grounds and forests can be managed sustainably

> how biotechnology can help in the development of new products

> how genetic screening works and some of the issues raised by these techniques

> why stem cells are so important to medicine and how they might enable treatments for a range of diseases

> how nanotechnology can help to produce packaging that keeps foods fresher for longer

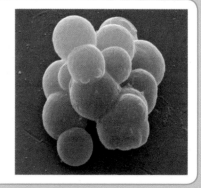

How the body moves

We are learning to:

> understand why we need a skeleton

> understand how muscles create movement

> understand what is meant by 'an antagonistic pair of muscles'

Do you have to be strong to be a dancer?

Strictly Come Dancing is one of the UK's most popular TV programmes. Over 14 million people watched the 2010 final – that's about one in four of the total population. All the movement involved in dancing is made possible by muscles and bones.

FIGURE 1: Just how strong do you have to be to be a winner?

Posture

Our skeleton acts rather like a coat-hanger, supporting our flesh. Bone is rigid. Because the different bones of the skeleton are held together with joints and muscles, we remain upright.

The skeleton has other functions, too:

> protection, e.g. the skull protects the delicate brain

> blood production – the marrow inside large bones makes blood

> movement – long bones are essential for movement.

When a dancer bends their knee they depend on muscles pulling on bones to make the movement. Muscles can only pull, not push. To straighten the leg again, another muscle has to pull it back into position.

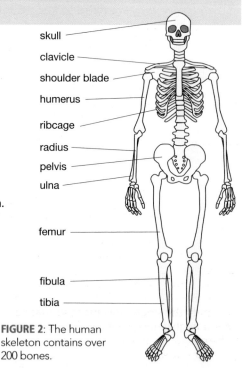

skull
clavicle
shoulder blade
humerus
ribcage
radius
pelvis
ulna
femur
fibula
tibia

FIGURE 2: The human skeleton contains over 200 bones.

QUESTIONS

1 What is the name of the group of bones that protect the heart and lungs?

2 Which two types of body tissue are holding a dancer upright when they stand in a particular pose?

Antagonistic pairs

Muscles **contract** when proteins in their cells react together. This pulls the two ends of the muscle closer together. Muscles with a large cross-sectional area can pull with a greater force than muscles with smaller cross-section. Muscles that are used often can grow thicker. This is why many athletes and dancers have very large muscles.

However, muscles cannot push. They can relax, which allows them to be pulled longer. The **biceps** muscle bends the arm at the elbow joint (Figure 3). The **triceps** muscle straightens it again when the biceps relaxes. These two muscles are called an **antagonistic pair** because they work in opposite directions.

human skeleton   functions of bone

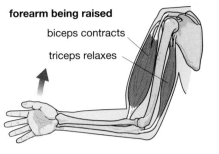

forearm being raised
biceps contracts
triceps relaxes

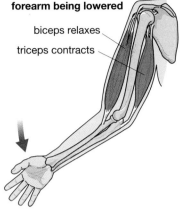

forearm being lowered
biceps relaxes
triceps contracts

FIGURE 3: The muscles that move the arm at the elbow work as an antagonistic pair.

Watch out!
Muscles cannot push on bones, they can only pull. Never use the word 'push' when describing how a muscle works.

Most of the muscles in your body are organised in antagonistic pairs. To straighten your leg at the knee joint, the muscles on top of your thigh contract while those underneath relax. To bend the knee, the pattern of contraction and relaxation reverses.

QUESTIONS

3 Explain, in your own words, what is meant by: 'contract', 'relax' and 'antagonistic'.

4 What is the name of the muscles that cause the arm to bend at the elbow?

5 Draw a simple diagram of the muscles and bones that bend your leg at the knee.

Did you know?

The rhinoceros beetle is the strongest creature in the world and can lift 850 times its own body weight. If Hossein Rezazadeh, an Olympic weightlifting champion (2004), could do the same he could lift a stack of seven London buses above his head (all full of passengers!).

Bones as levers

Muscles can only contract by about 10% of their total length. The biceps muscle, which bends your arm at the elbow, is about 30 cm long. It can shorten to about 27 cm. However, your arm moves much more than that. The biceps is joined to the bones of the lower arm by a **tendon**. When the biceps contracts, the bones of the lower arm are pulled upwards. The elbow acts as a pivot. The rigid bones magnify the small movement so that your hand might move by more than a metre. The bones act as **levers** to magnify the distance moved.

QUESTIONS

6 Do you think the biceps and triceps muscles have to have the same strength? Give a reason for your answer.

7 Plan an investigation to find out the strength of the biceps and triceps muscles.

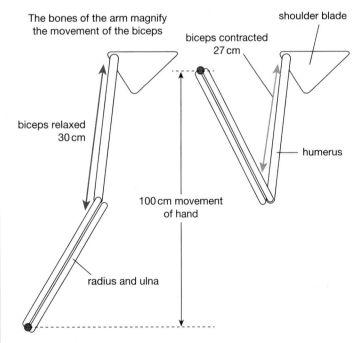

The bones of the arm magnify the movement of the biceps

shoulder blade

biceps contracted 27 cm

biceps relaxed 30 cm

humerus

100 cm movement of hand

radius and ulna

FIGURE 4: Long bones act as levers to magnify the distance moved.

Joints

We are learning to:
> recall the structure of joints
> relate the structure of the components of joints to their function
> assess the risk of an activity

How important is a ligament?

Damage to one of the **ligaments** of the knee has kept many a footballer off the pitch for weeks – or even months. This happened to Rio Ferdinand, for example, who was due to captain England in the 2010 World Cup.

Why are ligaments so important?

FIGURE 1: Rio Ferdinand – a torn ligament forced him out of the 2010 World Cup.

Did you know?

David Beckham insured his legs for £100 million! If he was injured, his insurance would pay for his lost earnings.

Bending – not breaking

The knee is a good example of a **synovial joint**. A synovial joint holds bones together but allows them to move. Most of the joints in your body are synovial joints. Shoulders, elbows, hips, knees and even the tiny joints in your fingers are synovial joints. All these joints have the same parts.

● QUESTIONS

1 List four synovial joints in your body.

2 Articular cartilage is smooth and hard. How does this help it to do its job?

FIGURE 2: The parts found in every synovial joint.

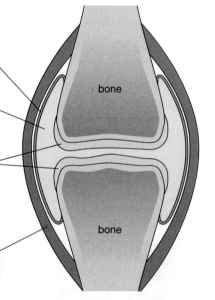

Synovial membrane lines the inside of the joint and encapsulates it. It produces a slippery fluid called synovial fluid.

synovial fluid

bone

Articular cartilage is shiny, smooth and hard. It stops the ends of bones being worn away as they press against each other.

bone

Ligaments join the knee bones together and help to keep the joint stable. Ligaments can bend and stretch slightly.

Keeping it stable

When muscles in the thigh contract they pull on bones with a great force. **Tendons** connect muscles to bones. When the muscle contracts, it pulls the tendon to move the bone. Ligaments are elastic but tendons do not stretch at all.

The leg should bend backwards but not forwards. The shape of the surface of the bones that meet at the knee allow this movement. This is rather like the hinge on a door. If the bones are not held firmly together the joint becomes too flexible and the lower part of the leg could move from side to side. This would be very painful and dangerous. In the worst case, the kneecap could pop out of its normal position and the person could be crippled.

Watch out!

Don't confuse tendons with ligaments. Tendons are always tight but ligaments are elastic.

Muscles, the shape of the ends of the bones and the ligaments all help to stabilise a joint. However, the ligaments have the toughest job. They act rather like shock absorbers. A sudden force will make them stretch slightly, which stops the force breaking the joint. When the force passes, the elasticity of the ligaments pulls the bones back together again.

In the hip joint, a ball of bone at the top of the femur fits neatly into a socket in the pelvis. It is very rarely damaged. The shoulder joint has a much shallower socket and many sportspeople have suffered with dislocated shoulders. In a dislocated joint the bones do not fit together in the correct way.

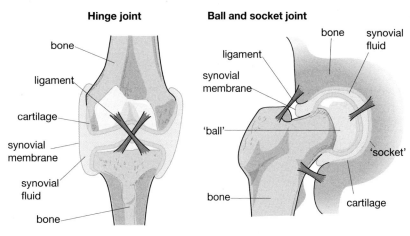

FIGURE 3: The knee has a **hinge joint**, whereas the hip and shoulder have **ball and socket joints**.

Sportspeople take **risks** when they compete. A risk involves something that *might* happen, for example, if you run across a road there is a risk that you could be hit by a car. Some risks are more likely than others. You can reduce the risk of injury in a sporting activity by wearing proper safety equipment, warming up before competing and avoiding dangerous play.

QUESTION

3 Give two reasons why the hips are less prone to injury than the shoulders.

Measuring risk

Rugby and hot-air ballooning would generally be accepted to be riskier than badminton – but how can we measure this risk? The two key factors are:

> how likely an injury is to occur

> how serious the injury is likely to be.

QUESTIONS

4 a Which of the groups of rugby players in the table had more injuries?

b Why might the answer for part **a** be misleading with respect to the likelihood of injury for young and old players? Use data from the table to explain your answer.

Injuries in one year to rugby players in Scotland.

Age group (years)	Players	Hours played	Players injured
under 16	204	7036	22
over 34	55	1081	11

Data from Garraway and Macleod, *The Lancet*

5 Describe the data you would need to collect to compare the risks of hot-air ballooning or scuba-diving.

FIGURE 4: Hot-air ballooning over hills in Guilin, China. In 2009, four Dutch tourists died when the balloon in which they were travelling crashed.

Exercise and health

We are learning to:

> recall the important factors for planning an exercise regime

> calculate the body mass index

> (Higher) understand the importance of repeatable data

New Year: new you?

Every year many people make resolutions to become fitter. This might mean losing weight, giving up smoking or drinking, getting more exercise, a change of diet or even learning a new sport. But how can we measure how fit we really are? And can anything help us to keep those resolutions beyond a few days?

FIGURE 1: Happy New Year!

Body size

Your **body mass index (BMI)** gives an idea of how appropriate your weight is for a healthy life. The formula here shows how the BMI is worked out.

$$BMI = \frac{body\ mass\ (kg)}{[height\ (m)]^2}$$

Guideline BMI and health risks.

BMI value	How is your body weight affecting your health?
17.5 or under	Seriously underweight, significant health risks
17.5 to 19	Underweight, some health risks
19 to 25	Normal, healthy weight
25–30	Overweight, some health risks
More than 30	Obese, significant health risks

FIGURE 2: Naim Suleymanoglu was a Bulgarian weightlifter who won three Olympic Championships, seven World Championships and held 46 world records. He was 1.5 m tall and weighed 64 kg. Was he overweight?

Proportion of fat

People often use the word 'fit' when they mean thin. **Fitness** depends on much more than just body weight. Some people who appear to have a normal body size can be unhealthy because they have too high a proportion of fat to muscle in their body.

To gain a more complete picture of your body and how fit you are, you also need to know the proportion of your weight that is made up of fat. Muscle is denser than fat and so weighs more than an equal volume of fat.

Watch out!
These are general guidelines – the divisions cannot be taken as exact for everybody.

Percentage body fat and fitness status.

Body type	Percentage of body weight that is fat (%)	
	Female	Male
Athlete	14–20	6–13
Generally fit amateur sportsperson	21–24	14–17
Average	25–31	18–24
Obese	32+	25+

Q body mass index   exercise programmes

QUESTIONS

1 a Work out the BMI for these people.
Andrew: 120 kg, 1.93 m; Naomi: 67 kg, 1.85 m; Precious: 52 kg, 1.8 m

 b What would your advice be to each person about their weight?

2 Calculate Naim Suleymanoglu's BMI. The proportion of fat in his body was 9%. Do you think he was unfit? Give reasons for your answer.

Key factors

If you have decided your BMI and body fat proportion are too high you could consider an exercise regimen. Before you start you need to think about the questions shown here.

Doctors stress that any exercise programme should start gently and build up over time. This allows your heart, muscles and joints time to get used to any new strains you put on them.

A Are you taking any medicines?

B Do you drink alcohol? How much per week?

C Do you smoke? How many a week?

D How active are you physically?

E Has anyone in your family suffered from heart attacks or high blood pressure?

QUESTIONS

3 Suggest a reason for each of the questions given in the speech bubbles.

4 Explain why doctors recommend a slow start to an exercise programme.

Likely improvements (Higher tier only)

Many magazines and TV programmes promise 'miracle results' from diets or exercise regimes. Is this possible? The table shows data for people who seem to have managed to keep to their New Year's resolutions. However, we need to look at the numbers in the table in more detail.

Does your heart always beat at the same rate when you are resting? There will certainly be slight variations. And is the blood pumped exactly 120 ml per beat? Could it be 121 ml? Or 119 ml?

The figures in the table are **averages**. This is one way to summarise a lot of numerical data. The more individual results collected, and the better the accuracy of the measuring device, the more confident we can be in the final average data. The ultimate test is to repeat the tests to see if the same results are produced. Scientists use the word **repeatability** if data is consistent when other researchers repeat the same tests. If different researchers get different results from the same tests this suggests that one of the researchers used poor methods or has biased the results in some way.

Changes in key data following training.

	Before training	After 6 months' training	An international athlete
Heart rate at rest (beats per minute)	72	58	36
Blood volume pumped by heart at rest (ml per beat)	64	79	128
Blood volume pumped by heart during vigorous exercise (ml per beat)	120	140	200
Size of heart (ml)	750	820	1200

Watch out!
A result may be repeatable but wrong, possibly because the measuring system is wrong.
A **reliable** result must be repeatable and accurate.

QUESTIONS

5 Give two ways to increase the reliability of a set of results.

6 Explain why repeatability is important for scientists.

Exercising safely

Could you run 26 miles inside a rhino costume?

The London Marathon is one of the biggest running events in the world, with well over 30 000 people taking part. Some are professional athletes and the winner usually completes the 26-mile course in just over 2 hours. Many others run for charity and may take 6 hours or more. Just how fit do you need to be to compete in the marathon?

FIGURE 1: Many people trying to raise money for charity dress up in elaborate costumes for the race.

Heart rate and exercise

When you do any exercise your heart rate and blood pressure go up. This increases blood supply to the muscles. Blood delivers glucose and oxygen to the muscle cells for respiration and takes away carbon dioxide.

Cells need energy to do work. Respiration converts glucose and oxygen to carbon dioxide and water and gives out energy, which the cells use. Muscle cells use energy to contract.

Maximum heart rate

If your heart rate rises too much, the muscles of the heart are strained and blood pressure rises. This rise can cause delicate blood vessels in the eye or brain to burst. For safe exercise, your heart rate should be between 70% and 90% of the maximum rate your heart can actually achieve (Figure 2).

The formula for your approximate maximum heart rate (in beats per minute, BPM) is:

220 minus your age in years

So, a 45-year-old competitor in the marathon will have a maximum heart rate of 220 − 45 = 175 bpm.

After a period of exercise has finished the heart keeps beating at a higher rate than normal for a while, to clear waste products from the muscles. This is called the **recovery period**. Fitter people tend to have shorter recovery times than unfit people.

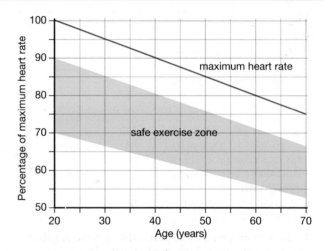

FIGURE 2: Safe exercise rates and ages.

QUESTIONS

1 Write out the word equation for respiration.

2 Give two reasons why your heart rate changes during exercise.

3 What is the maximum safe heart rate for a 30-year-old marathon runner?

4 What happens to the body during the recovery period?

safe exercise zone   maximum heart rate

Injuries

The table shows the percentage of runners treated in one London marathon and the reasons for their treatments. You can see that sprains, dislocations, torn ligaments or tendons are very common injuries.

Treatments for London marathon runners, as a percentage of the number of runners who completed the race.

Reason	Percentage (%)
General lack of fitness	1
Blisters	4
Sprains, dislocations, torn ligaments or tendons	20
Total	25

The bones forming a joint are connected to each other and kept stable by ligaments. A **sprain** occurs when the ligaments are stretched too much. The joint becomes more wobbly. It is often painful, swollen and inflamed. In severe cases the ligament is torn.

A **dislocation** is more much serious. When the hip is dislocated the ball at the top of the femur comes out of the socket formed by the pelvis. The body cannot cure this with rest – a medical practitioner will have to push the joint back together so that the bones are properly located.

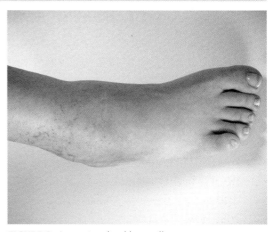

FIGURE 3: A sprained ankle swells up.

 QUESTION

5 a Which joint of a runner is most vulnerable to a sprain?

b Give a reason for your choice.

Treatment

The most common treatment for a sprain is:

Protect – to stop the sprain getting worse
Rest – to stop more strain being put on the damaged ligaments
Ice – to reduce swelling and pain
Compression – packing the joint tightly to help the ligaments to return to their normal shape and length
Elevation – to drain any excess fluid away from the joint.

A **physiotherapist** can help an athlete to strengthen any damaged joints by providing exercises.

Watch out!
A good way to remember the treatment for a sprain is to learn the acronym PRICE.

QUESTIONS

6 The organisers of the marathon are considering using the percentage of finishers who needed treatment to work out how many medical staff are needed for the next year's race. Would there be any problems using this percentage figure? Explain your answer.

7 What might a physiotherapist do to help an athlete with a sprained ankle:

a immediately at the race

b a few days after the race had finished?

Did you know?

The word marathon comes from a town in Greece, which was 26 miles from Athens – the length of modern marathon runs.

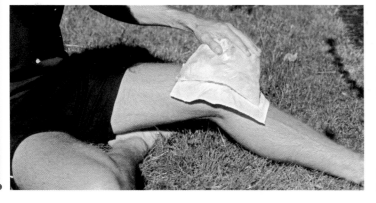

FIGURE 4: This athlete is using an ice pack to reduce swelling and joint pain caused by a sprain.

Preparing for assessment: Planning and collecting

To achieve a good grade in science you will need to be able to use your skills and understanding to understand how scientists plan, run and evaluate investigations.

These skills will be assessed in your exams and in Controlled Assessments. This activity supports you in developing the skills of considering the factors that may affect results, choosing factors to investigate and making decisions about the data to be collected.

✴ The Ten Tors Team

The Ten Tors event happens every year on Dartmoor in May. 400 teams of six have to cover routes of up to 55 miles in two days. All contestants are teenagers and completing the course demands considerable fitness. The rules state that the teams must carry everything they need for the two days – this is not just a leisurely stroll to a hostel where

someone will cook you a hot meal for the evening. This is survival camping.

A school wants to enter a team and asks for volunteers. They get offers from 45 students and decide to do some tests to see who is the fittest and so most likely to complete the challenge safely.

Task 1

> Suggest the kinds of conditions the team will meet on Dartmoor.

> Predict the changes that are likely to occur in the body during the race.

 ## Task 2

> Describe how you will measure a volunteer's fitness.

> List any equipment you will need for the measuring activity.

> Explain how long your tests will last and how much data you expect to collect.

 ## Task 3

> Identify any risks in the activity you are suggesting. How serious are these risks and how will you minimise them for your test?

 ## Task 4

> Explain why you think the data you collect will be reliable and accurate enough for your analysis.

> Explain how the data you collect will help you to identify the fittest volunteers.

 ## Maximise your grade

Use these suggestions to improve your work and be more successful.

E

To be on target for grade E you need to:
> make a prediction about what will happen

> predict the sorts of data you will need to collect to check your prediction.

C

To be on target for a grade D or C, you also need to:
> use scientific ideas to explain why you think your prediction is correct

> select equipment and plan a method that will allow you to test your prediction

> modify your equipment, or your method, as you go along to make sure the data is accurate and reliable enough.

A

To be on target for a grade B or A, you also need to:
> choose a range of conditions to test that will produce data useful to test your prediction

> identify any hazards that may occur as a result of your experiment and plan for ways to minimise them

> explain how the data will be used to answer the original question and so be able to concentrate on collecting the key, relevant data points to answer the question.

How the heart works

How long can you survive if your heart stops beating?

Occasionally people's hearts stop and they are resuscitated, or brought back to life. When a person's heart stops beating, doctors may use a special machine, called a defibrillator, to restart it with an electric shock. If the heart is not restarted within four minutes, it's too late.

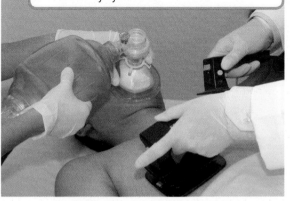

FIGURE 1: Using a defibrillator to restart someone's heart.

Heart structure

The human heart has four chambers joined together within one large block of muscle.

The four tasks of the heart are to:

> collect deoxygenated blood at low pressure from the body

> pump deoxygenated blood to the lungs

> collect oxygenated blood at low pressure returning from the lungs

> push oxygenated blood at high pressure to the rest of the body.

Each of these tasks is done by a separate pumping action.

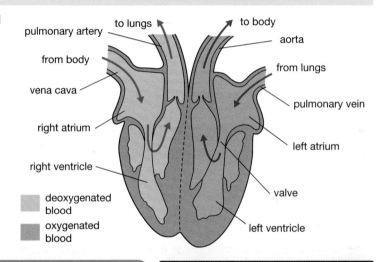

FIGURE 2: The human heart.

QUESTIONS

1 Which side of the heart collects blood from the body?

2 Which artery takes blood to the lungs?

3 What is the heart made from?

Did you know?

In a resting adult human, the heart beats roughly 70 times per minute, and will complete 25 000 000 000 (25 billion) beats in an average lifetime.

Double circulation

Humans have a **double circulation system**. This means that the heart pumps the blood twice for each trip round the body. Blood enters the heart on the right side and is pumped to the lungs. In the lungs the blood gives up carbon dioxide and takes in oxygen. The blood slows down to do this, so when it comes back to the heart along the pulmonary vein it is at low pressure. It comes back to the much larger left side of the heart, which then gives the blood another pump before it leaves at high pressure along the **aorta**. This means that the blood can travel quickly, about 1.2 metres every second, in the aorta. When it reaches the capillaries it slows down to only 1.1 centimetres every second.

Q arteries   veins   double   circulation   heart structure

The table shows the differences between arteries, capillaries and veins. Their different structures reflect the different jobs they have to do.

Arteries, capillaries and veins.

	Arteries	Capillaries	Veins
Walls	Thick, with layers of muscle and elastic fibres	Thin, single celled	Thin with no muscles
Direction of blood flow	Away from the heart	Through tissues	Towards heart
Blood	Oxygenated	Oxygenated at start, deoxygenated at end	Deoxygenated
Valves	Not present	Not present	Present

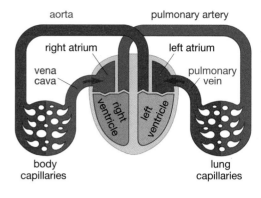

FIGURE 3: The human circulatory system.

QUESTIONS

4 How many times does blood go through the heart for every trip around the body?

5 What is the main advantage of a double circulation system?

Did you know?

A blood cell can get around the complete circulatory system in less than 15 seconds during vigorous exercise.

Valves

When the muscle of the left ventricle of the heart squeezes, it pumps blood along the aorta, but what stops blood being pushed back into the left atrium and going around the body the wrong way? A flap of skin-like tissue blocks off the entrance to the atrium when the ventricle pumps. This is a **valve**, called the mitral valve.

Valves open to let blood go one way but snap shut so that it can't go the wrong way. You can hear the sound of the valves in the heart opening and closing if you use a suitable microphone.

Valves in veins

Valves in the veins do a similar job. In the legs, for example, blood can be pushed up the leg but valves then prevent it dropping down again between heart beats. Muscles moving the legs also tend to push against veins as they work. This squeezes blood up the legs, rather like toothpaste being squeezed out of a tube. The valves make sure that the blood can only go one way – towards the heart.

Some people suffer from varicose veins, particularly as they get older. This means that the valves in their legs do not work so well and the blood tends to pool in their legs when they stand up. The veins swell and are often visible as purple lines through the skin.

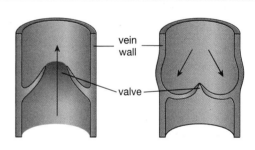

FIGURE 4: Backflow is prevented by valves that shut.

FIGURE 5: Varicose veins.

Watch out!

All veins have valves but only two arteries have valves – the aorta and the pulmonary artery, which both lead blood away from the heart.

QUESTIONS

6 Describe the function of valves in veins and explain why they are important.

7 Soldiers on guard outside government buildings are often told to wriggle their toes even if they are not allowed to move from their sentry box. This helps to stop them passing out. Explain why.

Did you know?

Scientists are working with genetically engineered pigs as a source of hearts for human transplants. A pig heart is about the same size as a human heart.

🔍 arteries   veins   double circulation   heart structure   valve

Blood components

We are learning to:
> recall the components of blood and their functions
> (Higher) understand how tissue fluid is formed and its function

Would you give blood?

At any one time there are about 45 000 to 50 000 pints of blood in the UK's blood banks. That may sound a lot but it's only enough to last a week – unless people continue to give more. Would you be prepared to give blood?

FIGURE 1: Blood saves lives every day.

What's in your blood?

Red blood cells:
> have no nucleus
> are full of a chemical called haemoglobin
> carry oxygen around the body for respiration in cells
> have a smooth shape to allow them to slip along narrow capillaries.

White blood cells come in different types:
> some recognise invading cells, such as those from a virus, and swallow them up
> some produce antibodies that destroy foreign cells.

Platelets:
> help blood to clot at injury sites.

Plasma:
> is a fluid that carries nutrients, antibodies, hormones and waste substances around the body.

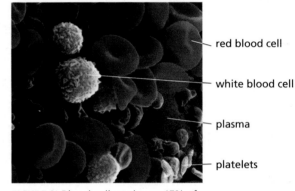

red blood cell

white blood cell

plasma

platelets

FIGURE 2: Blood cells make up 45% of blood; plasma makes up 55%.

Did you know?

The Human Immunodeficiency Virus (HIV) kills a type of white blood cell called a T4 cell, so the body cannot defend itself against infections.

QUESTIONS

1 a What is the liquid part of the blood called?
  b What proportion of the blood is made up of cells?
2 a What job do the red blood cells do?
  b What job do the white blood cells do?

Chemicals to make the body function

The plasma, which is the fluid part of the blood, contains many different chemicals. It is 90% water. The remaining 10% consists of:
> **glucose** to provide energy for all body cells
> amino acids and fats as nutrients for the cells
> proteins such as antibodies to help to protect the body
> salts to keep the blood at the right concentration
> hormones (in very small amounts) to help control a range of functions in the body, such as growth, puberty and blood glucose level
> waste substances –
  > carbon dioxide is carried to the lungs
  > urea is carried to the kidneys.

Watch out!

A useful way to remember the components in blood is to remember you are looking for one R (red blood cells), one H (hormones), two Ws (white blood cells, wastes), two Ss (salts and sugar) and three Ps (plasma, proteins, platelets), RH2W2S3P.

Q blood transfusions   human blood cells   haemoglobin

The platelets in the blood also have an important function. When the skin is wounded, blood comes into contact with the air and platelets start a series of reactions in the blood that produce a mass of protein called fibrin. This stops the bleeding.

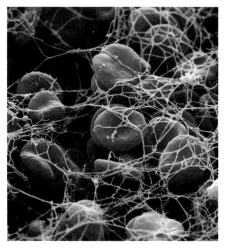

FIGURE 3: Fibrin is a bit like a mass of sticky microscopic spaghetti; it traps red blood cells in its fibres to make a clot.

QUESTIONS

3 The adult human body contains roughly 4.5 litres of blood.

a From the table, calculate the lowest number of red blood cells in a healthy adult human.

b A transfusion of one unit of blood is about 0.5 litres. What percentage of the body's total blood supply is this?

c The column heading in this table says 'Normal range'. Why is it impossible to give an exact figure for the level of these chemicals in the blood?

Blood levels in an adult male human.

Factor	Normal range
sugar	70–110 mg/100 ml
red blood cells	$4.5–6.5 \times 10^{12}$/litre
protein	60–80 g/litre
urea	8–25 mg/100 ml

4 Some people are born unable to make fibrin because they do not have one of the chemicals needed in their blood.

a What dangers are people with this condition likely to face?

b Suggest a way to help people with this condition.

Tissue fluid (Higher tier only)

When the blood reaches the capillaries the liquid part leaks out between the cells of the capillary walls. Capillary walls are only one cell thick and very leaky but they keep red blood cells inside the capillary. White blood cells can escape by squeezing through gaps between the cells of the capillary walls. The fluid that escapes from the capillaries is rich in oxygen and foods and is called **tissue fluid**. Tissue fluid is very like the liquid in a blister. Essential foods and oxygen diffuse into cells from the tissue fluid and wastes such as carbon dioxide and urea diffuse into the fluid.

Some of the tissue fluid passes back into the blood vessels but most passes along tubes called lymph vessels. These tubes lead the fluid back to the blood system.

QUESTION

5 a Explain how tissue fluid is formed.

b What does tissue fluid do?

c How does it get back into the blood stream?

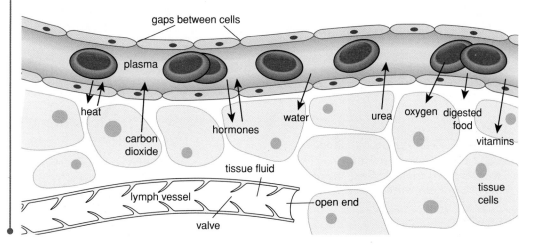

FIGURE 4: Tissue fluid (shown in yellow).

Blood as a transport system

We are learning to:
> understand how the blood carries oxygen
> understand that many chemicals are transported in the blood
> understand how red blood cells are adapted to their function

Can we make artificial blood?

Scientists at Sheffield University have made artificial blood from plastic. This blood carries oxygen, just as normal blood does. It can be stored without refrigeration and can even be carried around as a thick paste and then mixed with water, just before it is given to the patient.

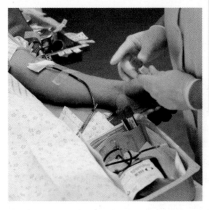

FIGURE 1: The NHS needs people to give blood regularly because the blood donated can only be kept for 42 days.

Carrying oxygen

Red blood cells are packed full of a chemical called **haemoglobin**, which contains iron.

In areas of high oxygen concentration, such as the capillaries of the lungs, haemoglobin reacts with the oxygen to form **oxyhaemoglobin**.

haemoglobin + oxygen → oxyhaemoglobin

In certain conditions, oxyhaemoglobin breaks down again to form oxygen and haemoglobin.

When the blood reaches areas of low oxygen concentration, such as the cells of an active muscle, the oxyhaemoglobin breaks down so that it releases oxygen to the part of the body where it is needed.

As well as taking oxygen from the lungs to the rest of the body, the blood carries carbon dioxide waste from every cell in the body back to the lungs. The carbon dioxide is dissolved in the plasma.

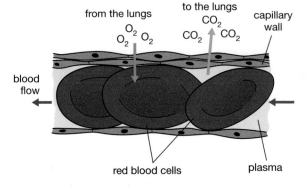

FIGURE 2: Gas exchange in the lungs.

QUESTIONS

1 What mineral does haemoglobin contain?

2 a What controls whether red blood cells take up oxygen or release oxygen?

 b Suggest why active muscles always have a low oxygen concentration.

Did you know?

$100 \, cm^3$ of fresh blood can absorb roughly ten times the amount of oxygen that ordinary water can.

Much more than an oxygen carrier

Sheffield's artificial blood carries oxygen but real blood does much more than that.

White blood cells in the bloodstream protect against infections. Some white blood cells engulf invading microorganisms. Some release antibodies that destroy invading microbes.

Watch out!

People often say carbon dioxide is made in the lungs – in fact, it is made all over the body and taken to the lungs to be removed.

Q haemoglobin   blood plasma

The blood plasma transports essential chemicals around the body. Glucose, for example, is taken around the body to feed the cells, providing muscles with energy.

The waste product urea, made in the liver from protein the body does not need, dissolves in the blood and is taken to the kidneys. The kidneys move it from the blood into the urine to pass it out of the body.

Plasma also carries hormones around the body. These are chemicals that control the way the body, or part of it, works. The hormone insulin is made in the pancreas but affects the way cells all over the body take up sugar from the blood. The hormone adrenaline is made in the adrenal glands near the kidneys and prepares the body for vigorous activity.

The table summarises the chemicals that are carried in the blood, where they come from and go to, and why they must be moved around the body.

FIGURE 3: White blood cell engulfing bacteria.

Substance	Taken from	Taken to	Why?
Oxygen	Lungs	All tissues	Needed for respiration in all cells
Hormones	Endocrine glands	Target organs	To regulate the way the organs work
Carbon dioxide	All cells	Lungs	To be removed in exhaled air
Urea	Liver	Kidneys	To be removed in the urine
Food substances such as glucose and amino acids (from protein)	Gut	Liver and other cells	To be used for energy or growth
Antibodies	Lymph glands	All tissues	To attack foreign cells

Substances carried in the blood.

QUESTIONS

3 There is only one type of red blood cell but there are more than one type of white blood cell. Explain why.

4 When someone has a stroke, a blood vessel in the brain is blocked. The cells supplied by this blood vessel are damaged and, after four minutes, are probably dead. Give two reasons why the cells are so quickly damaged.

Why are red blood cells so effective? (Higher tier only)

Red blood cells are perfectly adapted to carry oxygen. They have no nucleus so the whole of the space inside the cell can be packed with haemoglobin. This means that no space is wasted.

Even the shape of the red blood cell is a perfect compromise.

> If the cell was 'fatter' or more rounded some parts of the inside of the cell would be too far away from the outside for oxygen to get into it when the cells pass through the lungs.

> If the cell was more frilly around the edges it would have a greater surface area but cells would not slide smoothly past each other in small blood vessels.

QUESTION

5 Sickle-cell anaemia is a disease that changes the shape of red blood cells, as shown in Figure 4. Give two effects this might have on someone with the disease.

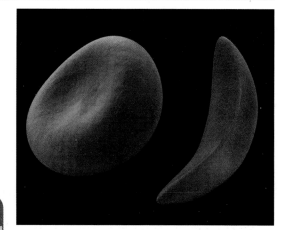

FIGURE 4: The shape of the red blood cell is perfect for exchanging gases with its environment. It is called a biconcave disk. In the 'sickle cell' the haemoglobin is damaged and this pulls the cell into the sickle shape.

Keeping cool

Why do people ride motorbikes across the desert?

In 1977, Thierry Sabine got lost on his motorbike in the Libyan Desert. Did a near-death experience put him off motorbike racing in the desert? Not so – he felt inspired to create the Paris to Dakar Rally. It is still a huge challenge for machines and humans – and it's water that's the biggest problem.

FIGURE 1: The Dakar Rally.

Controlling body temperature

Humans need to keep their body temperature at about 36.9°C. If it goes higher, chemical reactions in the body start to go faster, which can lead to serious problems, even death. The temperature in part of the Dakar Rally route can rise above 50°C, at which point even resting in the sunshine will make your temperature rise. If you are working hard it will be worse. Respiration, which is essential to supply energy for the body, also produces heat as a waste product.

In order to reduce body temperature:

> blood is diverted towards the skin, allowing heat to be radiated away from the skin surface

> sweat is produced, which cools the body as it evaporates.

Dehydration

Sweating cools the body very effectively but, in the worst conditions, especially during strenuous exercise, a human can lose 2.5 litres of fluid every hour. Since sweat is a solution of urea and salts in water, the person also loses sodium and potassium. Both these are essential for healthy muscle and nerve functioning. If the missing salts and water are not replaced, the body becomes **dehydrated**. Sweating will be reduced to save body water and will eventually cease. This allows the body to get hotter, leading to greater strain on the organs of the body and, in due course, death.

QUESTIONS

1 What are the symptoms as the body temperature rises from 36.9°C to 45°C?

2 What are the main factors that will increase body temperature?

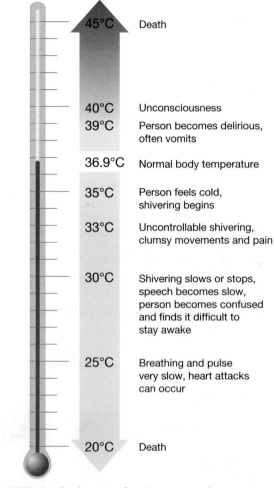

Temperature	
45°C	Death
40°C	Unconsciousness
39°C	Person becomes delirious, often vomits
36.9°C	Normal body temperature
35°C	Person feels cold, shivering begins
33°C	Uncontrollable shivering, clumsy movements and pain
30°C	Shivering slows or stops, speech becomes slow, person becomes confused and finds it difficult to stay awake
25°C	Breathing and pulse very slow, heart attacks can occur
20°C	Death

FIGURE 2: What happens if you become too hot or too cold.

human body temperature   dehydration of tissues

Sweating and water loss

Sensors in the skin detect external temperatures very quickly. You can feel the warmth of the sun on your skin, or a cold draft from an open door, almost immediately. This gives the brain advance warning of very warm or very cold conditions. Another sensor located deep in the middle of the brain detects body temperature by the temperature of the blood. This gives the brain information about the inner body temperature.

When body temperature rises, the brain sends nerve impulses to the sweat glands, telling them to produce sweat. As the water evaporates it cools the skin because it needs energy (in the form of heat) to change from liquid water to water vapour.

FIGURE 3: Sweating is essential for a professional athlete in training.

QUESTIONS

3 How does sweating cool the body?

4 After six hours in the hot sun without anything to drink, a competitor in the Dakar Rally stops sweating even though he still feels very hot. He thinks this is because he is getting used to the heat.

   a Why is his condition now even more dangerous?

   b Predict three things that will happen to him if he does not get medical treatment.

Did you know?

The body of an average adult male is about 70% water, that's just over 100 litres or 160 pints!

Vasodilation (Higher tier only)

As the body temperature rises, blood is shunted to the outer layers of the skin. Small blood vessels that supply the capillaries of the skin become wider to allow more blood to flow. This is called **vasodilation**. It is controlled by the brain and makes the skin look redder and feel much warmer.

When the body is too cold, the opposite happens. The small blood vessels get narrower, restricting blood flow through the skin capillaries. This is called **vasoconstriction** and it reduces heat loss.

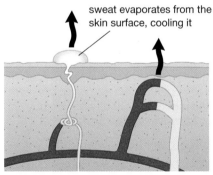

sweat evaporates from the skin surface, cooling it

Vasodilation

When the body is too hot: blood capillaries in the skin dilate and so blood flow increases, bringing more blood to the surface where it loses heat

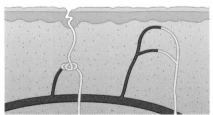

Vasoconstriction

When the body is too cold: blood capillaries in the skin constrict and so less blood flows through them, reducing heat loss

QUESTION

5 Vasodilation is often the first response by the body in its attempt to lose heat – before excessive sweating. Why is this an advantage to the body?

FIGURE 4: Vasodilation and the opposite process, vasoconstriction.

🔍 sweat glands and heat loss   vasodilation   vasoconstriction

Keeping warm

We are learning to:

> understand how the body controls temperature

> understand how the body generates heat

> interpret data about the best way to warm up someone suffering from hypothermia

Ice swimming... would you?

Winter 2012, Riga, a frozen lake. The perfect place for… the World Winter Swimming Championships. The rules are simple, cut a swim lane, 25 m long, in the ice, swim (only breaststroke allowed) along the course and the person with the fastest time wins. But what happens to the swimmers' bodies in temperatures just above zero?

FIGURE 1: The World Winter Swimming Championships.

Core and shell temperature

The temperature of the central core of the body needs to remain constant, at about 36.9° Celsius. The **shell**, which includes legs and arms, can get much cooler. Skin temperature can drop below 25 °C with little or no damage – although this does not mean the water will not feel very cold for the winter swimmers! Sensors in the skin pass impulses to the brain to warn of low temperatures.

The brain responds by:

> causing the muscles to start shivering

> diverting blood away from the cold shell into the warm body core

> stopping any sweating.

QUESTIONS

1 What is normal body temperature? Why does it depend on where in the body the temperature is taken?

2 State two ways in which the body responds to a drop in temperature.

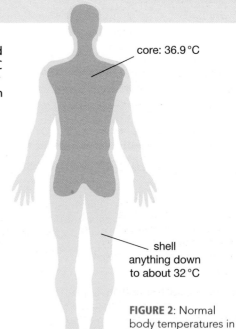

core: 36.9 °C

shell
anything down
to about 32 °C

FIGURE 2: Normal body temperatures in the core and shell.

Controlling responses

The part of the brain that controls responses to changes in temperature is located very near the centre of the skull, at the base of the brain. The brain analyses inputs from sensors in the skin and temperature measurements of its own blood flow. The brain then sends out impulses along nerves to **effectors** such as the muscles or the sweat glands. All of this happens without us having to think about it.

Q core body temperature

The diagram shows the complete temperature regulation system and how it responds to increases and decreases in temperature.

Blood cooler than normal

Reduce heat loss from body by:
- not sweating
- skin blood vessels narrowing to keep warmer blood deep in the body
- wearing more clothes
- moving to a warmer area

Increase heat production in body by:
- shivering
- respiration of extra sugar to release heat

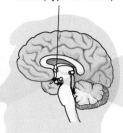

temperature receptor in brain (hypothalamus)

Blood warmer than normal

Increase heat loss from body by:
- sweating
- skin blood vessels dilating to take warmer blood nearer the skin's surface

Reduce heat production in body by:
- resting
- removing clothing
- fanning body
- moving to a cooler area

FIGURE 3: Temperature regulation in the body.

QUESTIONS

3 Draw a flow chart to show how the body responds to a rise in temperature.

4 Draw a flow chart to show how the body responds to a fall in temperature.

Hypothermia

When the core body temperature falls below 35 °C, the person suffers from **hypothermia**. An estimated 300 people die each year from hypothermia in the UK. In young people it is likely to be caused by an accident, perhaps through getting lost while walking in the mountains or as a result of swimming in cold lakes. In older people, who suffer from it more easily, it may be due to lack of money to pay fuel bills in the winter or because they do not 'feel' the cold as much as younger people and so do not dress accordingly. Young babies and older people cannot regulate their body temperature as well as other people can.

FIGURE 4: Danish soldiers administer aid to a comrade suffering from hypothermia during Arctic training.

In someone suffering from hypothermia, blood has moved away from the shell towards the core. The best treatment is slow, gentle warming, such as wrapping the patient in a blanket and covering the head. (Body heat is lost most quickly through the head.) If the person is warmed too quickly, for example, by sitting them in front of a fire, blood is drawn from the core to the skin to warm up. At the same time, cold blood from the skin passes to the core, causing a sudden and possibly lethal additional drop in body temperature.

Clever control (Higher tier only)

The **hypothalamus** in the brain is constantly monitoring blood temperature and using regulatory systems to raise and lower it. By carefully balancing these systems, it can make sure the temperature does not vary beyond safe limits. Effectors such as muscles and sweat glands can work **antagonistically** – they have opposite effects on body temperature.

QUESTIONS

5 Why is sudden warming dangerous for someone suffering from hypothermia?

6 Explain how sweat glands and muscles could act antagonistically to raise or lower body temperature.

Diabetes

What is diabetes and why is it getting more common?

The number of people in the UK with diabetes is increasing, particularly in a type of diabetes linked to obesity and poor diet (known as type 2). What is diabetes and is it really that serious? What are the chances of getting it?

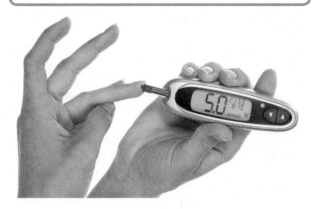

FIGURE 1: Testing blood glucose levels using a glaucometer.

Sugar levels in the blood

When carbohydrates are broken down in the gut they produce a sugar called **glucose**. This sugar passes quickly into the body and can cause sugar levels in the blood to rise. This causes:

> blood pressure to rise

> glucose to leak into the urine.

Neither of these effects is good.

> The increase in blood pressure can cause problems for the kidneys, the eyes and the circulation in general.

> The loss of glucose in the urine is wasteful.

Highly processed foods often contain high levels of sugar and this is rapidly absorbed into the blood. An oat-rich biscuit from one famous diet company was 20% sugar. This sugar rushes rapidly into our bloodstream – some even gets in through the lining of our mouths as we chew.

The body usually reacts to a rise in blood sugar levels by producing a hormone called **insulin** in the **pancreas**. Insulin encourages cells in the body to take glucose out of the blood and convert it into other substances for storage.

When glucose levels drop, insulin production is switched off again. Cells now control of blood sugar levels doesn't function properly so the levels of blood sugar change very widely, sometimes rising too high and sometimes falling dangerously low. When the level falls too low the person can go into a very deep sleep called a **coma**. They can die if their blood sugar level is not raised.

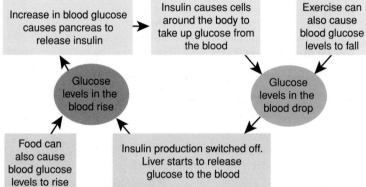

FIGURE 2: How insulin regulates blood sugar level.

- Increase in blood glucose causes pancreas to release insulin
- Insulin causes cells around the body to take up glucose from the blood
- Exercise can also cause blood glucose levels to fall
- Glucose levels in the blood rise
- Glucose levels in the blood drop
- Food can also cause blood glucose levels to rise
- Insulin production switched off. Liver starts to release glucose to the blood

QUESTIONS

1 a Which factors tend to increase blood sugar levels?

b Which factors tend to decrease blood sugar levels?

2 What is the hormone that causes cells to take up sugar?

3 What is dangerous about high blood sugar levels?

4a What is a diabetic coma?

b How do you think you could treat someone who fell into a diabetic coma?

diabetes   insulin   diabetic coma

Two types of diabetes

There are two types of diabetes, as the following table shows.

	Type 1	Type 2
How common is it?	10% of all cases	90% of all cases
When does it start?	Usually in childhood	Often after 40 years of age
How is the body affected?	Body cannot produce insulin	Body cannot produce enough insulin or the body cells stop responding to the insulin produced
What causes the disease?	Not sure, there may be a genetic component	It seems to be linked to a high-sugar diet or being overweight
Treatment	Injections of insulin	Improving the diet and taking more exercise

Types of diabetes.

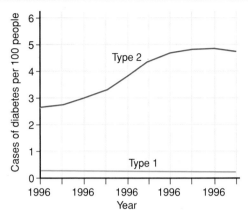

FIGURE 3: Levels of diabetes cases in the UK, 1996–2005 (data from the *Journal of Epidemiology and Community Health*).

The graph in Figure 3 shows the change in the number of people with diabetes in the UK over 10 years. As you can see, the number with type 1 was stable but there was a marked increase in the number with type 2. Doctors suggest that this rise is caused by increasing levels of obesity.

The chances of developing type 2 diabetes depend on the number of risk factors you have. Look at the list of risk factors. The more of these you can tick, the more likely you are to contract type 2 diabetes.

Risk factors for type 2 diabetes
- [ ] Being overweight
- [ ] Taking little or no exercise
- [ ] Being over 40 years of age
- [ ] High blood pressure
- [ ] Members of your family having diabetes
- [ ] Unhealthy diet: too much fat, not enough fibre

Watch out!

Although there are two types of diabetes, the effects are the same. The difference is in what seems to cause them, not the way they affect the body or how they are treated.

QUESTIONS

5 Sort the risk factors for type 2 diabetes into two groups: those you can control and those over which you have no control.

6 Why do people suffering from diabetes need to know their blood sugar levels before they inject themselves with insulin?

Feedback mechanisms

The control of body temperature and blood sugar levels are example of **negative feedback** loops. In negative feedback, a system will respond to any change by doing something that reduces the effect of that change. For example, when you start to feel cold your body shivers to raise your body temperature.

Most biological systems show negative feedback – it keeps them safely within healthy limits. A positive feedback system tends to increase the effect of any change that produces it. For example, an increase in the temperature of the oceans forces more carbon dioxide out of solution, which further encourages temperature rise.

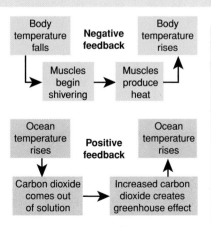

FIGURE 4: Negative and positive feedback loops.

QUESTION

7 An increase in body mass can often mean people take less exercise, which leads to further increase in body mass.

a Is this a positive or a negative feedback loop?

b Why are positive feedback loops rare in biological systems?

Cycles in nature

We are learning to:
> recognise the differences between open loop processes and closed loop cycles
> understand the importance of closed loops in natural ecosystems

What does it mean to be environmentally friendly?

Many shops sell recycled products. They are presented as 'more environmentally friendly'. It seems better to use a paper cup, which can be recycled into new products, than a plastic cup made from oil, which is then thrown away. Or is it even better to use a china cup, wash it and use it over and over again?

FIGURE 1: Paper is easily and economically recycled.

Open and closed loops

You are probably using a plastic pen to write notes. This will have started out as crude oil. Products from the oil were used to make the plastic, which was then made into a pen. When you have finished with your pen, you will throw it in the bin and it will be buried in landfill or incinerated. It cannot be re-used. Its usefulness has come to an end. This is called an **open loop process**.

The paper you write on is different. It started as wood, which was pulped. The wood pulp was made into paper and, after you have finished with it, it can be collected and recycled. Either it will be processed to produce more paper, or it could be composted and used to provide soil for more trees to grow. This is an example of a **closed loop process**.

FIGURE 2: The plastic items shown here can be recycled economically but many other plastic items cannot.

Open loops	Closed loops
In open loops wastes from one part of the process leave the loop. They cannot be used again.	In closed loops wastes from one part of the process become the raw materials for the next part. The loop can keep going round and round for ever.

Crude oil from wells → Crude oil is processed to make plastic for pens → Pen is thrown away or burnt after use

Trees grow taking in carbon dioxide to produce wood → Paper is made from woodpulp → Paper recycled as compost to help grow more trees or burnt to release carbon dioxide

FIGURE 3: Comparing open and closed loops.

QUESTIONS

1 List two things that you use regularly that are part of:

a an open loop

b a closed loop.

2 Give two reasons why closed loops are more friendly to the environment.

Closed loops in nature

There are many closed loops in the natural world. Here are some examples.

1 Carbon dioxide in the atmosphere is taken in by plants and used in photosynthesis to make sugar and other compounds containing carbon. These compounds are called **organic matter**. The waste from this process is oxygen, which is used by living organisms for respiration.

Q loop theory   ecosystems

2 Animals eat the plants and use the organic matter for energy. The plants become an **input** for the animals. Animals produce carbon dioxide and **faeces** as waste or **output**. The carbon dioxide provides an input for the plants. Faeces contains a range of chemicals that provide an input for microorganisms in the soil.

3 When plants and animals die their dead bodies provide a source of food for microorganisms. Digestive enzymes in microorganisms break down this organic matter for energy and give out carbon dioxide and mineral nutrients. Plants need these nutrients for healthy growth.

In ways such as these, materials are cycled in closed loops throughout the natural world. Nothing is wasted. The energy to drive the loops comes originally from the Sun.

Closed loops develop between organisms living in a particular area. A group of plants and animals that are able to form sustainable loops is called an **ecosystem**. A rainforest, a lake, a moor and an oak forest are all good examples of ecosystems. Ecosystems can be large or small but they all are:

> powered by energy from the Sun

> local, for example, a forest or a lake but not a whole country

> stable over many years.

Watch out!

Ecosystems do not have sharp boundaries, e.g. grassland may change gradually into forest, but must be roughly self-containing or they cannot establish closed loops.

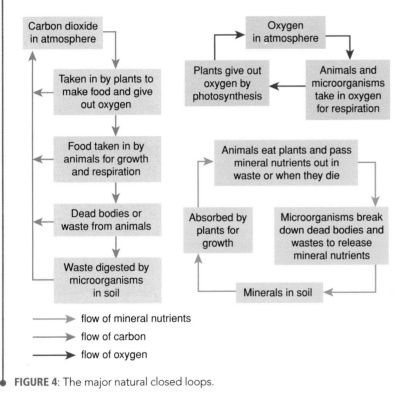

flow of mineral nutrients

flow of carbon

flow of oxygen

FIGURE 4: The major natural closed loops.

QUESTIONS

3 a List the waste products mentioned in Figure 4.

b Why might it be unfair to describe these items just as 'waste'?

4 Explain how microorganisms help to keep loops closed.

5 Some farmers add extra mineral nutrients as fertiliser to their fields to help the grass grow to feed their cows. Why doesn't the level of minerals constantly rise in the soil?

Dangerous loops

Crude oil was formed when plants and animals were buried millions of years ago. Over this long time scale, these organic remains changed into crude oil. Oil provides most of the energy used by human populations and, when it is burnt, the original organic material is output to the atmosphere as carbon dioxide and water. This loop may seem closed but in fact it is lop-sided. We are producing much more carbon dioxide per year than is being used up by the growth of plants in the same time.

QUESTION

6 Explain why burning oil is not considered part of a sustainable closed loop, even though the oil was produced from carbon dioxide in the first place.

Cycling in rainforests

We are learning to:

> recognise the energy costs of seed and fruit production

> understand how closed loops in stable ecosystems lead to sustainability

> understand that decisions need to be made about the human impact on ecosystems

Fancy some rainforest fruit?

Durian fruit tastes wonderful – but smells awful! Some people have said it's like eating your favourite flavour of ice cream while sitting on the smelliest toilet in the world! Would you want to eat it?

FIGURE 1: Durian fruit.

Fruits and energy

A fruit is a structure that develops from a fertilised flower. It contains seeds that can grow into a new plant. It usually has a good energy store to help the seeds to germinate. We eat fruits because they tend to hold more energy than the other parts of the plant do.

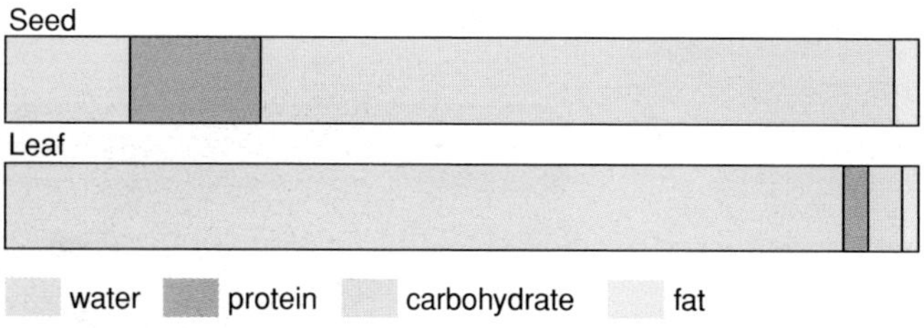

Seed

Leaf

water   protein   carbohydrate   fat

FIGURE 2: Nutrient composition of plant parts.

Did you know?

An average mango contains about 500 J of energy but the energy needed to transport it from the farm to your table is about 600 times greater!

QUESTIONS

1 Why is it important to the plant that fruits have a good store of energy?

2 Where does the energy to make the fruits come from?

Over production

Brazil nut trees are native to Amazonia. They live for 500 to 800 years. During that time they will produce about 150 pods of nuts every year and each pod will contain an average of 15 nuts.

Most of the nuts do not germinate. They will be eaten by animals, damaged by fungi or insect attack or may just fail to germinate. Of those that do germinate, not all will survive long enough to become adult trees.

This pattern is repeated in many animals and plants. A lot of energy is invested in **reproductive structures** to try to make sure that the plant produces the maximum possible number of seeds or the animal has a large number of offspring. The seeds that do not germinate, or the young animals that die, rot down in the rainforest and the mineral nutrients they contain are recycled.

FIGURE 3: Why does a brazil nut tree produce so many seeds that could lead to so many competing trees?

QUESTIONS

3 Why do animals and plants produce more offspring than they need just to replace themselves?

4 a How many seeds will a typical brazil nut tree produce if it fruits every year for 600 years?

b What happens to the energy and materials in the brazil nuts that do not germinate?

Keeping it in the forest

Materials in the rainforest cycle through closed loops to produce a **stable system**. Leaves fall from trees and decay quickly in the moist, warm conditions to release mineral nutrients to the soil. These nutrients are taken up by the plants to produce more leaves.

Similarly, oxygen released by photosynthesis is taken in by animals and carbon dioxide given out by animals is taken up by plants. Rainforests also cycle water very effectively. Water is collected from the soil by trees and evaporates into the air. As it rises the water vapour cools and turns back to liquid, which falls as rain. Inputs to the rainforest are broadly balanced by outputs to give a stable system. This balancing is essential to any stable ecosystem, including chilly coniferous forests in Russia or hot, dry grasslands in Tanzania. It's not just about rainforests.

However, no real system is a perfect closed loop. There are natural changes, for example, as animals leave an ecosystem or a river carries in mineral nutrients from an uphill area. All ecosystems have slightly 'leaky' borders.

Humans have a huge impact on natural closed loops. People use rainforests for timber, for agriculture and even as places to live. Forest products bring money to the local economy. Some of these uses unbalance the inputs and outputs for the rainforest cycles. Trees removed from the forest to make furniture or build houses take away a link in the cycle – the circuit is broken. If enough trees are left, the system can cope, although it will change. However, if the loss from the system is too great over several years this could lead to the destruction of the ecosystem. But people need to eat and to earn a living. What is the right thing to do?

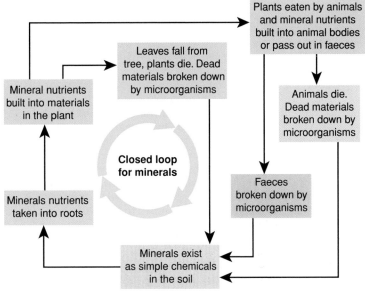

FIGURE 4: There may be many routes around this mineral cycle but it always gets back to where it started from.

FIGURE 5: Protestors in richer countries often complain about logging in rainforests – but they don't rely on money from rainforest products.

Watch out!

Ecological closed loops often mention elements such as carbon, oxygen or nitrogen being cycled. The chemicals are not usually present as simple elements but built into a range of chemicals in different parts of the cycle.

◉ QUESTIONS

5 a Draw a closed-loop diagram to show the flow of carbon through a rainforest.

b Modify your diagram from part **a** to show the trees in the forest being removed and exported to other countries.

c Predict what might happen in time if the trees are removed.

6 Identify some of the costs and benefits to local people of logging a region of a rainforest.

Feeding the world

The world grows more wheat every year – but not quite enough more to keep up with increased demand. The rising world population makes greater and greater demands on wheat. The increasing wealth of Southeast Asia and China mean that people can demand more Western-style diets with large amounts of wheat and meat (with meat-producing animals often fed on wheat). The United Nations Food and Agriculture Organisation (FAO) monitors prices of foods. It noted that their index of food prices rose 37% from May 2010 to May 2011.

Scientists are trying to help by breeding crops that can survive in cooler climates. A new breed of wheat has been produced that has:

> increased germination and initial growth rates

> tolerance of lower temperatures during the crucial initial stages.

This would allow growth of wheat in some of the cooler plains to the north of Kiev in the Ukraine that currently are not used for agriculture.

To test these claims, samples of seeds were germinated in dishes in the laboratory. Each dish contained a supply of seeds, water and mineral salts and percentage germination was noted after five days. The investigation was repeated at five different temperatures, with five data sets collected at each temperature.

The data collected is shown in Table 1. The researchers were also keen to investigate the initial growth of the seedlings. To do this they suggested selecting seeds that had germinated from the samples above and growing them on in potting compost. After seven days the height of the seedlings would be taken as a measure of early growth.

TABLE 1: Percentage germination rates at different temperatures.

Temperature (°C)	1	2	3	4	5	6	7	8	9	10
0	0	0	0	0	0	0	0	0	0	0
3	0	5	3	6	8	11	7	6	9	14
6	27	34	29	48	53	29	55	49	61	55
9	56	53	66	76	83	79	73	88	79	81
12	62	66	59	85	90	88	93	87	92	84

Columns 1 to 3 are traditional wheat seedlings, 4 to 10 are the improved variety.

TABLE 2: Average temperatures (°C) for Kiev, Ukraine.

J	F	M	A	M	J	J	A	S	O	N	D
–6	–5	0	8	15	19	21	19.5	15	8	2	–3.5

Wheat is planted in March–April and harvested in September.

Task 1

> How sensible was the original germination experiment? Is it likely to produce reliable data?

 ## Task 2

> Calculate the means for each for the data sets for each temperature in Table 1.

> Draw a suitable graph to show the results from the datasets.

> Were the experimental temperatures chosen appropriate for the question being investigated?

 ## Task 3

> Identify any strange or unexpected results in the data. Give reasons for your choices.

> How confident are you in the data provided for the germination experiments? Are there any sets you would like to repeat? Give reasons for any choices.

 ## Task 4

> How confident are you that the experimental temperatures chosen are suitable for generating useful data?

> Will growing on the seedlings produced from each treatment give reliable data about the cold tolerance of the strain? Give reasons for your answer and suggest any improvements you might want to see in the data collected.

 ## Maximise your grade

Use these suggestions to improve your work and be more successful.

E

To be on target for a grade E you need to:
> comment about any problems you see in the way the data was collected

> make some comment about how accurate you feel the data collected will be

> identify any particular results that you feel are unreliable because they are far away from other datapoints in the set.

C

To be on target for a grade D or C, you also need to:
> suggest ways to improve the data collection – in terms of accuracy or reliability

> show how the treatments chosen are appropriate to the problem being investigated, and suggest ways to improve the relevance of data collected if you feel the results do not allow you to answer the question originally posed.

A

To be on target for a grade B or A, you also need to:
> suggest explanations for some of the data that lies outside the expected range and suggest ways to test to see if this data is important and unexpected or just a simple error in technique.

Protecting soil

What is a dustbowl?

Areas of the USA that once were fertile are now deserts because of farming practices during the 1900s. These areas are still called the dustbowl or badlands. Can this ever happen again?

FIGURE 1: Parts of the USA have become what is called a 'dustbowl'.

Desertification

The farmers in the dustbowls of the USA were unlucky. They had ploughed up prairies, thinking that they were flat and good for crops such as maize and sugar cane. Unfortunately, the soil was very poor and when the plants were harvested the soil was washed away by floods or blown away by wind. Without constant vegetation cover the soil was too easy to dislodge. Once the soil had gone it was almost impossible to replant crops so the farms were abandoned.

Protecting the soil

Soil that is covered by vegetation is much less likely than bare soil to be eroded. Growing plants have three effects:

> their leaves and stems slow down the rain so that it hits the ground with less force

> vegetation cover acts as a sponge, soaking up water from the soil

> the roots hold the soil together.

A healthy soil also helps to prevent floods. The soil absorbs the water and releases it slowly so that the rivers and streams can drain away safely.

FIGURE 2: A farm in the USA in the 1920s.

QUESTIONS

1 List the ways in which plants can protect soil from erosion.

2 a What is desertification?

   b What factors make it more likely to happen?

Q desertification   dustbowls

Managing the weather

Rainforests are very complex ecosystems that help to protect the soil by covering it with many layers of foliage and by having roots that bind it together. This effect is so good that – even on the steepest slopes – water flowing out into the rivers at the base of the hills is often quite clear. When the rainforest is logged this protection is lost and soil washes into the rivers. These muddy rivers often become clogged and flood, causing further damage.

Rainforests also influence the weather. When water falls onto an area with a lot of vegetation, such as a rainforest, some of it is taken up by the plants through their roots. This water passes up the plant to the leaves where it evaporates back into the air. This evaporation is called **transpiration**. It helps to put some of the water back into the atmosphere. It never gets to the rivers. In this way the huge areas of rainforest in the world help to make clouds and then rain. As more and more rainforest is cut down, so weather becomes more unpredictable and extreme.

FIGURE 3: Logging in a rainforest can lead to soil erosion and muddy streams.

QUESTIONS

3 State three effects rainforests have on the water systems around them.

4 Draw a diagram to show the movement of water through an area densely covered with healthy rainforest. Include the water flowing into and out of the rainforest in rivers and the rain that falls onto it.

Ecological services

Ecological services are functions that the ecosystem provides for all members of the system. Soil protection is an example. Humans normally look at four broad areas of services:

> supporting services – nutrient cycling, oxygen production, pollination and soil formation and protection

> provisioning services – food, fibre, fuel and water

> regulating services – climate regulation, water purification and flood protection

> cultural services – education and recreation.

Ecosystem services are not provided by a single species. They come from the different elements of the ecosystem working together. The services help the whole ecosystem to flourish. Human beings take advantage of these ecosystems, for example, benefiting from the provision of food or clean water. We must be careful not to damage the ecosystem so much that these services become unavailable.

FIGURE 4: An allotment garden in an inner city area.

QUESTION

5 Suggest four ecosystem services provided for city dwellers by a large set of allotment gardens.

Ecological services

We are learning to:

> recognise the fragility of rainforests and other ecosystems

> understand the significance of sustainability in natural systems

> recognise that different people might have different opinions about a scientific issue

What is a 'tree-spiker'?

Tree-spikers hammer nails or spikes into trees in areas where logging is banned. If the trees are cut down and passed through a sawmill, the spike gets caught in the machinery and damages it.

FIGURE 1: Some people call tree-spikers 'ecoterrorists'. What do you think?

What are ecological services?

Your home is probably connected to the mains for electricity, water, gas and maybe cable television and telephone. These are called services. Organisms living in the rainforest also depend on services to survive. These are called **ecological services** and here are some examples.

> A plant may depend on an insect to pollinate its flowers so that it can produce seeds and offspring.

> A bird may need certain kinds of plant to build its nest.

> Many microorganisms provide services for plants by breaking down dead organic matter so that the valuable minerals can be absorbed through the plants' roots.

QUESTION

1 **a** Explain what the term 'ecological services' means.

b Give two examples of services a plant may depend on to survive.

Did you know?

Apple-growers often keep beehives in their orchards because the bees pollinate the apple flowers to give a good fruit crop. This is a useful ecological service.

Poor soils, great cycling

The warm, wet, sunny environment of the **tropics** helps plants to grow very fast. It also means that fungi and microorganisms in the soil can break down dead plants and animals very quickly to release minerals. As a result, minerals enter the soil very quickly. However, the conditions are also excellent for the growing plants and they remove the minerals very rapidly as they grow. So most of the minerals that usually make a soil fertile are contained within the growing plants. The UK has a cooler environment, called a **temperate** climate, and the minerals tend to stay in the soil for a long time because the plants grow more slowly.

Temperate forest

Minerals built into plants

Uptake by roots ↑   ↓ Breakdown by microorganisms

Mineral nutrients in the soil

Rainforest

Minerals built into plants

Uptake by roots ↑   ↓ Breakdown by microorganisms

Mineral nutrients in the soil

The wider the arrow the faster the process
The larger the box the bigger the store of materials

FIGURE 2: The different stores of minerals in temperate forests and rainforests.

Although the rate of movement around the cycle may be different in tropical and temperate forests, the inputs to the soil, and outputs from it to the plants, are balanced. This input–output balance gives a stable ecosystem. What happens when one of the inputs is lost? Some methods of timber harvesting show the problem very well.

Slash and burn

The **slash-and-burn** process of agriculture involves cutting down trees to make fields. The best trees are taken away for timber. What is left is burnt. Grass grows in the space created by the logging and cows can eat the grass to produce beef. For the first year or two this works well. The grass grows and the cows get fat. However, the milk and meat products are taken away to be sold in other areas. The minerals they have absorbed are not returned to the soil. In a few years the minerals in the soil are exhausted and the grass is replaced by low-value plants or even bare soil. The farmers then move on to clear another patch of rainforest.

Over a few years this technique:

> replaces a complex rainforest with a simpler grassland ecosystem – many of the ecological services provided by the rainforest are lost

> blocks rivers as fragile rainforest soil is washed into watercourses

> leads to desertification as the protective vegetation layer is lost from the soil.

QUESTIONS

2 a Explain why cycling of minerals is faster in temperate forests than in tropical forests.

b Give one implication of this difference for organisms living in the area.

3 State three problems with the slash-and-burn approach to developing the rainforest.

Sustainable forestry

Biodiversity is a measure of the variety of organisms living in an area. Rainforests are the most diverse ecosystems on the planet. For this reason, rainforests have never been replanted – we just do not know which varieties of trees and other organisms to gather together to plant. Once rainforest is gone it is lost for ever. The only way to carry out **sustainable** forestry in the rainforest is to take out less per year than the natural processes can produce in the same time.

In the UK, conifers grow quite quickly and are easy to plant. However, in some plantations they are planted so close together that other living things cannot survive. The forests may be sustainable, if considered simply in terms of wood production, but some of the other organisms living there have been lost.

FIGURE 3: In Wales many natural forests have been cleared and planted with conifers. Is this sustainable?

QUESTIONS

4 a A more biodiverse area is more likely to offer more ecological services. Explain why.

b Give two reasons why it is impossible to replant rainforests on land damaged by slash-and-burn agriculture.

c Suggest one problem that may occur with coniferous forests as they mature.

5 Tree-spikers say that rainforests are so valuable they must be protected at all costs. Do you agree? Give arguments for and against spiking trees in the rainforest.

Q biodiversity   slash and burn   sustainability

Poisoned lakes

How clean is that lake?

Wild swimming is an increasingly popular sport. Rather than swimming in heated pools, wild swimmers prefer open lakes, rivers and the sea. They say it's better because there's no chlorine to make their eyes sting. But how safe is the water in lakes and rivers?

FIGURE 1: Wild swimming.

Human impact on the natural environment

Waste that is not recycled has to go somewhere. The table shows what happens to some common types of rubbish. Eventually the environment breaks down the rubbish or spreads it around so much that it becomes safe.

Fate of different waste types.

Domestic refuse	Faeces	Waste gases
Buried underground or burnt	Cleaned at sewage works and the remains passed into rivers	Passed into the atmosphere and spread out to safe levels

The damage done by waste depends on:

> how much is produced

> how dangerous it is

> how quickly the environment can deal with it.

Sometimes the environment cannot deal with the waste quickly enough and it builds up to harmful levels. Human faeces is a good example. It is easily broken down in the environment, but it takes time.

Sewage includes everything that gets flushed down the toilet. Sewage from London used to drain directly into the Thames. As the population of the city increased the sewage could not be cleared away by the river. This killed fish in the river. Some sewage even got into drinking water supplies, which spread diseases such as cholera and typhoid fever.

Did you know?

The London sewers still dump raw sewage into the Thames during heavy rainfall. During one week in June 2005 one billion litres of raw sewage entered the river.

QUESTIONS

1 **a** Give three examples of waste materials that are not recycled.

b Suggest which of the wastes you mentioned in part **a** is most dangerous. Give a reason for your answer.

2 Human faeces is a natural input for an ecosystem. Why did it cause so much of a problem as the population of London increased?

Input-output balance

Human sewage is a mixture of complex chemicals. It provides an input to the ecosystem of nitrogen-rich compounds. Figure 2 shows what happens if the input and output are balanced or unbalanced.

Q sewage treatment

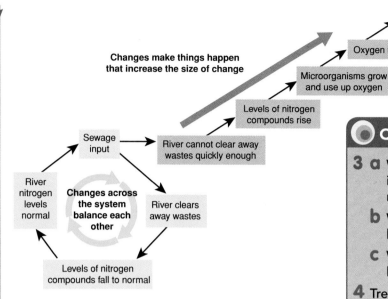

Changes make things happen that increase the size of change

Organisms in the river die and start to decay → Levels of nitrogen compounds rise further

Oxygen levels fall

Microorganisms grow and use up oxygen

Levels of nitrogen compounds rise

River cannot clear away wastes quickly enough

Sewage input

River nitrogen levels normal

Changes across the system balance each other

River clears away wastes

Levels of nitrogen compounds fall to normal

FIGURE 2: Sewage is not toxic unless the level of wastes unbalances the loops in the ecosystem.

QUESTIONS

3 a What are the nitrogen-rich compounds in the sewage used for by microorganisms and plants?

b What would be visible in the river if the levels were within safe limits?

c What would be visible in the river if the levels were above safe limits?

4 Treating sewage is expensive. Give two reasons for doing it.

Eutrophication and bioaccumulation (Higher tier only)

When a large amount of organic wastes enter a lake there is a sudden rise in the number of algae growing in the water. This sudden rise is called a bloom and can be seen in the summer in the UK. All **algal blooms** cause problems by using up oxygen in the water; this is called **eutrophication**. Some blooms are actually poisonous. Walkers around Rutland Water reservoir in Leicestershire are warned not to let their dogs swim in the water because some have been killed by the poisonous algae.

Eutrophication occurs when natural chemicals that can be broken down get into a water source. Over time the water system can clear itself. However, many of the chemicals used to kill pests are not broken down in the environment for many, many years.

Research done in the 1950s and 1960s showed how the levels of a pesticide called DDT cause change in the environment. In the USA, low levels of DDT were sprayed onto a lake to kill mosquitoes. This was a success but green plants absorbed some of the DDT. These plants were eaten by small animals that, in turn, were eaten by fish, which were eaten by small birds, and so on up to the large predatory birds including ospreys. At every step in the chain the levels of DDT detected in the organism rose because the organisms did not have the enzymes to break down the DDT in their bodies. This increase in concentration is called **bioaccumulation**.

FIGURE 3: The green sludge is an algal bloom that has been dragged out of a lake in Central Park, New York. The nitrogen-rich compounds in this pond may come from food waste and dog faeces.

QUESTIONS

5 a What is eutrophication?

b Why is it dangerous?

6 a Give one difference between the way naturally occurring nitrogen compounds and artificial compounds such as DDT pass through the environment.

b DDT was banned in the UK in 1984 but is still detectable in animals living in areas where it was used. How can you explain this?

c Discuss why DDT wasn't banned until 1984, although evidence of bioaccumulation of DDT was found decades before this date.

Sustainable fishing

How many fish are left in the sea?

Over the last few years a controversy has broken out about fish stocks in the North Sea. Some writers warn of the collapse of the numbers of cod in the North Sea while others say that the stocks have recovered. What are the real stock levels and has the traditional British meal of cod and chips had its day?

FIGURE 1: A quick meal on the way home on Friday? Or will it soon be so rare that it becomes an expensive delicacy?

Chinese ponds

The Chinese depend on fish as a source of protein. Traditionally, the fish are grown in ponds, as shown in Figure 2. The green colour in the water comes from water weed. Carefully measured amounts of run-off from the fields are used to fertilise the growth of this weed. The weed is an excellent food source for the fish.

The ponds are also re-stocked with young fish every year. This means that the fishermen know how many fish are in the pond and how many they take out. The ponds often have a very high **biomass** of fish. The biomass is the total weight of fish in the pond.

QUESTIONS

1 State three things that the water weed needs in order to grow.

2 a Why do the ponds need to be re-stocked with fish every year?

b How is fishing in the ponds different from fishing in rivers?

FIGURE 2: Fishing is a hobby and a great source of food in China. These men are busy catching their lunch in giant concrete reservoirs that are stocked every year with new fish.

Scottish lochs

In Scotland, salmon farmers keep fish in giant tanks, in lochs. These tanks are made of a net-like mesh that keeps the fish in but allows the loch water to pass through. Food is added and the fish are harvested when they have reached a suitable size. To stock the farm, eggs and sperm are removed from adult fish and mixed in the laboratory. The eggs are hatched in tanks of gently flowing water and the young fish, called fry, are added to the tanks in the lochs.

Q sustainable fisheries   fish farming

The **yield** is the amount of useful fish produced every year. The tanks are densely stocked with salmon, so the yield is excellent. However, keeping such a large number of fish close together makes infection more likely, so the farmers add pesticides to prevent this happening. These **pesticides** can leak out into the environment beyond the tanks and can damage other wildlife in the loch.

Fish produce waste. In ocean systems this is washed away naturally – but not in enclosed systems like the Chinese ponds. This means that the ponds have to be drained, cleaned and re-stocked roughly every six years.

FIGURE 3: Farming salmon in giant net tanks may have undesirable impacts.

QUESTIONS

3 Give two differences between water flowing into the net and water flowing out.

4 List the ways in which salmon farmers increase the yield of salmon from the farms.

5 Are fish farms sustainable? Give a reason for your answer.

Fishing in the open sea

When scientists talk about **stock biomass** they mean the mass of fish that are old enough to produce eggs, leading to the next generation of fish. Figure 4 shows the stock biomass of cod in the North Sea since 2002. The stock declined from 2002 to 2006 and this trend continues. The cause of the decline may be **overfishing** or rising sea temperatures.

Overfishing means that more fish are being taken from the sea than can be replaced during the breeding season. To prevent overfishing, governments have agreed **quotas** for fishing fleets. A quota controls:

> the number of days on which a fishing fleet can go out to work every year

> the minimum size of fish that can be taken (smaller ones must be thrown back into the sea).

The restrictive quotas (see Figure 4) mean that there is less work for fishermen. In fishing ports such as Grimsby this has led to a significant rise in unemployment. Conserving natural systems may need one course of action; the local populations that depend on those systems may need another. These problems are made worse when a number of countries need to agree and work together on conservation strategies, but each country also wants to protect its own workers.

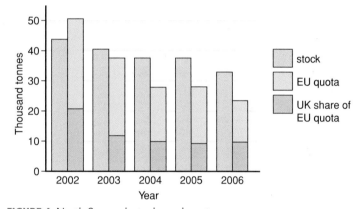

FIGURE 4: North Sea cod: stocks and quotas.

QUESTIONS

6 a How does setting the number of days fishermen work help to reduce the catch?

b What happens if the efficiency of the fishing boats increases?

7 How does the size of fish taken affect the growth of the fish population?

8 Describe the feelings the following people might have about quotas for the North Sea cod stocks:

a a fish conservation officer

b a local fisherman from Grimsby.

Farming microbes

We are learning to:

> recognise the benefits of using microorganisms in industry

> understand how penicillin manufacture was increased

> explore the factors that control microbial growth

How can you farm in a chemistry lab?

Some of the most profitable 'farmers' in the UK now work in small factory units near Basingstoke. These hi-tech labs farm microorganisms to produce a range of expensive biochemicals for industries as different as drugs, food and washing powders. But how does a microbial farm work?

FIGURE 1: Is this the new face of farming? Researchers are growing microorganisms in laboratories to harvest valuable chemicals.

Farming with microorganisms

Microorganisms can be used to make many useful products. The table gives some examples.

Microorganisms, such as bacteria, have a number of useful features for the modern hi-tech farmer.

> They have relatively simple biochemistry.

> They reproduce very rapidly.

> They can be farmed on a large scale to produce complex, useful molecules.

> They can be **genetically engineered** to produce further valuable chemicals.

> There are few ethical concerns about the way that a bacterium is treated.

Useful products made by microorganisms.

Product	Produced by	Use of product
Vitamin B12	*Streptomyces*	Vitamin supplements
Protease	*Bacillus subtilis*	Enzymes for biological washing powders
Pectinases	*Aspergillus* sp.	Increasing the amount of juice that can be extracted from fruit
Ethanol	*Saccharomyces* (yeast)	Making alcohol to use as a biofuel
Chymosin	*E. coli*	An enzyme used to make vegetarian cheese from milk
Penicillin	*Penicillium chrysogenum*	A common antibiotic

QUESTION

1 a Give two reasons why microorganisms are used for producing complex chemicals.

b Give one use of yeast that has not already been mentioned in the table.

Q biotechnology   single cell protein

Protein and penicillin

Bacteria can produce proteins very quickly. Could this be a way of feeding the growing world population? However, bacteria are difficult to harvest because the cells are very small. People also associate bacteria with illness rather than food. Yeasts are easier to harvest but grow more slowly and produce lower-quality protein. Figure 2 shows how much faster yeast can produce useful protein than beef cattle can. The only large-scale production of single-celled protein (SCP) is based on a fungus. In the UK it is marketed as the vegetarian food *Quorn* and can be made into meat-like pieces or mince.

Watch out!

Penicillium is the name of the fungus that makes the drug penicillin – take care to spell the words correctly.

Output of protein in 24 hours

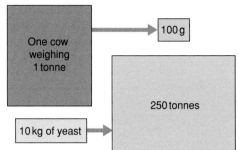

One cow weighing 1 tonne	100 g
10 kg of yeast	250 tonnes

FIGURE 2: The output of protein from microorganisms is much more efficient than that from animals.

Did you know?

The fungus in *Quorn* comes from a sample found in a field of cows near Marlow in Buckinghamshire over 20 years ago!

FIGURE 3: *Quorn* is made from single-celled protein (SCP). This packet contains *Quorn* treated to look like chicken fillets.

QUESTION

2 a List the main advantages of producing food from microbes rather than from raising cattle.

b List some of the problems a company manufacturing SCP might have selling it to customers.

c Suggest ways in which the company might overcome these problems.

Fermentation

The fungus *Penicillium chrysogenum* produces the valuable drug penicillin. Drug companies now use large steel vessels called **fermenters** to hold the mixture of the fungus and the food it needs.

Fermenters can be used to grow many different types of microbe on a large scale. Inside the fermenters, the conditions such as temperature and pH are very carefully controlled. This enables the manufacturers to produce large amounts of useful product as rapidly and cheaply as possible.

QUESTION

3 a Why is the stirrer needed in a fermenter?

b Fermenters are shut down and cleaned out if a microorganism other than *Penicillium* gets into it. Suggest why.

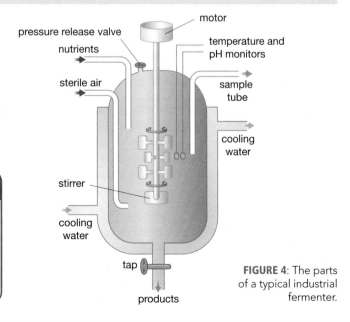

FIGURE 4: The parts of a typical industrial fermenter.

$\mathbb{Q}$ microbial drug production   plasmid

Genetic modification

We are learning to:

> recognise that genes can be transferred between species

> understand how genetic engineers move genes between species

> consider possible applications of gene technology and its implications

How can we control weeds?

Weeds are a problem. They can significantly reduce the yield of crops. What can be done? Herbicides can clear a field of weeds with just one spraying. Unfortunately, they can also damage the crops.

FIGURE 1: Spraying a soya bean crop with a herbicide.

Breeding stronger crops

Weeds can reduce the yield of crops by anything from 35% to 100%.

A **selective herbicide** kills certain plants but leaves others untouched. In 1975 over 80% of the USA soya-bean crop was resistant to certain selective herbicides. This meant that you could spray a field of soya beans and weeds and only kill the weeds. Unfortunately, the weeds hit back. They evolved resistance to the herbicides. By 2006 there were over 290 resistant types of weed. This is an increasing problem, as shown in Figure 2.

Research chemists produce new herbicides every year. Unfortunately, these chemicals often kill the crops as well as the weeds. Genetic engineers find genes that give plants resistance (often from plants on other sides of the world) and add these to the crop plants. This gives a new, powerful and safe herbicide.

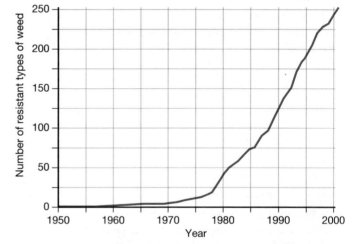

FIGURE 2: Rising numbers of weeds resistant to herbicides (data from www.weedscience.com).

QUESTIONS

1 How much damage can be done by a weed in a field of wheat?

2 What does the word 'herbicide' mean?

3 Why is it important for chemists and biologists to work together to produce each new herbicide?

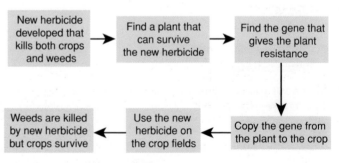

FIGURE 3: How a new herbicide is developed.

Q genetic engineering   herbicide resistance

Producing insulin

Insulin for people with diabetes used to be extracted from the pancreases of pigs or cows. It was an expensive process and the insulin needed to be purified very carefully to avoid problems with any contaminants from the pig or cow.

There were other disadvantages.

> Some religious groups regard cows as sacred and others think of pigs as unclean. They object to material from these animals coming into contact with humans.

> Other people regard animals as having the same rights as humans. They will not eat them or use them for medical research.

In 1982 human insulin that had been made by bacteria became available. A method of genetic engineering was used to produce this insulin by taking a human gene and inserting it into the bacterium *E. coli*. People do not usually have any strong feelings about using microorganisms in this way.

> ### QUESTION
>
> **4 a** Give two scientific problems associated with producing insulin from a pig.
>
> **b** Give one factor, not related to the science, that causes some people to complain about producing insulin from pigs.

Recombinant DNA

The technique used to produce both herbicide-resistant crops and human insulin from bacteria is the same. It is called **recombinant DNA** because it *combines* DNA from different sources. A **vector** is used to transfer a gene from one organism to another. There are two types of vector:

> plasmids   > **viruses**.

Plasmids are circular DNA molecules found in some bacteria. They can be modified with a useful gene and then inserted into another microorganism (Figure 4) where the gene is expressed. The human protein insulin is now almost entirely produced in this way. Scientists grow the microorganisms on a huge scale to produce large quantities of insulin.

Viruses are microorganisms, many of which cause diseases. Certain types of virus are able to inject DNA directly into another cell. The cell then duplicates the DNA from the virus as if it were part of its own genetic material.

Vectors that behave a little like viruses are being tested as a way to deliver a gene that can cure cystic fibrosis in humans. The gene is the code for the production of a protein that controls how fluid passes across a cell membrane. People with cystic fibrosis do not have this gene and cannot make this protein. This means that their lungs fill with fluid that interferes with their breathing. The virus-like particles are sprayed into their nose and pass down to the lungs. The gene is injected into cells and they are then able to make the protein they need to stay healthy.

Step 1: Find and multiply the gene

Gene is located and cut out of the original chromosome
↓
Enzymes are used to multiply the gene

Step 2: Insert the gene into a plasmid

Gene copies are mixed with plasmids
↓
Some of the plasmids open up and the gene is inserted into these plasmids
↓
Plasmids close up and can then be multiplied by more enzymes

Step 3: Insert the plasmid into the new cell

Plasmids inserted into bacterial or plant cell
↓
Gene is expressed when the modified cell develops

FIGURE 4: Using the process of recombinant DNA to transfer a gene.

> ### QUESTIONS
>
> **5** Interferon is a chemical, produced by human white blood cells, that kills many viruses. It is now produced by yeast cells that have been engineered to contain a gene for human interferon. Describe how the gene was transferred.
>
> **6** In the treatment of cystic fibrosis, it may be possible to spray the missing protein into a patient's nose, but this treatment does not last for ever. The genetic approach could give a permanent cure. Explain this difference.

Genetic testing

We are learning to:
> (Higher) understand how genetic testing works
> (Higher) understand the implications for society of this technology

Would you want to know?

In 2011 a survey of people's attitudes to testing for genetic illnesses looked at whether the tests would worry people – and if they would do anything to prevent the diseases happening. Of the people surveyed, 90% were not worried by the test results, even though they included information about the chance of getting very serious illnesses. Unfortunately, that meant that they also showed very little change in their lifestyle and diet.

FIGURE 1: These children are all the same age. Genetic testing could tell you about differences between them that may not appear for 40 years.

Genomic testing (Higher tier only)

Scientists use a technique called Fluorescence In Situ Hybridisation (FISH) to find particular genes in a person's cells. First, the researcher will prepare a length of DNA, called a **DNA probe**, that can bind to a particular gene. The probe can do this because the two strands of the DNA molecule are mirror images of each other – if you have one then only the matching opposite strand will be able to react with it. The probe is then 'labelled' with a chemical that glows in ultraviolet light.

The probe is mixed with a sample of DNA from the patient, usually collected from white blood cells. If the probe finds the matching gene it binds to it and, when it is exposed to UV light, glows. This glow tells the researcher that the gene is present.

The FISH technique is particularly useful for testing for the presence of genes we know make certain illnesses more likely. It is used particularly for testing before birth.

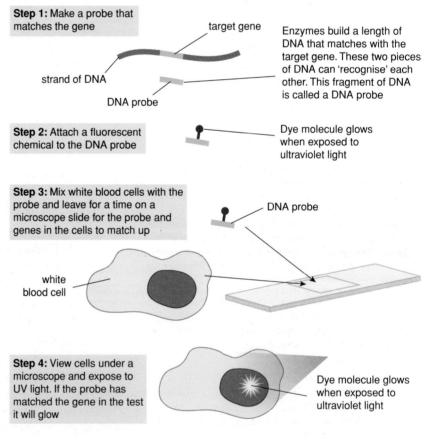

Step 1: Make a probe that matches the gene

target gene

strand of DNA

DNA probe

Enzymes build a length of DNA that matches with the target gene. These two pieces of DNA can 'recognise' each other. This fragment of DNA is called a DNA probe

Step 2: Attach a fluorescent chemical to the DNA probe

Dye molecule glows when exposed to ultraviolet light

Step 3: Mix white blood cells with the probe and leave for a time on a microscope slide for the probe and genes in the cells to match up

DNA probe

white blood cell

Step 4: View cells under a microscope and expose to UV light. If the probe has matched the gene in the test it will glow

Dye molecule glows when exposed to ultraviolet light

FIGURE 2: The FISH technique allows scientists to find genes that cause many genetic illnesses.

Q fluorescence in situ hybridisation   gene probes

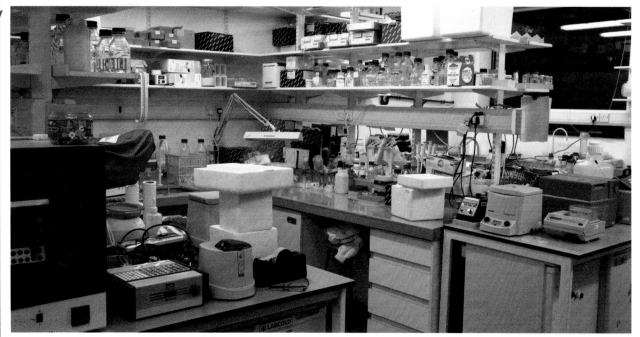

FIGURE 3: Work on DNA takes place in laboratories like this one below the Natural History Museum, in London.

Probability and chance

Is there a single gene for breast cancer? Or intelligence? Scientists have not found them yet. Most now believe that a combination of genes affects the likelihood of someone suffering from breast cancer. Intelligence is probably affected much more by the environment than by genes. These are very different from the inheritance of blue eyes in humans, which is controlled by a single gene and is much easier to track.

Ethical implications

Predicting possible illnesses creates some problems. If the tests are done before birth, should fetuses be aborted if they have an increased risk of contracting a disease in later life? And will fetuses be aborted because they have the 'wrong' eye colour? Will future fetuses have to pass a series of genetic tests before they are allowed to develop and be born? These are ethical issues that society has to face before gene-testing technology is adopted unquestioningly.

Even after birth, genetic tests could affect someone's life chances. Getting a job may be difficult if they had a gene that makes you more likely to suffer from an illness – or maybe even have the 'wrong' character traits.

In the future, will the rich and powerful be able to buy genetic superiority through gene transfer techniques? And if I have a gene that encourages musical talent do I own the rights to that gene? Can I sell my genes?

QUESTIONS

1 **a** Would you want to know if you were at an increased risk of a disease such as Alzheimer's or lung cancer? Give reasons for your answer.

b Do you think genetic testing should be voluntary or compulsory? Give reasons for your answer.

c If you know that you have an increased risk of a particular disease, should you be required to tell your doctor? Your employer? Or should you have the right to tell no one? Give reasons for your answer.

2 **a** What is a genetic probe?

b Explain why the probe can only bind to a particular area of DNA.

3 FISH is used to test for particular genes in unborn children. What things should a parent consider before asking for this test?

4 Explain why intelligence is not affected only by genes.

5 There are genes that increase the likelihood of developing breast cancer. Explain why this is not the same as saying that if you have a particular gene, or collection of genes, that you will suffer from breast cancer.

Nanotechnology

We are learning to:
> recognise the scale at which nanotechnology operates
> review the applications of nanotechnology

How small is small?

Imagine a machine that is as small as the tip of your finger. Imagine that it can make a copy of itself that is 100 times smaller. That copy can make a copy of itself that is 100 times smaller again. How many times could you do this before the machine was as small as an atom?

FIGURE 1: This tiny robot, called Mini-Alice, has been developed as part of research to develop artificial intelligence.

The scale of nanotechnology

The answer to the question above is six times.
Nanotechnology works at the scale of atoms and molecules. Materials at the nanoscale are usually between 0.1 and 100 **nanometres** (nm) in size. One nanometre (1 nm) is one billionth of a metre (10^{-9} m). Most atoms are 0.1 to 0.2 nm wide, strands of DNA are about 2 nm wide, red blood cells are around 7000 nm in diameter, while human hairs are typically 80 000 nm across.

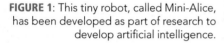
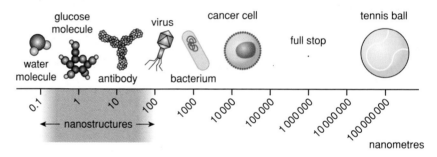

FIGURE 2: The relative size of nanostructures.

Did you know?

Your fingernails grow by about a nanometre every second.

QUESTION

1 a How many nanometres are there in a metre?

   b How many nanometres are there in the point at the base of the question mark at the end of this question?

   c A laboratory model of a glucose molecule measures about 10 cm across. How much bigger is it than the actual molecule?

Nanotechnology and food

In the UK, huge quantities of food are wasted every day because it has gone bad. Across the whole world, nearly 20% of food is wasted in this way. Most of the wastage is caused by the reaction between foodstuffs and oxygen in the air. You can see this reaction very quickly as the cut surface of an apple goes brown. Food packaging often lets oxygen seep through it, but new packaging with nanoparticles makes this much more difficult (Figure 3). It also reduces the rate at which water can pass through it the other way. This protects the food from spoiling for much longer, increasing its shelf life.

 nanoparticles   nanotechnology   nanometre

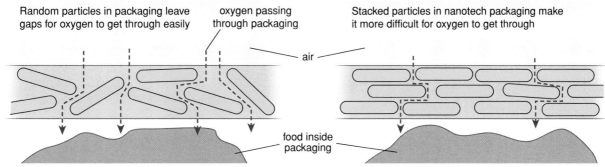

Random particles in packaging leave gaps for oxygen to get through easily

oxygen passing through packaging

Stacked particles in nanotech packaging make it more difficult for oxygen to get through

air

food inside packaging

FIGURE 3: Packaging containing nanoparticles reduces passage of oxygen to the inside.

Some food packaging now includes nanoparticles that change if the packaging is damaged or the temperature rises above a certain level. The colour of the packaging alters, to warn people that the food is not safe to eat. Some nanoparticles can even detect contaminants in the food and change colour if they are present.

QUESTION

2 a Explain how regularly ordered nanoparticles can reduce the speed at which oxygen can pass through a food wrapper.

b How does the reduction in oxygen permeability help to prevent the wrapped food going off?

c Give two factors that affect the rate that oxygen passes through food wrap.

FIGURE 4: This intelligent packaging contains nanoparticles which will cause it to change colour when the food has been exposed to damaging levels of oxygen.

Nanotechnology and medicine

Sticking plasters are now available with silver nanoparticles embedded in them. These particles have an antibacterial property to help stop the wound going septic.

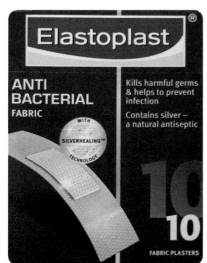

FIGURE 5: These sticking plasters incorporate nanoparticles of silver.

There are even more amazing uses of nanoparticles in medicine. Medical researchers in Rice University in Houston, USA, have used tiny, gold-plated nanobullets to seek out and destroy cancer cells. The scientists attach the particles to antibodies that only bind to cancer cells. When infrared light is passed into the body the gold particles heat up and kill the cells to which they are bound.

An American company called Nanobiotix uses similar technology. It embeds, in a special coating, a compound that reacts to X-rays by giving out electrons. This coating allows the compound to enter tumour cells. When the particles have collected in tumour cells, a small dose of X-rays produces a large supply of electrons. These electrons kill the cancer cells. Because the particles do not enter healthy cells, these cells are not damaged by the X-rays.

QUESTIONS

3 What kills the tumour cells in:

a the Rice University experiment

b the Nanobiotix technique?

4 What is the advantage of using nanoparticles and radiation as opposed to just radiation in the Nanobiotix treatment?

Q nanoparticles   nanotechnology   nanomaterials

Future medicine

Hoping for a new body?

In California, people known as cryonicists are paid a lot of money to preserve dead bodies in deep freezers. The 'patients' hope that, in the future, scientists will be able to bring them back to life. Sometimes only the head is preserved because this is cheaper. How close are we to being able to build new bodies for these people, should their brains ever be brought back to life?

FIGURE 1: Cryonicists from TransTime Inc., California.

We are learning to:

> recognise the difficulties of developing artificial body parts

> understand the importance of stem cells for medicine

> understand that stem-cell research is governed by legal frameworks and government bodies

Rebuilding the heart

The heart is an essential organ. Anything that interferes with its proper functioning can have very serious implications. For example, the valves in the heart can be damaged by disease and they do not tend to heal well. Rejection is the normal immune reaction to foreign tissues or parts in the body. If the transplanted part is rejected the body will damage it. However, surgeons can now replace a damaged heart valve with an artificial one. This can be made of metal or a type of plastic that blood does not stick to. Some surgeons prefer biological valves derived from pigs that have been specially bred to reduce the problem of rejection of the valve.

Pacemakers are devices that tell the heart when to beat. Human hearts should beat steadily but sometimes damage to the muscles and nerves of the heart wall can result in irregular beats. A pacemaker is sensitive to heart movement. If it does not detect a contraction within a certain time, will give the heart a small shock to make it contract.

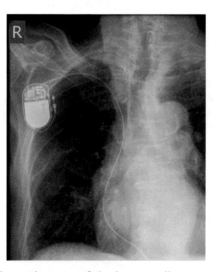

FIGURE 2: Surgeons can fit an artificial pacemaker just inside the chest.

QUESTIONS

1 Why is it important that blood does not stick to the surface of an artificial heart valve?

2 Pacemakers only give the heart a signal when they cannot detect a normal beat. Why not provide a constant series of signals?

Using stem cells

Making an artificial body part is not easy. In some instances it may be impossible. Would it be possible to grow a new, biological replacement? Some researchers think **stem cells** may be able to do exactly this.

Stem cells are undifferentiated (unspecialised) cells that can:

> reproduce themselves to give identical undifferentiated cells

> differentiate into any sort of cell when required to do so.

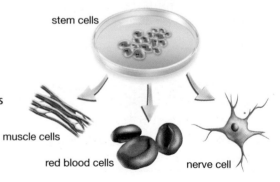

FIGURE 3: Stem cells can be induced to differentiate by giving them a biochemical 'signal'.

Q stem cell   replacement body parts

Stem cells injected into a damaged organ may be able replace dead tissues by developing into the cells that make up those tissues. There are four main sources and types of stem cell, as shown in the table.

Controlling research

Stem-cell research is tightly controlled by governments around the world. Researchers must get permission to harvest these cells and to use them in experiments. Different countries have different rules but all seek to license research that would provide the greatest benefits for the largest possible number of people. Sometimes the decisions taken are controversial. For example, some people believe that it is wrong ever to use cells from a human embryo, on religious grounds. Others believe that the potential cures that may come from this research are more important than other arguments. These disputes cannot be resolved by scientific argument alone.

Sources of stem cells.

Source	Type of stem cell	Notes
Cells from very young embryos (4 to 5 days old)	Embryonic stem cells	The embryo must be killed to extract the cells
Organs from a fetus	Fetal cells	These can be extracted from a fetus that has been aborted
Children and adults, often from the blood of the umbilical cord	Adult or 'somatic' stem cells	Available from many sites in the body, have been used to treat leukaemia
Amniotic fluid (the fluid that surrounds the growing fetus)	Amniotic stem cells	The fetus does not die when the cells are harvested so people are much less likely to object to this technique on religious or ethical grounds

QUESTIONS

3 What are the two characteristics of stem cells?

4 Explain why most of the work with stem cells has been done with adult stem cells over the last few years.

5 a What is amniotic fluid and where is it found?

b What is the main advantage of amniotic stem cells compared with embryonic stem cells?

What can stem cells be used for?

Since stem cells can differentiate into other types of cell, they have the potential to provide cures for many illnesses. For example, **leukaemia** is a disease of the bone marrow in which huge numbers of white cells are produced but not enough red blood cells. This means the blood cannot transport enough oxygen around the body. The first step in treating leukaemia is to use powerful drugs and radiation to kill the diseased bone marrow. Stem cells are then squirted into the bone marrow space and these develop into healthy bone marrow that can produce normal blood.

Stem cells are also being considered as a possible way to repair nerve tissue. Nerve cells do not usually repair themselves so a break in the spinal cord will be permanent. The first human trial of stem cells for patients with nerve damage was approved in 2009.

QUESTIONS

6 Why are stem cells so useful to doctors?

7 What are the key stages in treatment of leukaemia by stem cells?

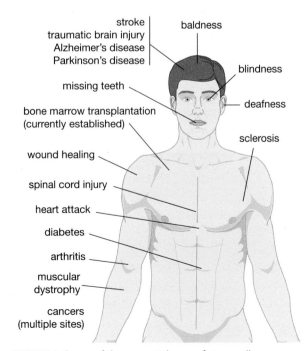

FIGURE 4: Some of the potential uses of stem cells.

B7 Checklist

To achieve your forecast grade in the exam you'll need to revise

To achieve your forecast grade in the exam you'll need to revise.

Use this checklist to see what you can do now. Refer back to pages 10–55 if you're not sure. Look across the rows to see how you could progress – **_bold italic_** means Higher tier only.

Remember you'll need to be able to use these ideas in various ways, such as:

> interpreting pictures, diagrams and graphs

> applying ideas to new situations

> explaining ethical implications

> suggesting some benefits and risks to society

> drawing conclusions from evidence you've been given.

Look at pages 206–212 for more information about exams and how you'll be assessed.

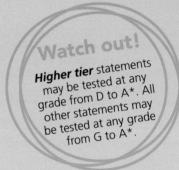

Watch out!

Higher tier statements may be tested at any grade from D to A*. All other statements may be tested at any grade from G to A*.

To aim for a grade E

To aim for a grade C

To aim for a grade A

understand that movement depends on bones and muscles working together

explain how joints are arranged to allow them the right degree of movement but still keep the bones attached to each other

explain how the properties of different tissues at a joint make them suitable for their function

understand that factors such as diet, smoking, drinking alcohol and amount of exercise taken can affect the chances of becoming ill

calculate body mass index (BMI); understand the use of BMI, along with other factors, in the assessment of physical fitness

suggest changes in lifestyle to improve health and ways to measure the improvement; explain how natural variation in experimental subjects has to be allowed for in such measurements

list the main components of blood; state what each of the main components of blood does; explain how red blood cells are adapted to carry oxygen around the body

describe how tissue fluid is formed; describe how tissue fluid helps to move carbon dioxide, oxygen, foods and wastes between the body cells and the blood

list the factors that will:
- increase body temperature when it is too low
- decrease it when it is too high

explain why it is important to the body that core body temperature does not vary too much; describe in detail the mechanisms used to control heat loss and gain by the body

understand that too much sugar in the diet is unhealthy; explain how high sugar levels in food and obesity in the population is linked to a rise in occurrence of type 2 diabetes

explain how the hormone insulin controls blood sugar levels; explain how injections of insulin are needed by some people with diabetes to control their blood sugar levels

appreciate the importance of closed loops in nature; distinguish between a closed loop system and an open loop system, give examples of closed loops in nature; explain how closed loops help to sustain the living world

understand that closed loops always involve some leakage; understand that all ecosystem loops eventually link up to form the biosphere; appreciate the significance of energy from sunlight energy in driving these closed loops

appreciate the potential threats of human activity to the environment; give examples of ways in which humans have damaged the environment; explain in those examples the damage occurred

understand the processes of bioaccumulation and eutrophication; use these as examples of long-term damage to ecosystems by humans

give examples of products of the natural world required by humans to survive, e.g. food, timber for fuel and building, certain plants for medicines, etc.; explain how the extraction of materials from the natural world can be managed to ensure long-term sustainability for human society

explain that different people will have different perspectives on the changes needed to make human society sustainable

To aim for a grade E

recall that bacteria and single-celled fungi are often used in the manufacture of useful chemicals

To aim for a grade C

explain why bacteria and fungi are used, rather than more traditional laboratory techniques, to produce some complex chemicals

To aim for a grade A

understand how genetic modification can make bacteria and single-celled fungi much more useful

understand that genetic testing can detect genes that might cause diseases; understand that scientific research is often controlled by government rules, especially in the field of human genetic modification

explain how genetic testing is carried out and appreciate some of the social and ethical issues surrounding its use

Watch out!

Higher tier statements may be tested at any grade from D to A*. All other statements may be tested at any grade from G to A*.

Exam-style questions

Foundation

AO1 1 The following statements are about muscles. Choose the correct term for each sentence.

a Muscles are joined to bones by *tendons / ligaments / cartilage*. [1]

b Muscle needs a *high / medium / low* blood supply during strenuous exercise. [1]

c Antagonistic muscles contract *in opposite directions to each other / in the same direction as each other / in both directions*. [1]

[Total 3]

2 A university has developed a new type of plastic. The body tolerates this plastic very well so researchers are looking at ways of using it to build replacement parts for damaged organs in the body. The plastic comes in different forms with different properties, as shown below.

Property	Plastic A	Plastic B	Plastic C	Plastic D
How flexible is it?	*****	****	*	*****
How easily does it stretch?	***	***	*	*
How strong is it?	***	***	****	****
What is its natural colour?	black	grey	grey	grey

Key: * indicates the plastic does not exhibit a property and ***** indicates it strongly exhibits a property

AO3 a Choose the best formulation for each of the jobs listed below. Give a reason for your choice in each case.
i   artificial tendon
ii artificial ligament
iii artificial bone [3]

AO1 b Which of the properties listed above is of no importance when making your choices? [1]

[Total 4]

AO2 3 The Fosse Memorial Health Clinic offers a series of 'health MOTs' for local residents. People can turn up at the centre, then the medical staff will ask them questions and perform tests to assess their health. The list gives some of the data collected. For each piece of data (a–e), explain why it is useful to a doctor giving advice to a local resident.

a BMI [1]
b Body fat percentage [1]
c Age [1]
d Number of cigarettes smoked per day [1]
e Number of units of alcohol drunk per week [1]

[Total 5]

4 Read this extract and answer the questions.

Is our Hyperfabric™ really a miracle? Or just heavenly to wear? Some of our customers find it almost impossible to believe! Our new Hyperfabric™ jacket keeps out the worst that the weather can throw at you but lets water out and keeps you dry and cool. This can make all the difference on long walks. The magic depends on three layers – an inner soft fleece, a thin layer of a fabric containing nanoparticles bonded to the outside with a tougher water-porous polymer fabric on the outside. The nanoparticle fabric lets water pass one way – but not the other. And the miracle jacket comes in so many colours you'll be sure to find one that matches your devilish good looks!

AO1 a What does the word 'nanoparticles' mean? [1]

AO2 b Why might a completely waterproof jacket make you feel wet on long walks over the mountains, even if it was not raining? [2]

AO2 c How does the jacket help to keep you cool? [2]

AO1 d Hillwalkers can get quite hot when hurrying to their campsite, even on a cool autumn day. What produces this heat? [1]

AO1 e Give two ways the body tries to get rid of this excess heat. You're not allowed just to take your jacket off! [2]

[Total 8]

AO1 5 My friend has diabetes and always carries two things with him: a small medal around his neck, which tells people he is diabetic and gives some important medical details about him, and an ordinary sachet of sugar from a coffee bar. His diabetes is usually well controlled but he has had a few scares when he passed out.

a What is likely to make a person with diabetes pass out? [1]
b Why would the sachet of sugar help prevent a person with diabetes from passing out? [1]
c When do you think the medal would be particularly useful? [1]

[Total 3]

AO1 recall the science AO2 apply your knowledge AO3 evaluate and analyse the evidence

Worked example

Foundation

Parkinson's disease affects about 120 000 people in the UK. It over-stimulates certain areas of the brain, leading to strain on the cells. This kills the cells, leading to difficulty in moving. Researchers know about an enzyme called GAD, which is able to calm down the overactive cells and give damaged cells time to recover.

Some researchers have identified the gene for GAD and placed it in a specially modified virus. To see if the gene would help with the treatment, they selected 45 patients with Parkinson's disease. Their movement skills were noted. 22 of the group were operated on and the virus was passed into their brains. The other 23 were operated on but were not given any virus. Neither the patients nor the surgeons knew who was in which group.

After six months the group who had received the gene had a 23% improvement in the score for their movement control.

AO2 **a** i What vector was used in the research above? [1]

   The virus particle ✔

   ii Why is a vector needed? [1]

   To get the gene into the cells. ✔

AO1

AO2 **b** What is a placebo and how was it used in the study above? [3]

A placebo is a dummy treatment in a drug trial. It contains none of the important drug under test ✔ *and provides a way to check that it is the drug and not the treatment process that is important in any cure.*

AO2 **c** The surgeons could have just injected the enzyme directly into the bloodstream. Why did they not do this? [2]

The body's defence mechanisms would react to the foreign protein ✔ *and, even if the enzyme was tolerated, it would run out after a while.* ✔

How to raise your grade

Take note of the comments from examiners – these will help you to improve your grade.

> Correct answers.

> This is a reasonable description of what a placebo is and gains 1 mark, but it would be better to use scientific terms, such as 'control', rather than everyday language such as 'dummy treatment'. The answer does not explain how the placebo was used in the investigation. For the second mark, a sentence is needed stating that the surgery alone, rather than surgery plus the use of the virus, should have no effect on the patient. For the third mark the point should be made that neither the patients nor the doctors doing the surgery knew whether they were in the active or control group. This is to prevent any effects occurring because they believe – or don't believe – they will occur. Always check that you have answered every part of a question.

> A good answer, showing the student drawing ideas from beyond the immediate module.

Higher

6

The Tibetan Plateau collects rain and snow and then channels it to rivers such as the Yellow and Yangtze in China, the Tsangpo in Bangladesh and the Mekong in Vietnam. In 1959 there were 25.2 million hectares of forest in Tibet. By 1985 this had dropped to 13.57 million hectares. In 1998, China suffered its worst ever flood on the Yangtze, affecting 223 million people. Floods have also become much more common in Bangladesh.

AO2 a What is the percentage fall, to one decimal place, in forest cover from 1959 to 1985? [2]

AO2 b Explain how the fall in forest cover would make flooding more likely. [2]

AO2 c The lack of tree cover means less waste wood is available for fuel. More and more yak manure is being dried and used as fuel for stoves and heaters (it burns slowly and gives off a lot of smoke). Farmers used to spread the manure on their fields. Describe how the change in the use of yak manure will affect the ecosystem. [3]

[Total 7]

7

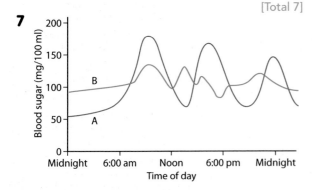

AO3 a Which colour curve on the graph above shows blood sugar for a patient with diabetes who is not currently receiving treatment? Give a reason for your answer. [2]

AO2 b The other curve shows blood sugar for a person without diabetes. When did he/she eat:
i breakfast   ii lunch   iii dinner? [3]

AO3 c One trace shows a slight rise in blood sugar at about 3.30 in the afternoon. What might have caused this? [1]

AO3 d The person shown by the green line played tennis for an hour at some point during the day. When do you think the match started? Give a reason for your answer. [1]

AO1 e How would an injection of insulin affect the level of blood sugar? [1]

[Total 8]

AO2
AO3 8 The data below is from a salmon farm in Scotland.

Fish per tank	Growth rate (g per fish per day)
250	0.032
500	0.026
750	0.020
1000	0.014
1500	0.008

People are divided on the idea that fish farms are sustainable. Give arguments on both sides of this debate and state if you think, on balance, fish farms are sustainable. Use the data in the table to support your answer.

The quality of written communication will be assessed in your answer. [6]

[Total 6]

9

AO1 a Give three reasons why red blood cells are good at carrying oxygen around the body. [3]

AO2 b i Leukaemia is a cancer of the bone marrow where the ratio of white blood to red blood cells increases massively. One of the symptoms of leukaemia is feeling very tired. How can you explain this? [1]
ii Leukaemia-sufferers are likely to get infections. What does this tell you about the massive number of white cells they are producing? [1]

AO2 c Some faulty gas fires do not get enough oxygen to burn the gas completely to carbon dioxide and water vapour. They produce small amounts of carbon monoxide as well. Carbon monoxide reacts with haemoglobin to make a chemical called carboxyhaemoglobin. This is very stable and does not break down to haemoglobin. Explain why this can kill someone, even if there is plenty of oxygen in the room where they are sitting in front of the gas fire. [1]

[Total 6]

AO1 recall the science   AO2 apply your knowledge   AO3 evaluate and analyse the evidence

Worked Example

Higher

The graphs show the conditions downstream from a sewage outflow. Normally the sewage is treated before being released but during a recent storm the storage tanks overflowed and raw sewage was passed into the river.

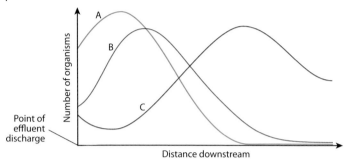

AO2

AO3 **a** Match the graph traces to the organisms, as described below. Give reasons for your choices. [3]

Organism	Curve	Reason
Sewage fungus: digests raw sewage	A	The fungus will grow most rapidly near to the sewage outfall. As the sewage is reduced the food supply falls and the fungal mass drops. ✔
Bloodworms: can survive in low-oxygen environments	B	These will thrive in the low-oxygen conditions as the sewage fungus starts to use up oxygen to digest the sewage. This will be slightly further away from the sewage outfall than the sewage fungus peak. ✔
Green algae: photosynthetic organisms	C	

A reservoir suffers from a sudden growth of algae. The growth is so rapid that the water looks like a thick green soup and users are warned to stay out of the water as the algae may be poisonous. The water board officials believe that the increased algal growth is caused by runoff of water from the surrounding fields which the farmer has recently fertilised.

AO2 **b** Explain why the water board officials think the sudden growth in algae might be connected to the fertiliser on the fields. [1]

Fertiliser helps plants to grow and algae are plants.

AO2 **c** A river that runs through the same area does not show this sudden growth of algae. Suggest a reason why this is so, giving a justification for your suggestion. [2]

The river brings a constant supply of clean water into the area and carries away the mineral nutrients downstream. ✔

How to raise your grade

Take note of the comments from examiners – these will help you to improve your grade.

2 marks out of 3. Clear justifications have been given for some of the choices. When asked to justify choices or explain answers, give as many reasons as possible from the data provided. The lack of a reason for the third section may be that the student ran out of time or did not know the reason but put the answer down because it was the only choice left. This is a good idea – it may be worth a mark. What is required here is that the green algae grew because of the rich supply of minerals available from the breakdown of the sewage.

This statement is correct but does not merit a mark, because it does not explain how the fertiliser on the fields produced the growth in algae. The answer needs to show how these are connected, with a sentence like 'Water picks up mineral nutrients from the fertiliser as it passes through the fields to the reservoir.'

This answer is good but not complete; 1 mark only. It's necessary to include the idea that the reservoir is a much more stable body of water with less chance for the minerals to leave the ecosystem. If you are comparing two situations you will not get full marks if you refer to only one in your answer.

C7 Further chemistry

What you should already know...

The chemical industry produces a wide variety of products

The synthesis of chemicals, such as fertilisers, involves choosing the reactants and the conditions for the reaction, estimating the risks, calculating the quantities, separating and purifying the product and calculating the yield.

 How can the choice of reactants affect the yield?

Chemical reactions involve energy changes

Reactions may be exothermic or endothermic. The energy changes can be shown by an energy diagram.

Catalysts do not change a reaction or the amount of energy involved but they speed up reactions.

 The decomposition of hydrogen peroxide is exothermic and is catalysed by manganese dioxide. Draw an energy diagram for the reaction.

Hydrocarbons are compounds with chains of carbon atoms

The simplest hydrocarbon is methane, CH_4. Other hydrocarbons have carbon atoms joined together by covalent bonds. Carbon can form covalent bonds with hydrogen, oxygen and atoms of other elements.

Hydrocarbons burn to form carbon dioxide and water. Crude oil is a vital but non-renewable source of hydrocarbons.

 What properties depend on the number of carbon atoms joined together in a hydrocarbon?

Analysis provides important information about substances

We can use chemical tests or flame colours to identify the elements present in a substance. These are examples of qualitative analysis.

We can use the technique of titration to measure how much of a reactant is needed to react with another reactant.

 How can you find how much hydrochloric acid is needed to neutralise sodium hydroxide?

In C7 you will find out about...

> the difference between 'fine' and 'bulk' chemicals

> jobs in the chemical industry and regulations that prevent damage to the environment

> how scientists are looking at ways of producing chemicals more sustainably, for example using a sustainable feedstock

> the energy needed to start off a reaction

> the energy changes when bonds are broken and formed

> the effect of catalysts on the energy changes in a reaction

> the use of enzymes as catalysts

> the family of hydrocarbons called the alkanes

> the uses and properties of alcohols, particularly as fuels

> how ethanol is produced by fermentation of sugars using yeast

> the family of weak acids called carboxylic acids

> the reaction between alcohols and carboxylic acids to form esters

> the properties and uses of esters, for example, in fruit flavours

> how to make an ester in the laboratory

> reactions that are reversible and how some reactions reach an equilibrium

> how ammonia is manufactured by the Haber process, mainly for making fertilisers

> the choice of conditions in the Haber process

> other ways of making fertilisers that are more sustainable

> methods of handling samples for quantitative analysis

> the use of paper and thin layer chromatography in analysis

> the use of gas chromatography to analyse mixtures

> how to ensure quantitative analysis gives accurate and repeatable results

> how titration can be used to find the concentration of an acid or alkali

The chemical industry

What does the chemical industry do for us?

Lime (calcium oxide) has many uses, including to neutralise acid soils, to make mortar for building and whitewash for painting walls. It was once made in small stone lime kilns but now is made in huge rotary burners. There are thousands of other chemicals that we use which have to be manufactured.

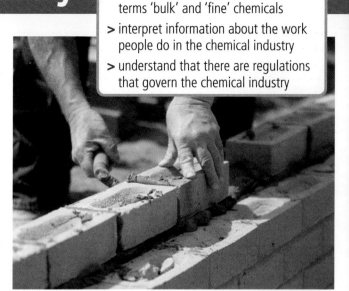

FIGURE 1: Lime for mortar needs to be manufactured using limestone.

Large and small

Some chemicals are produced in very large quantities. These are called **bulk chemicals** and include sulfuric acid, ammonia, sodium hydroxide and phosphoric acid. They are used in the manufacture of other products. For example, sodium carbonate is used to make glass.

Other substances are produced in much smaller quantities and are called **fine chemicals**. Fine chemicals include drugs, fragrances, and the flavourings, preservatives and additives used in food production. These substances are produced in amounts ranging from a few kilograms to a few tonnes. For example, ethyl vanillin is an artificial flavouring that is used instead of natural vanilla. A vanilla ice cream may contain several milligrams of ethyl vanillin.

FIGURE 2: A large chemical factory can produce millions of tonnes of bulk chemicals a year.

FIGURE 3: A worker supervises the production of a fine chemical.

QUESTIONS

1 Name a bulk chemical and a fine chemical.

2 Look at the pictures of chemical factories in Figures 2 and 3. What differences are there in the manufacture of bulk and fine chemicals?

Nice work

The chemical industry employs people with a wide variety of skills and qualifications. A typical large company will have people who:

A Supervise the processes, making sure the conditions are correct and that the product is being produced at a suitable rate and level of purity

B Make sure that the raw materials are supplied in sufficient quantity and quality

C Maintain the equipment

D Test the raw materials and products in laboratories

E Develop improvements to the process equipment

F Research and develop new products, or new uses for old products

G Look after the safety of workers, the public and protect the environment

H Market and sell the products

I Manage the company and the finances

J Recruit workers and look after employees

K Maintain the IT systems.

FIGURE 4: A researcher tests the smell of a perfume being developed by a cosmetics company.

QUESTIONS

3 Look at the list of what jobs people do in the chemical industry. Which jobs would need a knowledge of chemistry?

4 What skills do you think are needed by a researcher of perfumes for the cosmetics industry?

It's the law

There are laws and regulations which determine how a chemical factory is run. They cover the materials used, how they are transported, stored and used, the disposing of waste, the safety of employees and the people who live nearby, and the protection of the environment. Regulations vary between countries. In the UK, the Health & Safety Executive (HSE) monitors safety issues in the chemical industry. REACH is a European agreement on safety with chemicals. There are international rules about releasing pollutants such as carbon dioxide.

A lot of research is done to develop a new product or a new process, such as using a catalyst to produce a substance more cheaply. The research programme must take account of the laws regarding safety and environmental protection as well as the benefits of the product.

Watch out!

Manufactured chemicals may have important benefits, but the costs to the environment have to be considered as well.

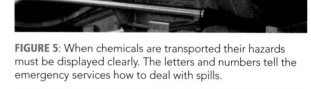

FIGURE 5: When chemicals are transported their hazards must be displayed clearly. The letters and numbers tell the emergency services how to deal with spills.

QUESTIONS

5 Why is it important to have international laws on the transport of chemicals?

6 Gold nanoparticles are suggested as the catalyst for new processes. What do researchers need to consider as they develop a new process?

Did you know?

Some of the most expensive chemicals are drugs. Soliris, a drug for a very rare blood disease, costs almost £1000 per daily dose. The costs are high because a lot of research has to be done before a drug can be used.

chemical industry careers   environmental health and safety

Green chemistry

Can the chemical industry be 'green'?

Visiting a fertiliser factory in the 1980s you would have noticed brown smoke emerging from chimneys. This smoke contributed to acid rain and it also meant the factory was wasting valuable resources. Today, no smoke can be seen leaving the chimneys of a fertiliser factory, showing that the process has become more efficient and sustainable.

FIGURE 1: A modern fertiliser factory in Cheshire, England. There is no smoke, only steam.

Making chemicals

Sulfuric acid is made by reacting sulfur with oxygen and adding water. There are five stages in manufacturing a chemical such as sulfuric acid. They are:

1 Getting and preparing the materials, called the **feedstock**, needed for the process.

2 Reacting the raw materials to make products. This is called **synthesis**.

3 Separating the useful products.

4 Dealing with unwanted **by-products** and wastes.

5 Checking the purity of the product.

Materials are used up in every chemical process. Most of the stages use energy. Some stages may release pollutants into the environment unless this is prevented. Chemical processes can have unexpected effects, for example, salt mining in Cheshire caused buildings in towns to collapse.

QUESTIONS

1 What is the feedstock in the manufacture of sulfuric acid?

2 Draw a flowchart for the stages in the manufacture of sulfuric acid.

FIGURE 2: Recycled waste is the raw material used for new products.

FIGURE 3: Materials from plants offer a renewable feedstock for the chemical industry (such as oil from sunflower seeds).

Sustainability

To be **sustainable** a chemical process should be able to continue without damage to the environment and without using up resources that cannot be replaced. To help bring this about there are various questions to consider:

> Is the feedstock renewable? Is it using recycled materials or materials produced by living organisms from simple, renewable sources?

> What happens to the by-products and waste materials? Can they be recycled in other processes?

> How much energy is needed and released? Is renewable energy used? Is the energy given out by reactions used elsewhere?

> What is the environmental impact of the process? How can it be reduced?

> Are there health and safety issues? What can be done to reduce risk?

> Are there social or economic benefits to the process? Do the products help people's lives?

Watch out!

Pollution and environmental damage are not intended effects of chemical processes but they must be dealt with for a process to be sustainable.

FIGURE 4: Mining sulfur from an active volcano is a dangerous and unhealthy job.

Did you know?

If everyone on Earth had the same standard of living as those of us living in developed countries, and were as wasteful as us, then we would need about three planet Earths in order to provide all the resources needed.

QUESTIONS

3 Sulfur is found near volcanoes and in underground deposits. Explain whether using sulfur from these sources is a sustainable process.

4 Why is using waste products from a process an important part of sustainability?

Atom economy

An important factor in making a process more sustainable is the **atom economy** of the chemical reaction. The atom economy is the percentage of the mass of atoms in the feedstock that end up in the useful product.

In an old process for making sulfur trioxide, sulfur was reacted with potassium nitrate.

$$6KNO_3(s) + 7S(s) \rightarrow 3K_2S(s) + 6NO(g) + 4SO_3(g)$$

The sulfur trioxide was dissolved in water to make sulfuric acid. However, this process has poor atom economy because a lot of the atoms are wasted in making the potassium sulfide (K_2S) and nitrogen oxide (NO).

In the modern process, sulfur is reacted with oxygen to make sulfur trioxide.

$$2S(s) + 3O_2(g) \rightarrow 2SO_3(g)$$

Here the atom economy is 100%. This is because there are no by-products and nothing is wasted. All the atoms end up in the sulfur trioxide.

QUESTIONS

5 Why is improving the atom economy of a process an important factor in making it more sustainable?

6 To make magnesium sulfate you could react magnesium or magnesium carbonate with sulfuric acid. Which would have the better atom economy? Explain your answer.

Energy changes

We are learning to:

> understand and use the terms exothermic and endothermic in energy diagrams

> understand that energy is needed to break bonds and is given out when bonds form

> understand that activation energy is needed to make a reaction take place

Why do explosives need a detonator?

A lighted splint 'pops' hydrogen in a test tube and the same reaction blasted the Space Shuttle into orbit. However, a mixture of hydrogen and oxygen can safely be kept in a balloon because the reaction needs a flame to start it off. Without a flame the reaction is prevented from starting.

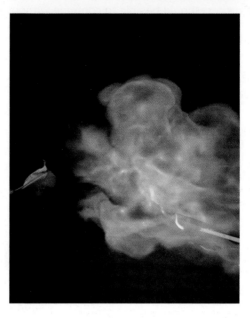

FIGURE 1: This fire ball was created when a lighted candle (bottom right) was applied to a balloon filled with hydrogen. The remains of the balloon are visible on the left of the photograph.

Energy out, energy in

We can investigate energy changes in chemical reactions by measuring temperature changes. An **exothermic** reaction gives out heat to its surroundings. The temperature rises. The heat is energy lost by the reactants. This can be shown in an **energy level diagram.** Burning the gas in a Bunsen burner is an exothermic reaction.

In an **endothermic** reaction the products have more energy than the reactants. They get this extra energy by taking heat from the surroundings. The temperature of its surroundings falls. The fizzing reaction of an Alka-Seltzer tablet in water is an endothermic reaction.

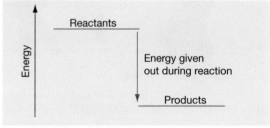

FIGURE 2: An energy level diagram for an exothermic reaction.

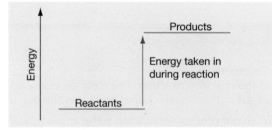

FIGURE 3: An energy level diagram for an endothermic reaction.

QUESTIONS

1 When magnesium reacts with hydrochloric acid in a test tube it feels warm. Is the reaction exothermic or endothermic?

2 When baking powder is mixed with water the temperature drops. Sketch an energy level diagram for this reaction.

Making and breaking bonds

We can measure energy changes in reactions and use our imagination to develop explanations of what is happening. Bonds between atoms change during reactions. Breaking bonds is an endothermic process. Energy is used to pull the atoms apart. When new bonds form the atoms are pulled together like a stretched spring contracting. Energy is released, so making bonds is an exothermic process.

energy level diagrams   exothermic   endothermic

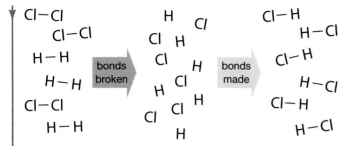

FIGURE 4: Bonds are broken and made when hydrogen reacts with chlorine.

The bonds in reactants have to be broken first before new bonds can be formed in products. This means that there is an endothermic stage at the start of all reactions. The energy that is put in at the start of the reaction is called the **activation energy.** We can show this in an extended energy level diagram.

Did you know?

The breaking and making of particular bonds in molecules can be followed using molecular beams. Individual molecules can be fired at each other and the results of the collision collected to find how much energy was involved in the change.

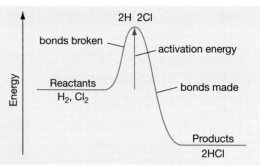

FIGURE 5: An extended energy level diagram showing activation energy.

QUESTION

3 Hydrogen molecules react with oxygen molecules to form water in an exothermic reaction.

a What bonds are broken and made during the reaction?

b Sketch an energy level diagram for the reaction showing the activation energy.

The energy barrier

If activation energy was not needed, hydrogen would explode in oxygen as soon as the gases were mixed together. This doesn't happen. Even in highly exothermic, explosive reactions, some energy is needed to start the reaction off. A spark will provide enough energy to break the bonds in a few reactant molecules. These can then react and release energy which breaks the bonds in more reactant molecules, and so on. Very quickly many molecules are reacting at the same time. The energy available at room temperature is enough to start some reactions off.

Some exothermic reactions require a very large activation energy to start them off and so the reaction does not take place under normal conditions.

Watch out!

Remember that breaking bonds is endothermic, making bonds is exothermic.

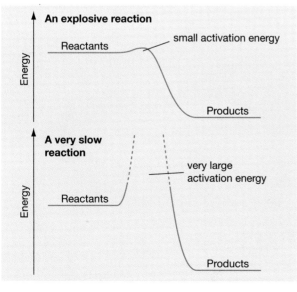

QUESTIONS

4 In the industrial process to make sulfuric acid, the reaction between sulfur dioxide and oxygen to form sulfur trioxide is exothermic but hardly any reaction takes place if the gases are just mixed together. What does this tell you about the reaction? Sketch an energy level diagram to illustrate your answer.

5 Magnesium will start to fizz as soon as it is put in hydrochloric acid at room temperature and quickly gets warm. Sketch an energy level diagram to show what happens.

FIGURE 6: The size of the activation energy can determine whether a reaction is fast or slow.

Catalysts and enzymes

How can catalysts help a murderer?

In a murder mystery by science-fiction writer Isaac Asimov, a speck of platinum oxide was used as the trigger of a murder weapon. The victim had taken great care to ensure that there was no spark to set off a hydrogen/oxygen explosion, but the platinum oxide catalysed the reaction. Usually catalysts are used for more beneficial purposes.

FIGURE 1: What brought the house down?

Catalysts good, enzymes better

Catalysts are used to speed up reactions in the chemical industry. They make some reactions possible that would otherwise be too expensive. Examples of industrial catalysts are:

> iron in the Haber process for making ammonia

> nickel for making margarine from vegetable oils

> vanadium oxide in the Contact process for making sulfuric acid.

In these processes the catalyst must be heated up in order to work well.

Enzymes also make certain reactions go faster. They are protein molecules found in cells. We have used the enzymes in yeast cells for making bread rise and brewing alcoholic drinks for a long time. Now the chemical industry is using enzymes as catalysts. For example, enzymes are used to change cheap corn starch into sugars for foods.

Watch out!

Enzymes are catalysts, but they work only under certain conditions because of their complex structure.

QUESTIONS

1 Why are catalysts useful to the chemical industry?

2 Give examples of an industrial process that uses:

a a catalyst containing metal

b an enzyme found in living cells.

FIGURE 2: Bread making uses the enzymes in yeast to turn sugars into carbon dioxide gas.

Q enzyme uses

What do catalysts do?

Catalysts and enzymes speed up chemical reactions. They do this by providing an alternative route for a reaction. Instead of having to react with each other the reactants first react with the catalyst. This reaction has a lower activation energy than the route without the catalyst. Less energy is needed to start the reaction and more of the reacting particles can react. For many reactions one particular substance is a better catalyst than others. This is especially true of enzymes. In living cells each enzyme has its own particular reaction which it makes happen.

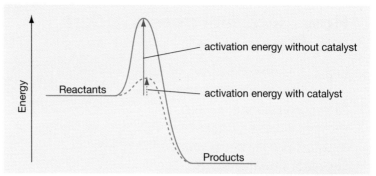

FIGURE 3: An energy level diagram for a reaction with and without a catalyst.

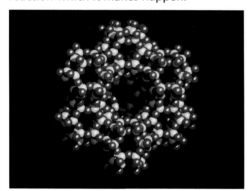

FIGURE 4: Zeolites are naturally occurring minerals that act as catalysts. Reactant molecules fit into the holes in the zeolite structure where they can react.

Did you know?

Enzymes can turn carbon dioxide and water into methanol. Methanol is a useful fuel but a zeolite catalyst can turn it into petrol. Chemists are working to turn these reactions into industrial processes that could replace fossil fuels.

QUESTION

3 A zeolite catalyst is used in the oil industry to break up large molecules into smaller ones for use as petrol.

a What will be the first stage of the reaction?

b Why does the reaction take place faster with the catalyst than without?

c Why does using the catalyst make the process more economical?

Limits of enzymes

Catalysts make reactions with good atom economy possible for the chemical industry. This improves the sustainability of the process. Enzyme catalysis is particularly attractive for the chemical industry. Whereas in the past we used the enzymes present in whole organisms such as yeasts or bacteria, now the enzymes are being extracted and used on their own.

Enzymes are very sensitive to reaction conditions. If the temperature rises too high they will **denature**. This means they lose their unique shape that allows the reactant molecules to combine with the enzyme molecule. For a similar reason enzymes also only work for a narrow range of pH. The fact that enzymes work best at low temperatures benefits the sustainability of a process. Less energy is needed to heat up the reactants than was needed for older catalysts. Enzyme-catalysed reactions also produce fewer by-products, which is another boost to sustainability.

QUESTIONS

4 Give two reasons why catalysed reactions are more sustainable than non-catalysed reactions.

5 Why is it both an advantage and disadvantage that enzymes generally work best at close to normal body temperature?

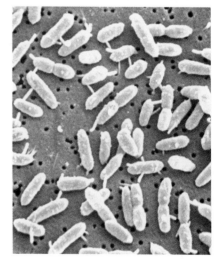

FIGURE 5: Extremophile bacteria live in unusual conditions and have enzymes which catalyse useful reactions. This example lives in strong acids and can extract iron from waste.

catalyst activation energy

Energy calculations

How much fuel does a rocket need?

If a rocket doesn't carry enough fuel it won't reach orbit. If it carries more than is needed then some will be wasted. Luckily if we know the reactions taking place when the fuel burns and the energy of the bonds, then we can calculate exactly how much energy each gram of fuel will release.

FIGURE 1: The amount of fuel must be calculated carefully.

Energy calculations for an exothermic reaction (Higher tier only)

When you mix hydrogen gas and chlorine gas nothing much happens, but hydrogen can be ignited so that it will burn in the chlorine. It is an exothermic reaction and we can calculate how much energy is released by considering the bonds which must be broken and formed.

hydrogen + chlorine → hydrogen chloride
$$H_2(g) \ + \ Cl_2(g) \ \to \ 2HCl(g)$$

To start the reaction off we must break up the bonds in the hydrogen molecule. This requires 436 kJ/mol.

The chlorine molecule must also be split up. This requires 243 kJ/mol.

We need a total of 436 + 243 = 679 kJ to produce the separate atoms of hydrogen and chlorine.

The hydrogen atoms join up with chlorine atoms to form hydrogen chloride molecules. The energy given out when the bond forms is 432 kJ/mol but the equation shows that for every H_2 and Cl_2 molecule two molecules of hydrogen chloride are formed. The total energy given out is $2 \times 432 = 864$ kJ.

This is shown by the energy level diagram in Figure 3.

The energy change in the reaction is:

(energy given out making bonds) – (energy put in to break bonds) = 864 – 679 = 185 kJ

This is the energy given out as heat by the reaction.

FIGURE 2: Hydrogen burns in chlorine.

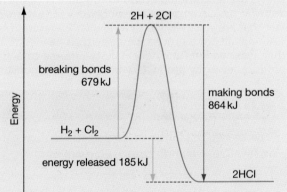

FIGURE 3: Energy level diagram for the hydrogen/chlorine reaction.

As another example, we can consider the reaction between hydrogen and oxygen.

hydrogen + oxygen → steam
$2H_2(g)$ + $O_2(g)$ → $2H_2O(g)$

The table on the right shows the energy needed to break each bond in the substances in the reaction.

Bond	Energy (kJ/mol)
H–H	436
O=O	498
H–O	464

The energy put in to break bonds in the reaction is:

$2 \times$ (H–H) = 2×436 = 872 kJ/mol (there are 2 molecules of hydrogen in the equation)
$1 \times$ (O=O) = 498 kJ/mol

Total energy put in = 1370 kJ/mol

The energy given out when bonds form is:

$4 \times$ (H–O) = 4×464 = 1856 kJ/mol (there are 2 molecules of water formed, each with two H–O bonds)

The energy change is therefore:

1856 − 1370 = 486 kJ/mol

This is given out as heat.

Watch out!
Remember to count all the bonds of each type on each side of the equation.

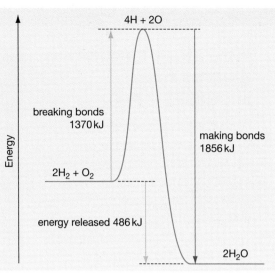

FIGURE 4: Energy level diagram for the hydrogen/oxygen reaction.

Did you know?

The energy released to form nitrogen molecules (N_2) is the largest for diatomic molecules. Reactions which produce nitrogen gas are thus amongst the most exothermic and have been used in powerful rockets.

QUESTIONS

1 How can we tell by looking at the energy from making and breaking bonds that the formation of hydrogen chloride from hydrogen and chlorine is an exothermic reaction?

2 Hydrogen reacts with bromine to form hydrogen bromide.

$H_2(g) + Br_2(g) \rightarrow 2HBr(g)$

The energy needed to break the bonds is shown in the table on the right.

Bond	Energy (kJ/mol)
H–H	436
Br–Br	193
H–Br	366

a What is the total amount of energy needed to break up the hydrogen molecules and the bromine molecule in the equation?

b What is the total energy given out by bonds formed in the reaction?

c Draw a labelled energy level diagram for the reaction.

d What is the energy change for the reaction?

e Is the reaction exothermic or endothermic? Explain your answer.

3 Use the data in the table on the right to calculate the energy given out when methane is burned.

$CH_4(g) + 2O_2(g) \rightarrow CO_2(g) + 2H_2O(g)$

Bond	Energy (kJ/mol)
C–H	435
O=O	498
C=O	805
O–H	464

Reacting masses

We are learning to:
> find the relative atomic mass of elements from the Periodic Table
> calculate the relative formula mass of substances
> (Higher) use balanced equations to calculate the mass of reactants and products in a reaction

How does calculating masses help sustainability?

About 200 million tonnes of sulfuric acid are produced each year. This uses about 64 million tonnes of sulfur. If we didn't know this we might not make enough sulfuric acid or we might turn spare sulfur into polluting sulfur dioxide gas. Sometimes doing calculations saves time and resources.

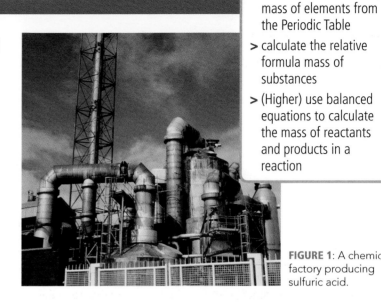

FIGURE 1: A chemical factory producing sulfuric acid.

Relative atomic mass

The number printed above the symbol of the element in the Periodic Table on page 215 is the **relative atomic mass (RAM)**. This is the mass of an atom of an element compared to the mass of an atom of carbon that is given a mass of 12. For example, the atoms of titanium are four times the mass of a carbon atom. This means that the relative atomic mass of titanium is $4 \times 12 = 48$.

	oxygen	fluorine
	8	9
	32 **S** sulfur 16	35.5 **Cl** chlorine 17
	79 Se	80 Br

FIGURE 2: The relative atomic mass of an element is the figure above the symbol.

QUESTIONS

1 Look at the Periodic Table on page 215. Write down the symbol and relative atomic mass of the following elements: oxygen, aluminium, potassium, phosphorus, bromine.

2 Krypton atoms are seven times heavier than carbon atoms. What is the relative atomic mass of krypton?

Relative formula mass

The **relative formula mass** (RFM) is the mass of a molecule or formula unit of a compound compared to the mass of a carbon atom which has a mass of 12. The relative formula mass is the sum of the relative atomic mass (RAM) of all the atoms in the formula.

Chlorine molecules (Cl_2) are made up of two chlorine atoms (RAM 35.5).

The RFM is $2 \times 35.5 = 71$

Sodium sulfate has the formula Na_2SO_4. (RAMs Na = 23, S = 32, O = 16)

The RFM is $(2 \times 23) + 32 + (4 \times 16) = 142$

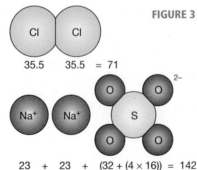

FIGURE 3

35.5   35.5 = 71

23 + 23 + (32 + (4 × 16)) = 142

QUESTION

3 Using the Periodic Table on page 215, calculate the relative formula mass of the following:

a molecules: fluorine, F_2; ammonia, NH_3; sulfur trioxide, SO_3; methanol CH_3OH

b formula units of ionic compounds: sodium bromide, NaBr; magnesium carbonate, $MgCO_3$; copper nitrate $Cu(NO_3)_2$.

Masses of reactants and products (Higher tier only)

Using the relative atomic mass and relative formula mass we can convert the number of reacting atoms in a balanced equation into a mass. Consider the reaction between hydrogen and chlorine.

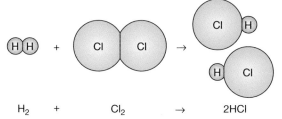

$$H_2 \quad + \quad Cl_2 \quad \rightarrow \quad 2HCl$$

FIGURE 4

> **Watch out!**
>
> The total mass of the reactants $2 + 71 = 73\,g$ is the same as the mass of the products. The masses of the reactants and products are always in the same ratio.

The RFM of a hydrogen molecule is 2, of a chlorine molecule is 71 and of a hydrogen chloride molecule is 36.5.

We can see that:

2 g of hydrogen will react with 71 g of chlorine to make $2 \times 36.5 = 73\,g$ of hydrogen chloride,
4 g of hydrogen react with 142 g of chlorine to make 146 g of hydrogen chloride,
0.2 g of hydrogen react with 7.1 g of chlorine to make 7.3 g of hydrogen chloride

Example

What mass of sulfur trioxide is formed when 6.4 tonnes of sulfur dioxide completely react with oxygen?

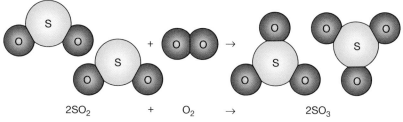

$$2SO_2 \quad + \quad O_2 \quad \rightarrow \quad 2SO_3$$

FIGURE 5

> **Watch out!**
>
> Make sure you multiply the RFM by the number in front of the formula in the equation, if there is one, to find the ratio of the reacting masses.

The RFM of $SO_2 = 64$ and that of $SO_3 = 80$

The equation shows that:

$2 \times 64 = 128\,g$ of SO_2 reacts to form $160\,g$ of SO_3,

so, 1 g of SO_2 forms $\dfrac{160}{128} = 1.25\,g$ of SO_3

and, 6.4 tonnes of SO_2 forms $6.4 \times 1.25 = 8.0$ tonnes of SO_3

Did you know?

A new balance has been designed that can measure the mass of particles as small as one femtogram ($1 \times 10^{-15}\,g$). It uses the principle of a ruler vibrating over the edge of a bench. The 'ruler' is about 0.1 mm long. The particles being weighed change the frequency of the vibration.

⬤ QUESTIONS

4 In the example given above, what mass of oxygen gas is needed to react with the 6.4 tonnes of sulfur dioxide?

5 Ammonia is manufactured by the Haber process.

$N_2(g) + 3H_2(g) \rightarrow 2NH_3(g)$

What mass of hydrogen will react completely with 14 tonnes of nitrogen gas?

6 What mass of ethanol (C_2H_5OH) can be produced by reacting 56 g of ethene (C_2H_4) with excess water by the reaction

$C_2H_4(g) + H_2O(g) \rightarrow C_2H_5OH(g)$?

🔍 reacting mass

Alkanes

What is organic chemistry?

Organic chemistry is the study of compounds based on carbon. Living organisms are made up of organic chemicals and we use them for fuels, plastics, drugs, dyes and many other products. Most of the organic chemicals we use are produced from hydrocarbons in crude oil but this is an unsustainable resource.

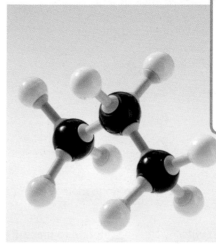

FIGURE 1: Hydrocarbon molecules such as propane are organic molecules containing only carbon and hydrogen atoms.

A family of hydrocarbons

A hydrocarbon is a compound of hydrogen and carbon only. There are many different hydrocarbons. Some are similar and are grouped together as a 'family' of compounds. One family of hydrocarbons is called the **alkanes.**

Like all hydrocarbons, the alkanes burn in plenty of air to form carbon dioxide and water

For example:

methane + oxygen → carbon dioxide + water

Alkanes do not dissolve in water. They do not react with reactants dissolved in water.

Name	Molecular formula
methane	CH_4
ethane	C_2H_6
propane	C_3H_8
butane	C_4H_{10}

Some members of the alkane family.

Watch out!

The names of all the alkanes end in -ane. Make sure you write the names clearly.

QUESTIONS

1 What is the name of the alkane that has three carbon atoms and eight hydrogen atoms in its molecular formula?

2 Write a word equation for the reaction that occurs when butane burns.

Patterns in properties

The alkanes have similar properties because of similarities in their structures. The bonds between the carbon atoms and between the carbon and hydrogen atoms are single covalent bonds. This is shown by single lines in the structural formulae and in 'ball and stick' diagrams.

During combustion the bonds in the alkane molecule are broken and new bonds formed in carbon dioxide and water. For example:

$CH_4(g) + 2O_2(g) \rightarrow CO_2(g) + 2H_2O(l)$

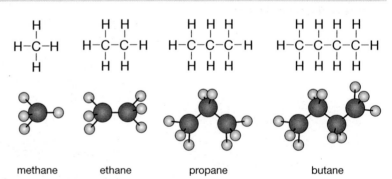

methane   ethane   propane   butane

FIGURE 2: Structural formulae show the bonds in the molecules, and 'ball and stick' models show how the atoms are arranged in 3D.

🔍 alkanes GCSE

The C–C and C–H bonds in alkanes are difficult to break. There is a large activation energy needed to make the alkanes react with other substances. For this reason their reaction with reactants dissolved in water (aqueous solutions) are very slow. The alkanes are said to be unreactive.

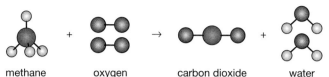

| methane | oxygen | carbon dioxide | water |

FIGURE 3

QUESTION

3 The balanced equation for the combustion of propane is:

$C_3H_8(g) + 5O_2(g) \rightarrow 3CO_2(g) + 4H_2O(l)$

a How many molecules of oxygen are needed to completely burn a molecule of propane?

b Explain why three molecules of carbon dioxide and four molecules of water are formed for every molecule of propane.

c The larger the alkane molecules the more oxygen is needed to make them burn completely. Is this statement true? Explain your answer.

FIGURE 4: An uncontrolled combustion of methane.

Saturated and unsaturated molecules

Alkanes are said to be **saturated** molecules because all the bonds between the carbon atoms are single bonds. Some other molecules have double covalent bonds between carbon atoms. These molecules are said to be **unsaturated.** Unsaturated compounds are more reactive because it is easier to break the double covalent bond.

When an alkane is ignited by a flame the energy given out by forming carbon dioxide and water heats up other alkane molecules sufficiently for the burning to continue.

The alkanes form a family of hydrocarbons because their molecular formula follows a pattern. The pattern is $C_nH_{(2n+2)}$. This gives the molecular formula of an alkane with the number of carbon atoms equal to the number n. Many other organic compounds have a chain of carbon atoms that resembles the alkanes.

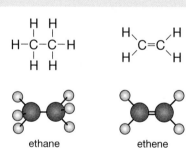

ethane   ethene

FIGURE 5: Ethane is a saturated alkane and ethene is unsaturated.

QUESTIONS

4 An unsaturated hydrocarbon makes an aqueous solution of bromine turn from orange to colourless. Explain why butane does not have this effect.

Higher tier only

5 Write a balanced symbol equation for the complete combustion of ethane, C_2H_6.

6 What mass of carbon dioxide is given off when 16 g of methane are completely burned? (RAM H = 1, C = 12, O = 16)

Did you know?

A vast amount of alkanes are used as fuels, but one other use is to protect alkali metals from reacting with the air. Alkali metals are stored in a liquid alkane because the alkanes are unreactive.

Alcohols

We are learning to:
> recall the names, formulae, structure, properties and uses of methanol and ethanol
> understand the cause of the properties of alcohols
> understand why alcohols burn
> (Higher) recall the reactions of alcohols with sodium

What is the alcohol in alcoholic drinks?

All around the world people use a drug that is called '**alcohol**'. Alcoholic drinks contain an organic compound called ethanol. Ethanol is one of a family of compounds called the alcohols. Other members of the alcohol family are even more toxic to drink than ethanol.

FIGURE 1: Alcohol is available in many varieties.

Sorting out the alcohols

Methanol and ethanol are the simplest members of the **alcohol** group of compounds. Alcohols are not hydrocarbons because they contain oxygen atoms.

Name	Molecular formula
methanol	CH_3OH
ethanol	C_2H_5OH

Methanol and ethanol are liquids at room temperature. Their uses include:

> Methanol is mixed with ethanol to form a fuel, methylated spirit. Methanol is very poisonous so methylated spirit cannot be drunk.

> Methanol is used as a raw material to make other substances such as plastics, drugs, and solvents.

> Ethanol is used as a fuel.

> Ethanol is used as a solvent, for example in perfume and medicines.

Alcohols burn in air forming carbon dioxide and water, for example:

methanol + oxygen → carbon dioxide + water

FIGURE 2: In Brazil ethanol is mixed with petrol so less of the expensive fossil fuels are needed.

Did you know?

When Henry Ford designed the first mass-produced car, the Model T in 1908, he expected it to be fuelled by ethanol. He said that ethanol was the 'fuel of the future' but oil companies made sure that petrol was used instead.

QUESTIONS

1 Write a word equation for the burning of ethanol in air.

2 Methanol is a solvent but cannot be used for medicines. Why not?

alcohols GCSE

Structure and properties

All alcohols have an oxygen and hydrogen atom linked together and attached to a carbon atom in the molecule. This –OH group is called the **functional group** of the alcohols and is responsible for the particular properties of alcohols. The rest of the molecule resembles the alkanes.

Alcohols are soluble in water because of the –OH group and have higher melting and boiling points than the alkane with the same number of carbon atoms. For example, ethanol is a liquid at room temperature and dissolves easily in water while ethane is a gas that is insoluble in water.

Alcohols burn well in air because they have a hydrocarbon chain, that is, a chain of carbon atoms with hydrogen atoms attached, like an alkane.

$$C_2H_5OH(l) + 3O_2(g) \rightarrow 2CO_2(g) + 3H_2O(l)$$

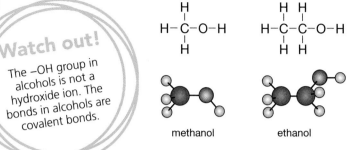

methanol   ethanol

FIGURE 3: Structural formulae and ball and stick models of simple alcohols.

Watch out!

The –OH group in alcohols is not a hydroxide ion. The bonds in alcohols are covalent bonds.

FIGURE 4: C–C, C–H and C–O bonds in the ethanol break when the molecule burns.

ethanol   oxygen   carbon dioxide   water

QUESTIONS

3 Which of the following formulae represents an alcohol? Give a reason for your answer.

A: C_3H_8 **B:** C_3H_7OH

C: C_2H_4 **D:** C_2H_3Cl

4 Give two examples of how the –OH group affects the properties of alcohols.

Reaction with sodium (Higher tier only)

A piece of sodium placed in ethanol fizzes. Hydrogen gas is given off. When excess ethanol is evaporated a white solid is formed which is a compound called sodium ethoxide.

sodium + ethanol → sodium ethoxide + hydrogen

$$2Na(s) + 2C_2H_5OH(l) \rightarrow 2C_2H_5ONa(s) + H_2(g)$$

The reaction is very similar to, but slower than, the reaction of sodium with water. This is because water, like the alcohols, has –OH groups. Sodium does not react with alkanes because they do not have an –OH group.

QUESTIONS

5 How does the reaction of sodium with ethanol resemble the reaction of sodium with water?

6 Write a balanced equation for the reaction of sodium with methanol.

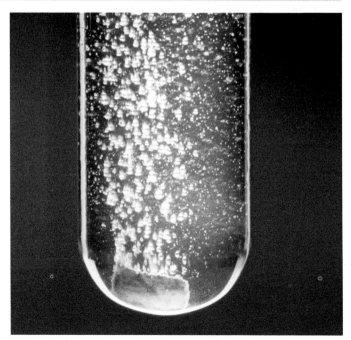

FIGURE 5: Sodium reacting in ethanol.

Preparing for assessment: Planning and collecting

To achieve a good grade in science you will need to be able to use your skills and understanding to understand how scientists plan, run and evaluate investigations.

These skills will be assessed in your exams and in Controlled Assessments. This activity supports you in developing the skills of considering the factors that may affect results, choosing factors to investigate and making decisions about the data to be collected.

✳ Alcohols as fuels

Spirit burners containing alcohols are often used as a source of heat.

Alcohols are a group of compounds in which an –OH group is attached to a hydrocarbon chain.

The alcohol series of compounds.

Alcohol	Formula
methanol	CH_3OH
ethanol	C_2H_5OH
propanol	C_3H_7OH
butanol	C_4H_9OH
pentanol	$C_5H_{11}OH$

All alcohols burn in air. Methanol and ethanol are the simplest members of the group and both are used as fuels. They can be burned in engines in cars or in spirit burners.

$$\text{methanol} + \text{oxygen} \rightarrow \text{carbon dioxide} + \text{water}$$
$$2CH_3OH + 3O_2 \rightarrow 2CO_2 + 4H_2O$$

Bond energies.

Bond	Bond energy (kJ/mol)
C–C	347
C–H	413
C–O	358
O–H	464
O=O	498
C=O	805

As the size of the molecule increases, there are more bonds to break when the molecule burns, but more molecules of carbon dioxide and water are formed.

Spirit burners are often used by campers to heat up a kettle or saucepan of water for cooking food or making a hot drink. A kettle full of water takes the same amount of heat to raise its temperature to boiling point, no matter what fuel is used or how long it takes. As all the alcohols in the table are liquids they are easy to carry and pour into the burner when it needs refilling. Alcohols light easily and burn with a smokeless flame.

✳ Task 1

> How do you think changing the alcohol may affect the amount of heat given off?

> How could you compare the amount of heat released by burning different alcohols in a spirit burner?

Task 2

> Make a prediction about how using a different alcohol may affect the heat produced.

> Explain the ideas behind your prediction.

> Your teacher may ask you to collect some data from burning alcohols in spirit burners. Follow the instructions carefully, including safety precautions.

 Task 3

> Write down a hypothesis that you can test by investigating the effect of changing the alcohol on the heat given out by a spirit burner.

> What factors would you need to consider, to test your hypothesis fairly?

> If you have been asked to carry out the practical, collect enough data to test your hypothesis.

> What should you do to make the data accurate and show that it is repeatable?

 Task 4

> Make sure you have considered all the factors that may affect your hypothesis and describe how they would be controlled.

> Make a quantitative prediction based on your hypothesis – suggest the amount of change that will happen when you change the factor in your hypothesis.

> Look at any data you have collected. What is the **range** of values collected?

> Are there any **outliers**? What should you do about them?

 Maximise your grade

Use these suggestions to improve your work and be more successful.

E
To be on target for grade E you need to:
> make a prediction based on something you have learned or experienced before
> use some scientific terms in your explanation
> record enough data to be able to test your prediction.

C
To be on target for a grade D or C, you also need to:
> consider factors that may affect the investigation
> write an hypothesis that can be tested that investigates the effect of one factor on the quantity you are measuring
> organise your report well and use some scientific terms
> collect sufficient data to test your hypothesis, repeating measurements where possible
> record your data clearly.

A
To be on target for a grade B or A, you also need to:
> consider all the factors that could affect your measurements
> make a quantitative prediction based on your hypothesis
> make sure your report contains no grammatical or spelling errors, and uses scientific terms well
> carry out preliminary tests to decide on an appropriate range of values for your measurements
> deal with any outliers that occur by carrying out a sufficient number of repetitions of the measurements
> make sure that your data is of high quality – that it provides a good test of your hypothesis.

Fermentation and distillation

What substances can be turned into ethanol?

People have been making alcoholic drinks for thousands of years. They have used yeast to feed on plant material containing sugars. Plants that have been used include grapes, barley, rice, potatoes and sugar cane.

FIGURE 1: Apparatus used to collect alcohol in the 17th century.

We are learning to:

> understand the process of fermentation of sugars by yeast

> understand how distillation is used to concentrate ethanol

> understand some of the consequences of ethanol production

Fermenting sugar

Fermentation is the process by which yeast produces ethanol from sugar. Yeasts are micro-organisms. They use the sugar to get energy to grow and reproduce. Ethanol is produced as a waste product.

Fermentation produces a dilute solution of ethanol. The solution is **distilled** to make it more concentrated. The mixture is heated to just above the boiling point of ethanol (78°C). The ethanol boils off leaving most of the water behind. The ethanol vapour is cooled and condenses to form the liquid. Distilled ethanol was called 'spirit'. Spirit drinks such as whisky, brandy, gin, rum and vodka are each made by distilling the ethanol from an ethanol solution. Distilled ethanol is also used as a fuel.

Methods of fermenting sugars and distilling ethanol industrially have developed. Alcoholic drinks have become cheap and very common but ethanol is poisonous. Drinks containing ethanol make people become drunk and can cause liver disease.

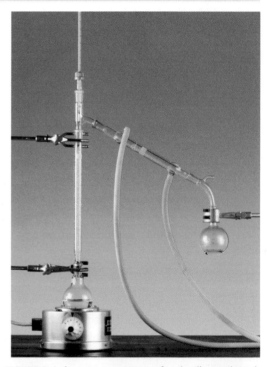

FIGURE 3: Laboratory apparatus for distilling ethanol.

FIGURE 2: To make whisky, ethanol is distilled in copper 'stills'.

QUESTIONS

1 Describe how you could obtain fairly pure ethanol from a solution of ethanol in water.

2 What undesirable effects have developments in fermentation and distillation of ethanol had?

fermentation yeast

Exploring fermentation

The fermentation reaction makes use of **enzymes** produced by yeast cells. There are many different types of yeast which have enzymes that work best under slightly different conditions. Most yeasts ferment sugar solutions fastest in the range 20 to 32°C. They are also most active in slightly acidic solutions, around pH 5. For this reason acids such as vinegar or even sulfuric acid are added to some fermentation solutions. Oxygen must be excluded from the mixture as the reaction is an example of anaerobic respiration.

sugar $\xrightarrow{\text{enzymes}}$ ethanol + carbon dioxide

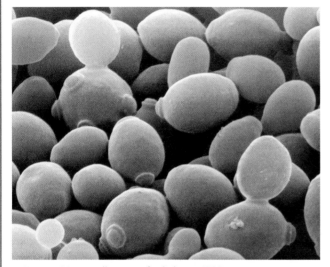

FIGURE 4: Yeast cells magnified about 4000 times.

FIGURE 5: In a modern brewery the conditions are monitored and controlled very closely. Fermentation takes place in the stainless steel vats behind the control desk.

Watch out!
Enzymes are not alive but the yeast cells which produce the enzymes are living organisms.

QUESTIONS

3 Look at Figure 6. Describe what the shape of the graph shows.

4 What would be the effect of adding too much acid to the fermentation mixture?

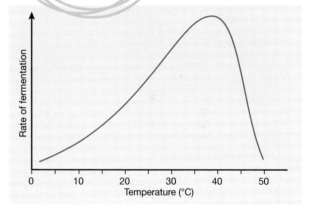

FIGURE 6: A graph of rate of fermentation against temperature.

Limits to fermentation

Ethanol is a toxic compound and is poisonous to yeast as well as to humans. As the ethanol concentration increases over two to three days the yeast cells start to die and fermentation slows. For beers and wines the limit of ethanol concentration is about 18% ethanol by volume. Drinks which contain a higher percentage of alcohol must either have been distilled or had distilled ethanol added to them. Ethanol for use as a fuel must contain as little water as possible as water can damage engines.

Did you know?

The Royal Navy used to test or 'prove' the strength of the rum given to sailors by seeing if gunpowder would burn in it. Gunpowder would not burn in rum with less than 57% ethanol (43% water) so this percentage was said to be 100% proof.

QUESTIONS

5 Why is the maximum ethanol content of beers and wine less than 18% ethanol?

6 Discuss the advantages and disadvantages of using fermentation of sugars by yeast to produce ethanol for use as a fuel.

Q ethanol distillation

Alternatives to fermentation

Why can't we make all the ethanol we need using yeast?

Fermentation of sugars using yeast produces carbon dioxide gas as well as ethanol. The carbon dioxide is a waste product. Yeast can only ferment simple sugars. These make up a small part of the plant material and could be used as food. Other processes for making ethanol may be more efficient and sustainable.

We are learning to:

> recall how ethanol can be produced from ethane

> understand how bacteria can be used to produce ethanol

> interpret data to compare the sustainability of processes for making ethanol

FIGURE 1: An experimental factory for producing ethanol from waste plant material.

Oil and biomass

Crude oil can be used as a raw material for making ethanol. Ethane, an alkane found in crude oil, is converted into ethene, which is also a hydrocarbon. Ethene reacts with steam to form ethanol. This reaction needs a catalyst. A distillation process is used to separate the ethanol from the reactants and to purify it.

A lot of plant material is left over from agriculture and logging. This is called **biomass**. Scientists have been searching for bacteria that can turn biomass into useful materials like ethanol. Bacteria have been genetically modified to do the job. In the future this may be an important source of ethanol for use as a fuel.

QUESTIONS

1 Describe two ways of making ethanol other than using yeast to ferment sugar.

2 What is biomass?

FIGURE 2: The crops have been harvested so these stalks could be burned or converted into ethanol fuel.

Q ethene ethanol reaction

Comparing processes

The process for obtaining ethanol from ethane takes place in two stages. Ethene is formed by removing hydrogen from ethane using a catalyst and high temperature. The reaction from ethene to ethanol takes place at high temperature (300 °C) and high pressure (50–70 atmospheres) with phosphoric acid as the catalyst.

ethene + steam → ethanol
$C_2H_4(g)$ + $H_2O(g)$ → $C_2H_5OH(g)$

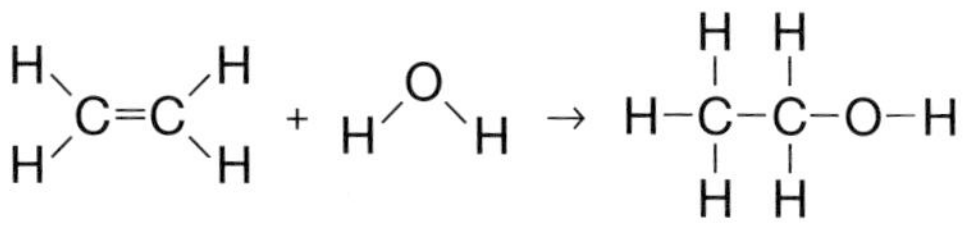

FIGURE 3

Biomass is largely made up of cellulose, the complex sugar that makes up plant cell walls. Genes from natural bacteria that attack cellulose have been transferred to a strain of *E. coli* bacteria. The biomass must be turned into a liquid by dissolving it in a mixture of acids and solvents. Then the genetically modified *E. coli* bacteria get to work, growing and multiplying while they convert the cellulose into ethanol. The process takes place at just above normal temperatures. There have been problems in carrying out the process on a large scale so it is still not a major producer of ethanol.

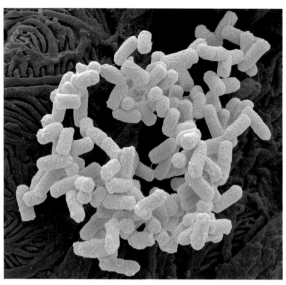

FIGURE 4: Electron microscope image of *E. coli* bacteria, used in the process of converting waste biomass to ethanol.

Did you know?

E. coli bacteria have also been genetically modified to convert biomass into other alcohols, hydrocarbons and biodiesel. Each of these processes could become a useful source of fuel for the future.

QUESTIONS

3 Why does the ethane to ethanol process use more energy than the process using genetically modified bacteria?

4 Why are the genetically modified bacteria preferred to yeast for producing alcohol?

Sustainable ethanol

Converting ethene into ethanol has a good atom economy as there are no by-products, and unreacted ethene can be recycled until it is nearly all converted into ethanol. The process has poor sustainability however, because it uses non-renewable crude oil and the conditions for the process require a lot of energy. It is not a process that could be used to provide ethanol for fuel.

Using *E. coli* bacteria to turn waste biomass into ethanol has many advantages for sustainability.

> It uses a renewable resource.

> It disposes of waste material.

> Potentially, about 90% of the cellulose could be turned into ethanol with a high level of atom economy.

> The conditions used require little energy.

The only disadvantage is the need for chemicals to turn the biomass into a liquid. Nevertheless, this process should be able to produce ethanol more sustainably than traditional methods using yeast.

Watch out!

Various bacteria are being investigated to produce biofuels but none yet has replaced fermentation by yeast.

QUESTIONS

5 The ethane process is used to produce ethanol as feedstock for the chemical industry. Why is it unlikely to be used to produce ethanol as fuel?

6 Give two reasons why the *E. coli* process is more sustainable than using yeast to ferment sugars.

Q *E coli* bacteria produce ethanol

Carboxylic acids

We are learning to:
> recall the names, formulae and properties of some carboxylic acids
> recognise that the –COOH group in carboxylic acids determines their properties
> understand the reactions of carboxylic acids

How are nettles like ants?

Nettles and red ants sting. The sting is a mixture of complex chemicals in an acid. It is the same acid in nettles, red ants and bees. The acid was called formic acid from the Latin name for ants (*formica*) but it is now known as methanoic acid, a carboxylic acid.

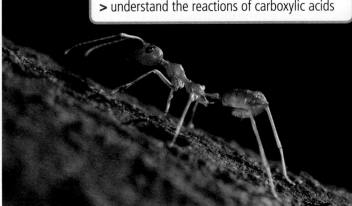

FIGURE 1: Methanoic acid was first obtained from crushed red ants.

What are carboxylic acids?

Methanoic acid and **ethanoic acid** are two of a group of organic compounds called **carboxylic acids**. They are liquids. Methanoic acid is found in some insect and plant stings. Ethanoic acid is found in vinegar. All carboxylic acids have a sharp, acidic taste. Many people like the taste of vinegar but other carboxylic acids have unpleasant smells and tastes. They are found in old sweaty socks and butter which has gone off or become rancid.

Indicators change colour in solutions of carboxylic acids. Reactive metals such as magnesium fizz in them.

Name	Molecular formula
methanoic acid	HCOOH
ethanoic acid	CH_3COOH

Names and molecular formulae of carboxylic acids.

FIGURE 2: Magnesium ribbon reacting with ethanoic acid.

QUESTIONS

1 What is the name and formula of the carboxylic acid found in vinegar?

2 How could you show that methanoic acid solution is an acid?

Structures and properties

Molecules of methanoic acid and ethanoic acid contain the carboxylic acid functional group –COOH. This group of atoms is found in all carboxylic acids and is responsible for the acidic properties of the compounds. The –COOH group is attached to a carbon chain like that in the alkanes.

methanoic acid

ethanoic acid

FIGURE 3: Structural formulae, and ball and stick diagrams of methanoic acid and ethanoic acid.

Carboxylic acids show the typical reactions of acids and form salts with the -oate ending in the name. For example, magnesium will react with ethanoic acid giving off hydrogen gas and forming a salt called magnesium ethanoate.

ethanoic acid + magnesium → magnesium ethanoate + hydrogen gas

Ethanoic acid is neutralised by sodium hydroxide solution.

ethanoic acid + sodium hydroxide → sodium ethanoate + water
$CH_3COOH(aq)$ + $NaOH(aq)$ → $CH_3COONa(aq)$ + $H_2O(l)$

Ethanoic acid also reacts with sodium carbonate.

ethanoic acid + sodium carbonate → sodium ethanoate + carbon dioxide + water
$2CH_3COOH(aq)$ + $Na_2CO_3(aq)$ → $2CH_3COONa(aq)$ + $CO_2(g)$ + $H_2O(l)$

Many useful compounds, such as the painkillers aspirin and ibuprofen, contain the carboxylic acid functional group –COOH. Compounds containing the carboxylic acid group are also used to make polyesters, nylon and Perspex.

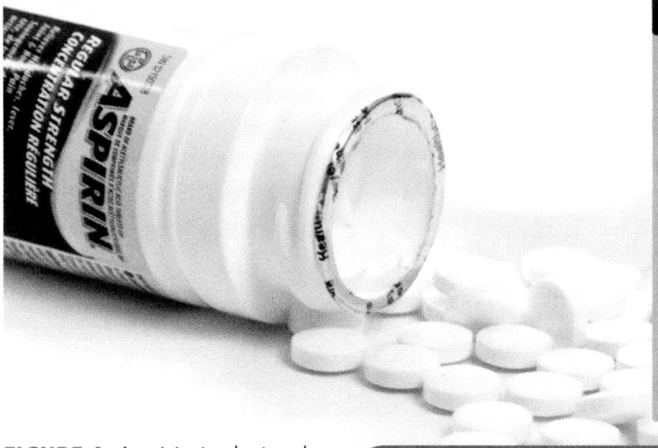

FIGURE 4: Aspirin is derived from salicylic acid found in willow bark that contains the –COOH group.

Did you know?

Three different carboxylic acids can be obtained from the fats in goats' milk.

FIGURE 5

QUESTIONS

3 Write word equations for the reactions of methanoic acid with:

a magnesium **b** sodium hydroxide **c** sodium carbonate.

4 Why do all carboxylic acids have similar reactions with metals and alkalis?

Why are carboxylic acids acids?

The hydrogen atom in the –COOH group behaves like the H atoms in hydrochloric acid and sulfuric acid. The acid molecule can lose the hydrogen ion, H^+, leaving a negative ion that forms a salt with a metal, such as sodium methanoate, $HCOO^- Na^+$.

Other naturally occurring acids such as citric acid in fruits also contain the –COOH group.

Watch out!

The carboxylic acids must be dissolved in water before they show the typical properties of acids.

QUESTIONS

5 Write a balanced chemical equation for the reaction of methanoic acid solution with sodium hydroxide solution.

6 a Which of the following is the formula of a compound found in rancid butter? Explain your answer.
C_4H_{10} C_4H_9OH C_3H_7COOH

b What would you expect to see if a mixture of rancid butter and water was mixed with egg shells? (Hint: Egg shells are largely calcium carbonate.)

Q ethanoic acid

Weak acids

We are learning to:

> recall that vinegar is a dilute solution of ethanoic acid

> understand that weak acids such as carboxylic acid are less reactive than strong acids

> understand that weak acids have higher pH values than strong acids

Is vinegar corrosive?

Even dilute solutions of sulfuric acid carry warnings to show that the solution is corrosive and could burn skin. But carboxylic acids found in foods are not considered harmful. The difference is not just because the amounts of acid in food may be small, but because acids can be described as strong or weak.

FIGURE 1: Vegetables pickled in vinegar.

How do you like your vinegar?

There are many different types of vinegar. Some types of vinegar are coloured and some colourless. All varieties of vinegar contain ethanoic acid. The ethanoic acid gives vinegar its sharp taste. The labels on bottles of vinegar may say it contains acetic acid which is an old name for ethanoic acid.

Vinegar is not harmful because it is a dilute solution and because ethanoic acid is a **weak acid**. But pure ethanoic acid is corrosive and containers must have warning signs.

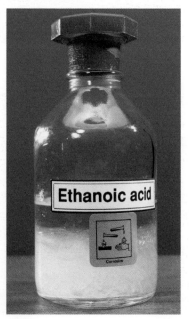

FIGURE 2: Vinegar can be made from wine, cider or fermented malt.

FIGURE 3: Pure ethanoic acid must not be confused with dilute solutions as it is corrosive.

Did you know?

Bacteria turn ethanol in cider, wine or ale (fermented malt) into ethanoic acid. The reaction is oxidation and the bacteria use it as a form of respiration to get energy.

QUESTIONS

1 How does the taste of vinegar tell you it contains an acid?

2 Why do bottles of vinegar not need warning symbols showing they contain an acid?

Q ethanoic acid   vinegar

What do we mean by a weak acid?

When a piece of magnesium is put in hydrochloric acid it fizzes violently. A similar piece of magnesium in a dilute solution of ethanoic acid fizzes much more slowly even if there is the same amount of ethanoic acid present as hydrochloric acid. The slower reaction shows that ethanoic acid is a weak acid. All carboxylic acids are weak acids.

The reaction of carboxylic acids with carbonates also gives off carbon dioxide gas more slowly than strong acids such as sulfuric acid, nitric acid and hydrochloric acid. Nevertheless, weak acids will neutralise alkalis.

The **pH** of a solution is a good indicator of strong and weak acids. If similar dilute solutions of strong and weak acids are compared the weak acids will have a higher pH than the strong acids.

Watch out!

Do not taste or even sniff chemicals if you are not sure what they are.

QUESTIONS

3 How is it possible to distinguish between bottles of dilute hydrochloric acid and dilute ethanoic acid which have lost their labels?

4 The pH of a dilute solution of hydrochloric acid is 1 and of a dilute solution of methanoic acid is 3. What would you expect to be the pH of similar dilute solutions of:

a sulfuric acid

b ethanoic acid

c nitric acid?

FIGURE 4: There is fizzing when vinegar is added to sodium hydrogen carbonate but it is less vigorous than with a strong acid.

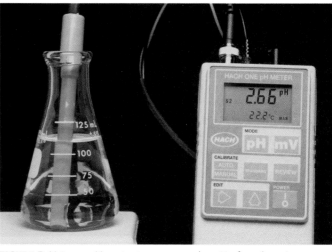

FIGURE 5: Using a pH meter to measure the pH of methanoic acid solution.

Explaining weak acids

All acids produce hydrogen ions, H^+, when dissolved in water. Strong acids split up completely in solution. For example, hydrochloric acid breaks up into hydrogen ions and chloride ions. In solutions of weak acids only some of the molecules break up into ions so there are much fewer hydrogen ions in the solution of the acid. On the pH scale, the more hydrogen ions in every cm^3 of solution, the lower the pH.

Watch out!

The equations for the reactions of weak and strong acids are similar and do not show whether the acid is strong or weak.

QUESTIONS

5 Solution A has a pH of 2, while solution B has a pH of 4. Which solution contains the most hydrogen ions in each cm^3 of solution?

6 Methanoic acid has a slightly lower pH than a similar solution of ethanoic acid. What does this tell you about methanoic acid?

Q weak and strong acids GCSE

Esters

We are learning to:
> recall that esters are compounds with distinctive smells found in foods
> recall the uses of esters
> understand that esters are formed by reactions between alcohols and carboxylic acids

Why do some substances smell?

Substances smell because gaseous molecules travel through the air to our noses. Some gases such as oxygen, nitrogen and methane have no smell. Some simple molecules such as hydrogen sulfide have strong unpleasant smells, whereas hydrogen cyanide, although toxic, has a pleasant almond smell. The appetising smell of foods is made up of a wide variety of compounds.

FIGURE 1: Something smells good.

Smells and flavours

Strawberries, apples, bananas – they each have their own smells and flavours. These are mixtures of chemicals including a group of compounds called **esters**. Esters are formed when alcohols react with carboxylic acids. Each ester has a different smell and flavour which we recognise as coming from a particular fruit or flower. Esters have low melting and boiling points and they evaporate quickly at room temperature. The air carries the ester vapour from the fruit to our noses so we are able to smell the fruit.

QUESTIONS

1 Why can we tell the difference between the smell and flavour of an apple and a pear?

2 Why is the low melting point of esters important?

FIGURE 2: The smells and flavours of many fruits contain esters.

Uses of esters

One of the simplest of esters is ethyl ethanoate. This has a pleasant smell and is a useful **solvent**. It is often used as a solvent for nail varnish and as nail varnish remover. It is safer and more pleasant to use than propanone, which is also used as nail varnish remover. Esters similar to ethyl ethanoate are used as solvents for paints, inks and other materials.

Other esters found in fruits are used as flavourings, for example in sweets. Esters which have been synthesised are often less expensive to use than those extracted from fruits. Esters are often used as the perfumes in cheaper shampoos and shower gels. They are not used in expensive perfumes as they can decompose on the skin.

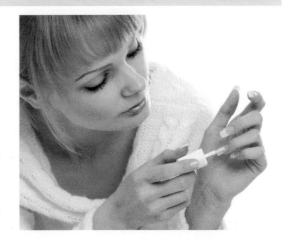

FIGURE 3: The solvent in nail varnish and in nail varnish remover is often ethyl ethanoate.

Q esters   flavourings

Esters are relatively unreactive molecules and some are used as plasticisers in polymers such as PVC. The plasticiser molecule separates the polymer molecules therefore making the polymer more flexible. The esters used are usually more complex than those used in flavourings. There has been concern that some esters used as plasticisers, known as phthalates, are a hazard to health.

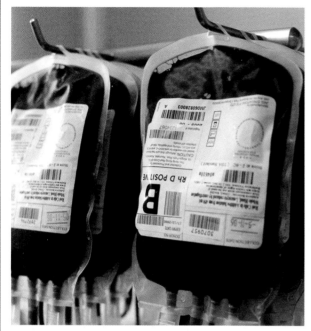

FIGURE 4: Bags for storing blood are made from PVC. They contain an ester as a plasticiser.

Did you know?

Pear drops are traditional boiled sweets usually coloured pink and yellow. They were among the first to be flavoured with a synthesised ester. The ester, 3-methyl butyl ethanoate, is found in bananas and pears.

FIGURE 5

QUESTIONS

3 State three uses of esters.

4 What properties does ethyl ethanoate have that make it a good solvent for nail varnish?

Making esters

An ester is made by combining a particular alcohol with a particular carboxylic acid. For example, methyl ethanoate is produced by reacting ethanoic acid with methanol.

| acid | + | alcohol | → | ester | + water |

ethanoic acid + methanol → methyl ethanoate + water
CH_3COOH + CH_3OH → CH_3COOCH_3 + H_2O

The reaction is very slow on its own so a catalyst is used. This is a strong acid, usually concentrated sulfuric acid or phosphoric acid. The reactants are also heated to increase the speed of reaction.

Watch out!

The first part of the ester's name comes from the alcohol it is from and the latter part ending in -oate is from the acid.

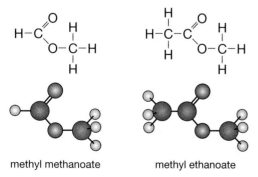

methyl methanoate   methyl ethanoate

FIGURE 6: Examples of esters.

QUESTIONS

5 Why are heat and a catalyst needed in the reaction to produce esters?

6 a Write a word equation for the formation of ethyl ethanoate ($CH_3COOC_2H_5$) from ethanol and ethanoic acid.

b (Higher tier only) Write a symbol equation for the reaction in part **a**.

Making esters

How much ethyl ethanoate do we use?

Most esters are used in small quantities as flavourings but ethyl ethanoate is also used as a solvent for many glues, paints and coatings as well as for nail varnish. Over a million tonnes is used worldwide every year and a factory in the UK city of Hull can produce over 200 000 tonnes a year.

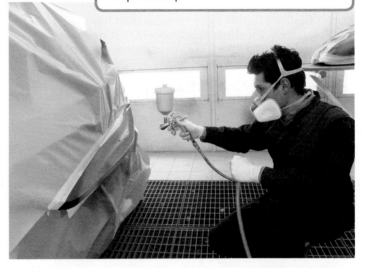

FIGURE 1: The motor industry uses paints dissolved in ethyl ethanoate.

Synthesising ethyl ethanoate (Higher tier only)

Esters can be synthesised by reacting an alcohol with a carboxylic acid. To make ethyl ethanoate the reaction is:

ethanoic acid + ethanol → ethyl ethanoate + water
$$CH_3COOH + C_2H_5OH \rightarrow CH_3COOC_2H_5 + H_2O$$

The equation shows that one molecule of ethanol reacts with a molecule of ethanoic acid. The relative formula masses (RFMs) are 60 for ethanoic acid and 46 for ethanol. Roughly equal amounts of the two reactants can be mixed together.

The reaction is slow, so concentrated sulfuric acid is needed as a catalyst. Only a relatively small amount of catalyst is required.

The reaction is still slow, so the temperature should be raised to speed the reaction. If the mixture was simply heated the ethanol would be lost as its boiling point is 78 °C. To stop this the mixture is heated under **reflux**. This means the mixture is boiled and the vapours cooled so that they fall back into the mixture.

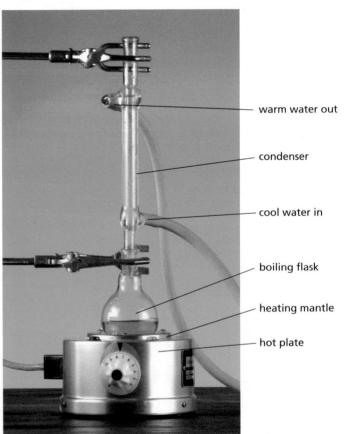

warm water out

condenser

cool water in

boiling flask

heating mantle

hot plate

FIGURE 2: Heating volatile reactants and products under reflux.

Did you know?

An alternative process for making ethyl ethanoate reacts ethene with ethanoic acid over a catalyst. Ethene is obtained from crude oil. As the price of crude oil rises the process is becoming more expensive to operate.

Q preparation ethyl ethanoate

After a suitable time the ethyl ethanoate that is formed can be separated from the mixture and purified, as in the following steps.

1 Distillation

The reaction mixture is boiled and the vapours directed into a collecting tube and cooled. This is done until about two-thirds of the mixture in the reaction flask has been distilled over. Unfortunately some water, as well as unreacted ethanol and ethanoic acid, will distil over with the ethyl ethanoate.

2 Removing acid

Sodium carbonate solution is added to the impure product. Sodium carbonate reacts with acids to give off carbon dioxide gas and forms salts which dissolve in the water and not in the ethyl ethanoate. The mixture is put in a **tap funnel**, shaken and allowed to settle. The ethyl ethanoate forms a layer on top of the water. The lower layer is then run out of the funnel.

3 Removing alcohol

Calcium chloride solution is added to the impure product. Any ethanol mixed with the ethyl ethanoate dissolves in the calcium chloride solution. The mixture is put into a tap funnel and the lower layer removed and discarded.

4 Drying

Pieces of anhydrous calcium chloride are added to the product. This absorbs any water from the product.

5 Second distillation

To separate the ethyl ethanoate from the solid drying agent it is distilled again. The boiling point of pure ethyl ethanoate is 77°C.

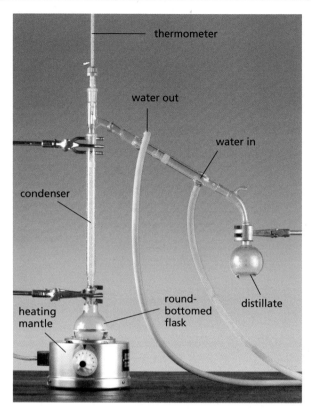

FIGURE 3: Distillation of a product from a reaction mixture.

FIGURE 4: Two liquids that do not mix separate in a tap funnel. The lower liquid can be run out from the bottom.

◉ QUESTIONS

1 Why does only a small amount of sulfuric acid need to be added to the reaction mixture?

2 Describe what happens to the reactants when a reaction mixture is refluxed.

3 How is distillation different to reflux?

4 a What impurities in the product will react with sodium carbonate solution?

b How can you tell that all the acid impurities have been removed?

5 How can you be sure that the ethyl ethanoate is pure at the final distillation?

6 Why is it very difficult to get a high percentage yield of ethyl ethanoate when doing the preparation on a small scale in the laboratory?

Watch out!
Reactions of organic compounds are slow and some of the reactants remain unconverted into products.

Fats and oils

Can you run an engine on chip fat?

Cooking oil made from plants is a very good source of energy and burns well in diesel engines. Chip shops use a lot of vegetable oil which has to be replaced regularly. Before being used as a fuel, it has to be filtered to remove any left-over pieces of chips, and it does have quite a distinctive smell!

FIGURE 1: As an experiment the St Mawes to Place ferry was converted to run on chip oil from a local hotel.

What are fats and oils?

Fats and oils are very similar substances and are a special group of esters. Oils are liquids at normal temperature, while fats are solids.

Organisms use fats and oils as a way of storing energy. Plant oils are often called vegetable oils and are found in nuts and seeds. Plants make oils as a store of energy mainly for their seeds. When the seeds become new plants they use the energy in the oil for growth.

Vegetable oils are a very good source of energy for animals. We eat oils from olives, rapeseeds, sunflowers, peanuts and many others. Animals store spare energy from foods as fats and oils. During the summer many animals build up a layer of fat. They use the fat as a source of energy during winter months when food is scarce. Eating too much food means that we store more fat and become overweight.

FIGURE 3: Brown bears lose up to a third of their body mass over winter when they use energy stored in their fat.

FIGURE 2: Nuts are a good source of vegetable oils.

Watch out!

Oils found in plants and animals should not be confused with the oils obtained from crude oil (petroleum). They are different chemical compounds.

QUESTIONS

1 Why do plants and animals make oils and fats?

2 Give one difference between a fat and an oil.

The structure of fats and oils

Like all esters, fats and oils are a combination of a carboxylic acid and an alcohol. The carboxylic acids are called **fatty acids**. They have the –COOH group of the acid at the end of a long hydrocarbon chain similar to the alkanes.

The alcohol in fats and oils is called **glycerol**. It is special because it has three –OH groups. This means that fats and oils have three fatty acid chains attached to the glycerol molecule.

carbon chains of various lengths

FIGURE 4: The molecular structure of a fat or oil.

Fats and oils from different sources have different fatty acids attached to the glycerol. The various fatty acids give the fats and oils different properties.

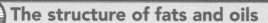

QUESTIONS

3 Why are fats and oils members of the esters group?

4 Are the following statements true or false? Write corrections for the false statements.

A olive oil is an ester found in olives

B olive oil is a mixture of glycerol and a fatty acid called oleic acid

C all vegetable oils contain oleic acid

Comparing fats and oils

The fatty acids that make up most vegetable oils are unsaturated. This means they have some carbon-to-carbon double bonds (C=C) in the fatty acid chain. Unsaturated substances make bromine solution change colour from orange to colourless.

Most of the fatty acids that make up animal fats are saturated. All the carbon-to-carbon bonds are single bonds (C–C). Saturated molecules do not affect the colour of bromine solution.

It is generally thought that unsaturated fats and oils are healthier to eat than saturated fats, although all fats and oils can contribute to making you overweight.

Did you know?

Liquid vegetable oils can be turned into solid fats by reacting the oil with hydrogen over a nickel catalyst. The hydrogen turns some of the double carbon bonds into single bonds making the molecule more saturated. The more saturated fats have higher melting points.

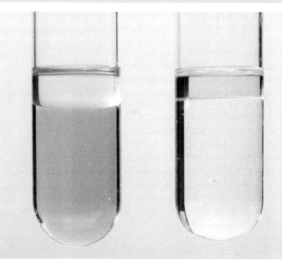

FIGURE 5: Testing oils for unsaturation. On the left an oil floats above bromine solution. After shaking, the solution turns colourless, indicating that the oil is unsaturated, as shown on the right.

Watch out!

There is usually some unsaturated fatty acid in animal fats although most will be saturated, but it means that animal fats will take the colour out of bromine solution.

QUESTIONS

5 Shaking fat with bromine solution causes its colour to change from orange to colourless. What does this tell you about the fat?

6 Polyunsaturated oils have more carbon-to-carbon double bonds than mono-unsaturated oils. How could you distinguish between sunflower oil and olive oil which have different amounts of each type of oil? (Hint: One molecule of bromine reacts with each double covalent bond in the fat.)

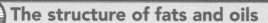

Q fats oils bromine   unsaturated

Reversible reactions

We are learning to:
> recognise that some reactions are reversible
> understand how reactions can be in a state of equilibrium
> (Higher) explain the dynamic equilibrium of reversible reactions

Can we make changes go backwards?

We can melt ice and we can freeze water to form ice. We can stretch an elastic band and let it go back to its original size. These are **reversible** changes. Once you've fried an egg, though, you can't change it back into raw egg. This is an irreversible change. We need to look more closely at the direction of change.

FIGURE 1: Some changes cannot be reversed.

Reactions that will go backwards

If you heat a piece of magnesium it burns with a bright flame and a white powder is formed. You cannot easily make the white powder turn back into the silvery metal. Most chemical reactions go one way.

Some chemical reactions can also go backwards. We say these reactions are reversible. For example, blue hydrated copper sulfate crystals turn white when they are heated. Water vapour is given off. The white powder is called anhydrous copper sulfate.

> **Watch out!**
> We use the ⇌ symbol instead of the usual one-way arrow → to show that the reaction can go both ways.

FIGURE 2: Heating hydrated copper sulfate (left) and adding water to anhydrous copper sulfate (right).

If water is added to the white powder when it is cool, the blue colour returns. The reaction is reversible. We can show this as a word equation:

hydrated copper sulfate (blue) ⇌ anhydrous copper sulfate (white) + water

QUESTIONS

1 If you see the ⇌ sign in an equation, what does it tell you?

2 The changing colour of an acid/alkali indicator such as litmus is a reversible reaction. How can you make blue litmus turn red, then back to blue?

Reaching equilibrium

If you heat solid ammonium chloride it splits up into two gases, ammonia and hydrogen chloride. This reaction is reversible; the two gases can combine to form the white solid.

ammonium chloride $\rightleftharpoons$ ammonia + hydrogen chloride

$NH_4Cl(s)$ $\rightleftharpoons$ $NH_3(g)$ + $HCl(g)$

If you keep all the substances in a closed container, after a short time the rate at which the solid is decomposing is the same as the rate at which the two gases are combining. The reaction reaches a state of **equilibrium**.

The symbol $\rightleftharpoons$ shows not only that the reaction is reversible but that the reaction can reach equilibrium, when the amounts of the reactants and products will each stay the same.

Watch out!

Reversible reactions can only reach equilibrium if all the reactants and products are kept enclosed in a container.

QUESTIONS

3 What two things does the $\rightleftharpoons$ sign mean?

4 Ethanoic acid reacts with ethanol to form ethyl ethanoate and water. The reaction is reversible.

a Write a word equation for the reaction.

b What evidence would show that the reaction is at equilibrium?

Going both ways (Higher tier only)

A reversible reaction that takes place in a closed container reaches equilibrium because the reaction goes both ways at once. The reactants react to form products and as soon as some products are formed they react to re-form the reactants. Even at equilibrium the forward and backwards reactions are still going on. This is called **dynamic equilibrium**.

Dynamic means 'moving'. We can imagine that in any mixture of reactants and products the particles are constantly moving, colliding and reacting. At equilibrium the forwards and backwards reactions are happening at the same rate so reactants and products are being formed as fast as they are being used up.

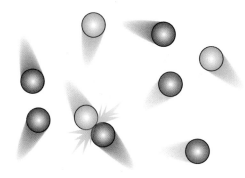

FIGURE 3: We can visualise particles of reactants and products constantly moving, colliding and reacting.

Did you know?

The Belousov–Zhabotinsky reaction is an unusual reaction because it oscillates forwards and backwards, changing from colourless to yellow and back again over and over again. The colour changes eventually slow down as the chemicals reach equilibrium.

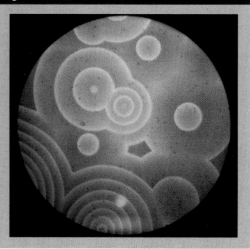

FIGURE 4: Waves of colour produced as the chemical changes oscillate in the Belousov–Zhabotinsky reaction.

QUESTIONS

5 Consider the reaction in question 4. What is happening to the reactants and products of this reaction in a dynamic equilibrium?

6 Why does heating hydrated copper sulfate in an open test-tube not produce an equilibrium?

The Haber process

Do we need synthetic fertilisers?

In the mid-20th century a rapidly growing world population meant that many people were starving. The so-called 'Green Revolution' of the 1960s and 1970s greatly increased the production of food. Synthesised fertilisers were one contributor to the improved growth of crops.

FIGURE 1: Farmers spread fertiliser containing synthesised ammonium nitrate on their crops.

Making ammonia

Nitrogen is the most important element needed by plants to help them grow. There is plenty of nitrogen in the air but plants cannot use nitrogen in the form of gas. They need to take it in as nitrates. Forming nitrate compounds from nitrogen is called **fixing** nitrogen.

In the early 20th century, farmers worried about getting enough fertiliser for their crops. Making artificial fertiliser meant first making ammonia. Fritz Haber, a German chemist, solved the problem of getting nitrogen gas to react with hydrogen.

nitrogen + hydrogen → ammonia

The reactants, nitrogen and hydrogen, are the feedstock for the process.

The ammonia produced is reacted with nitric acid to make the ammonium nitrate used in fertilisers.

Today, factories still make ammonia by the **Haber process**. Nitrogen is taken from the air. Hydrogen is produced by reacting natural gas (methane) with steam.

Did you know?

Fritz Haber won the Nobel Prize for his process, but ammonia produced by the process was also used to make explosives for Germany's weapons in World War 1. Haber also developed poison gases, also used in the war. His wife, Clara, who was also a chemist, committed suicide because of Haber's deadly inventions.

FIGURE 2: Fritz Haber (1868–1934).

QUESTIONS

1 Why was the Haber process important to farmers?

2 What are the sources of the feedstock for the Haber process?

ammonia fertilisers   Fritz Haber

Optimising the Haber process

The reaction used in the Haber process is exothermic, slow and reversible.

$$N_2(g) + 3H_2(g) \rightleftharpoons 2NH_3(g)$$

The reaction is speeded up by using a catalyst. Haber and his colleague, Carl Bosch, tested hundreds of different substances and found that iron was the most convenient. If potassium hydroxide is mixed with the iron the speed of the reaction is increased further. A high temperature (about 450 °C) and a high pressure (about 200 atmospheres) are also used to increase the speed of the reaction.

The high temperature and pressure also affect the amount of ammonia formed when the reaction reaches equilibrium. The number of molecules drops during the reaction (from four to two) so high pressure squeezes the molecules together, producing more ammonia. Heating the mixture encourages the endothermic backwards reaction, reducing the amount of ammonia that is in the equilibrium mixture.

The gases do not spend enough time in the reaction vessel to reach equilibrium and only about 20% of the nitrogen and hydrogen is converted into ammonia. This not a problem because after the ammonia is removed the hydrogen and nitrogen left over can be recycled and none is wasted.

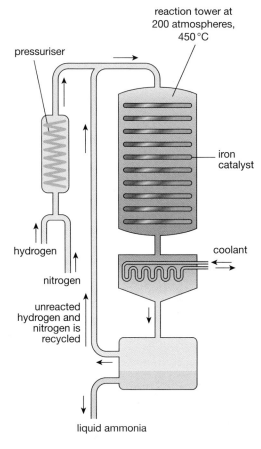

FIGURE 3: The Haber process for synthesising ammonia.

QUESTIONS

3 How do the temperature and pressure used in the Haber process affect the yield of ammonia in the reaction?

4 How has altering the iron catalyst changed the process?

5 Why doesn't it matter that only a small percentage of the reactants are turned into ammonia?

Choosing the compromise

The choice of the conditions for the reaction is a compromise between speed, yield and cost. Using a higher temperature would speed up the reaction but produce less ammonia and would cost more in fuel. Higher pressure would help the speed and the yield but the cost of maintaining the high pressure and preventing leaks would be too great.

Watch out!

The amounts of nitrogen, hydrogen and ammonia present when the reaction is at equilibrium depend on the temperature and the pressure but it can take a long time for the mixture to reach equilibrium.

QUESTIONS

6 Why aren't conditions in the Haber process chosen to produce the maximum possible yield of ammonia?

7 Explain what impact you think the Haber process has had on society.

Alternatives to Haber

We are learning to:

> understand the unintended impact on the environment of synthesised fertilisers

> understand that natural means of fixing nitrogen could be copied

> evaluate the sustainability of different forms of fertiliser

Are there other ways of making fertiliser?

Imagine holding a test-tube in which nitrogen from the air is reacting to make fertiliser. This alternative to the heat and pressure of the Haber process is a dream that is becoming a reality. It offers one alternative source of fertiliser for the crops of the future.

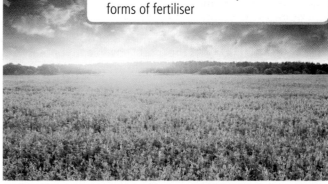

FIGURE 1: This crop of peas may hold the answer to the fertiliser of tomorrow.

Organic versus synthesised fertilisers

Synthesised or artificial fertilisers have increased the yield of crops but they do cause problems. If too much is put on crops, or the crops are sprayed at the wrong time, the soluble fertiliser can be washed into rivers and into the sea. Fertiliser helps algae to grow. The algae are eaten by bacteria, which take oxygen from the water. Fish and other animals cannot breathe and so they die.

Many people think that organic fertilisers such as compost and manure are better for crops. They are longer-lasting and less likely to be washed away. Other people think there is not enough organic fertiliser for all the crops needed to feed a world population of over seven billion.

QUESTIONS

1 Why has the use of synthesised fertiliser caused some rivers to die?

2 Name two sources of organic fertiliser.

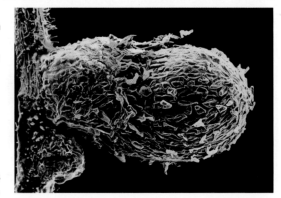

FIGURE 2: Spreading manure from cows, pigs, and chickens is one way of helping crops grow.

Copying bacteria

Bacteria that live in the soil and in the root nodules of legume plants (clover, peas and beans) naturally 'fix' nitrogen from the air. Traditionally, fields were left to lie fallow between crops, to allow the soil bacteria to replace fertilisers, or legumes such as peas were grown in between other crops. Now scientists are hoping to copy the action of the bacteria.

FIGURE 3: Nodules on the roots of pea plants contain nitrogen-fixing bacteria.

organic and artificial fertiliser

The bacteria produce special enzymes that catalyse the reaction of nitrogen from the air. Producing copies of these enzymes may make it possible to make fertilisers cheaply, at room temperature and pressure, instead of by the Haber process.

Alternatively, crops may be genetically modified so that either they produce the enzymes to fix nitrogen or they allow the bacteria to live in their roots, as legumes do. If this happened, then crops such as wheat and rice could be grown without needing fertiliser of any sort.

Watch out!

All plants need supplies of nitrogen compounds in the soil. These are formed by 'fixing' nitrogen in the air, either naturally or synthetically.

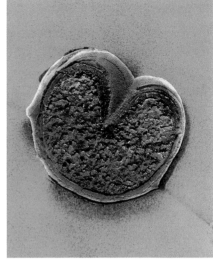

FIGURE 4: One of the bacteria involved in the sequence of reactions that converts nitrogen from the air into nitrates in the soil.

QUESTIONS

3 How is nitrogen 'fixed' naturally?

4 What is the advantage of using enzymes to make fertiliser instead of producing it by the Haber process?

Sustainable fertiliser

Most people agree that making fertiliser by the Haber process is not sustainable for the future. It uses natural gas, a non-renewable resource that has to be transported great distances to factories making fertiliser. The process uses a great deal of water, about 37 tonnes for every tonne of fertiliser. Also, it is only economic to build large fertiliser factories. Not many are needed (there are just two in the UK) so the fertiliser has to be carried a long way to the crops. The process uses a great deal of energy provided by fossil fuels. It is estimated that producing one tonne of fertiliser releases nearly seven tonnes of carbon dioxide, to contribute to global warming.

The alternatives – using organic fertiliser, bacterial enzymes and genetically modified crops – will use much less energy and resources and thus will be more sustainable.

FIGURE 5: Some of the millions of tonnes of fertiliser produced each year awaiting transport to a field.

Did you know?

Using global positioning satellites (GPS) and instruments that analyse the nitrogen content of leaves, farmers can instantly calculate how much fertiliser to spread on crops in each part of their fields. Less fertiliser is wasted, reducing costs and pollution of water courses.

QUESTIONS

5 About 230 million tonnes of fertiliser are produced worldwide annually.

a How much water is used to produce this fertiliser?

b What mass of carbon dioxide is released into the atmosphere?

6 Why do you think alternative sources of fertiliser are more sustainable than using the Haber process to fix nitrogen?

🔍 nitrogen-fixing bacteria

Analysis

We are learning to:
> understand that there are qualitative and quantitative forms of analysis
> recall that many types of analysis are carried out with solutions
> understand the methods of selecting, collecting, storing and preparing samples for analysis

Is analysis exciting?

'I want to find the identity of the killer,' said the famous detective, looking at the body in the conservatory.

'First, we'll have to do a sweep search for DNA samples,' replied the nervous young crime-scene investigator, 'then run a DNA fingerprint analysis on the victim and other room users, cross-match sources of the footprint and calculate the splatter pattern of the blood splashes.'

'When can I expect an answer?' the detective responded impatiently.

'Oh, in a month or two,' the scientist answered.

FIGURE 1: A crime has been committed.

Descriptions and numbers

Analysts carry out work in a variety of fields, including crime, food, rocks, fuels, metals and many others. They look for evidence to support an hypothesis. Some of the evidence collected will be descriptions or names of materials, such as the name of the mineral in a rock or the colour of a paint. This is called **qualitative data**.

On the other hand, any measurement that gives a numerical result is called **quantitative data**. For example, the amount of an impurity in a pot of yogurt is found by quantitative analysis.

FIGURE 2: A flame test is an example of qualitative analysis. The colour of the flame is evidence of the metal present in the sample.

FIGURE 3: The speed of a vehicle measured by a police radar speed gun is quantitative evidence.

QUESTION

1 Are the following qualitative or quantitative evidence?

  a A white precipitate is formed if barium nitrate solution is added to a solution containing a sulfate.

  b A sample of impure water boils at 102 °C.

  c A carbonate fizzes when acid is added to it.

Q forensic science

Selecting and collecting samples

The results of just one test or one measurement may be wrong so it is always a good idea to make several tests or measurements on any sample. The sample should be taken from the middle of the material being tested, to make sure it is typical. For example, if you want to know the temperature of water being heated in a beaker, you place the thermometer in the centre of the beaker, not close to the surface or the edge, where it may be cooled by the air, or at the bottom, where the heater is.

Because test results on samples from different sources may have to be compared, it is important that analysis procedures are standardised.

Samples must not become contaminated with impurities so precautions must be taken when collecting them. The chemical analyst wears gloves and perhaps a mask. They will use a clean spatula or pipette to collect each sample and place it in a clean container. The container itself must not contaminate the sample. In special cases, they use plastic containers without plasticisers, or envelopes made from acid-free paper.

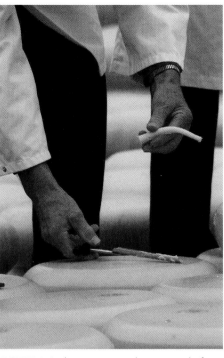

FIGURE 4: A cheese tester takes a sample from within the cheese instead of from the surface where air may have reacted with the cheese.

 QUESTIONS

2 A farmer needs to analyse the soil of a field to see whether it needs fertiliser. How many samples should she take and from where?

3 Why should an analyst wear gloves and a mask?

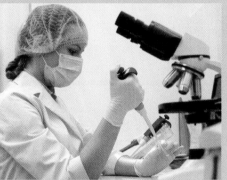

FIGURE 5: An analyst at work.

Did you know?

The Society of Public Analysts was formed in 1860 to make sure that food sold was not harmful to health. At the time sawdust or chalk used to be added to bulk out flour, and poisonous dyes were even added to meat to make it look fresh.

Storage and preparation

Samples can quickly deteriorate so they must be stored carefully; this usually means in a temperature-controlled environment. For example, most bacteria need a temperature above 5 °C to reproduce, so samples can be stored in a refrigerator for some time. Freezing may damage some samples, particularly plant or animal tissues, because ice crystals damage cells. Some samples have to be kept dry and some may have to be kept in an inert atmosphere of nitrogen or argon to prevent reaction with oxygen.

The analyst must also take care to avoid contamination when preparing the sample for testing. Tests are often carried out on solutions so the analyst must know the exact amount of sample and the volume of solvent used.

Watch out!
It is important to follow any analytical procedure very carefully and to keep a full record of results.

 QUESTIONS

4 A sample of magnesium chloride absorbs water from the air. How should it be stored?

5 An athlete suspected of taking drugs provides a urine sample to be tested by two analysts. How could the results from the analysts differ?

Principles of chromatography

We are learning to:

> understand the use of aqueous and non-aqueous solvents

> understand the distribution of a solute between two solvents

> understand how chromatography separates substances

How are ink stains used in analysis?

You might have noticed how ink stains spread out on a sheet of paper, a cotton shirt or a piece of chalk. In 1900 the Russian scientist, Mikhail Tsvet, used the idea to separate the coloured substances in green plants. He had invented the analytical method that he called **chromatography**.

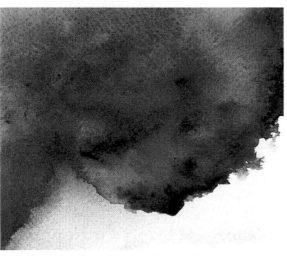

FIGURE 1: Ink spreading out on a wet surface.

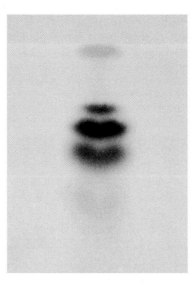

FIGURE 2: Tsvet found that by using chromatography he could separate different substances from the green dye in plants.

Colour writing

You have probably done an experiment where you put a spot of ink on a piece of filter paper and added drops of water. The spot of ink spreads out and may separate to form rings of different colours. This is a simple example of chromatography.

In any form of chromatography there are two parts. There is the fixed part or **stationary phase**. This is the paper in the example above. Then there is the part that moves, the **mobile phase**, which carries the sample along. In the example in Figure 3, the mobile phase is the water soaking up the strip cut in the paper.

A substance that dissolves in another substance is called a solute. A solution of a solute in water is called an **aqueous** solution. (Aqua is the Latin word for water.) Other liquids, such as petrol, ethanol or cyclohexane, can act as solvents. These are called **non-aqueous** solvents. Some substances may dissolve more and some less in non-aqueous solvents than in water. If you use a non-aqueous solvent in the simple chromatography experiment you may get a different pattern of colours from that resulting from using water.

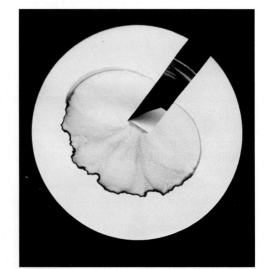

FIGURE 3: Simple paper chromatography using a filter paper, ink and water.

QUESTION

1 Explain what you understand by these terms:

   a stationary phase   b mobile phase   c non-aqueous solvent.

🔍 chromatography

Distribution between solvents

Two liquids that do not mix are said to be **immiscible**. After they are shaken together they settle out into two layers. If a solute is added to the two liquids it will dissolve in both solvents but may be more soluble in one than the other. The solute particles move from one solvent to the other and back again in a type of reversible reaction. After a short time a point is reached where the amount of solute in each solvent stays constant, although the swapping back and forth of particles still continues. This is called a dynamic equilibrium and the solute is said to be **distributed** between the two solvents.

QUESTIONS

2 Why is the distribution of a solute between two immiscible solvents said to be a dynamic equilibrium?

3 Look at Figure 5. What evidence is there that iodine is more soluble in the non-aqueous solvent than in water?

4 How does creativity and imagination help to explain the distribution of a solute between two solvents?

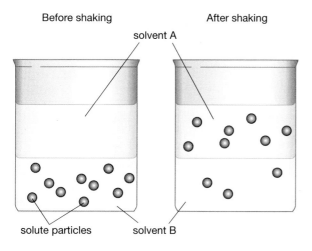

FIGURE 4: Distribution of particles between two solvents.

FIGURE 5: A solution of iodine in water has been shaken with a non-aqueous solvent, such as cyclohexane, which floats on top of the water. Iodine is distributed between the two layers.

Separating by distribution

In chromatography the components of a mixture are separated because they become distributed differently between the stationary and mobile phases. The substance that is most soluble in the mobile phase will be carried fastest through the stationary phase. On the other hand the substance that is least soluble in the mobile phase will tend to stick to the stationary phase and move more slowly.

QUESTION

5 A and B are two components of a mixture. A is more soluble in water than in cyclohexane while B is more soluble in cyclohexane. What will you see when the mixture is put on filter paper and:

a drops of water are added to the paper

b drops of cyclohexane is dripped onto it instead?

Watch out!

The stationary phase in chromatography may be solid or liquid and the mobile phase may be liquid or gas.

Did you know?

Useful substances in plant material can be separated by using column chromatography. A mixture of plant material is washed through a tube packed with a powder such as silica. This was the method first developed by Tsvet for separating different types of chlorophyll.

Q Tsvet chromatography

Paper and thin-layer chromatography

We are learning to:

> describe paper and thin-layer chromatography

> understand the use of reference materials and locating agents

> understand and use R_f values

How is chromatography used?

A driver involved in an accident is likely to be asked to give a blood sample to check for drugs. The blood plasma would be tested, by thin-layer chromatography (TLC), using samples of drugs for comparison. The chromatogram quickly shows whether the driver had taken drugs.

Making chromatograms

Paper chromatography is done with sheets of special paper similar to filter paper. The paper fibres have a coating of water. This is the stationary phase.

In thin-layer chromatography (TLC), used in many analytical laboratories, a plate of glass is coated with silica (silicon dioxide) or alumina (aluminium oxide). In this case, the silica or alumina is the stationary phase.

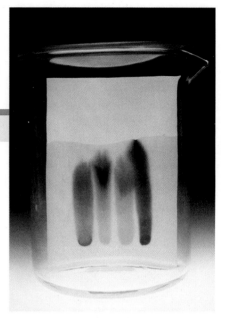

FIGURE 1: Paper chromatography of four different coloured inks.

Spots of the samples are put on a line about 1 or 2 cm from the end of the paper or plate. The paper or plate is then placed upright in a dish, with the marked end at the bottom. The dish contains a little of the solvent that is used as the mobile phase. The solvent slowly rises up the paper or plate. Different substances travel different distances with the solvent.

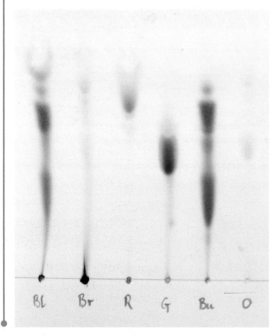

FIGURE 2: A completed paper chromatogram of six inks.

QUESTIONS

1 Why are the samples spotted a short distance from the end of the paper or plate?

2 Look at Figure 2. Do any of the coloured inks seem to have just one component? Which ones?

Seeing the results

If the same solvents are used, chromatograms can be compared. It helps to use **reference materials** to make sure that results are repeatable. A known substance is spotted onto the paper or plate next to the sample. If the sample contains the same substance as the reference material, the substance in both the sample and the reference material will travel up the chromatogram the same distance.

Did you know?

Paper chromatography was first used by the British scientists Archer Martin and Richard Synge in the 1940s. They used it to identify the amino acids that made up various proteins. Chargaff used the same method to identify the four bases in DNA.

Q paper chromatography   thin-layer chromatography

Most test materials are not coloured so the results of a paper or thin-layer chromatogram cannot be seen immediately. An ultraviolet (UV) light will show up the spots if the paper or plate has been treated with a fluorescent material. Another method is to spray the paper or plate with a **locating agent**, such as ninhydrin. This sticks to the substances and gives them a colour. Another method is to put the paper or plate in a closed container with some iodine crystals. Iodine vapour settles on the spots making them visible.

When using locating agents all the spots show up as the same colour, so it is important to use reference materials to enable you to identify the components of the test sample.

QUESTIONS

3 Why would a locating agent be needed to observe a chromatogram of samples of aspirin?

4 A criminal may have used one of three pens to write a letter. How could you use chromatography to identify which pen was used?

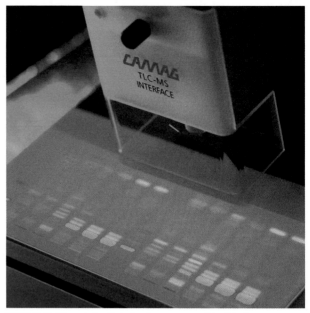

FIGURE 3: Ultraviolet light is shone on to this thin-layer chromatogram. The samples are fluorescent and give out light that reveals their positions.

R_f values

The **R_f value** of a substance is a measure of its position on a chromatogram.

$$R_f \text{ value} = \frac{\text{distance moved by sample}}{\text{distance moved by solvent}}$$

The R_f value for a substance in a paper or thin-layer chromatogram is always the same for the same solvent at the same temperature. Unknown substances can be identified from the R_f value if a list of values for substances with the same solvent is available.

Watch out!

To calculate the R_f value it is usual to measure to the top of a sample spot. This should be done a few times to get the best estimate of the true value.

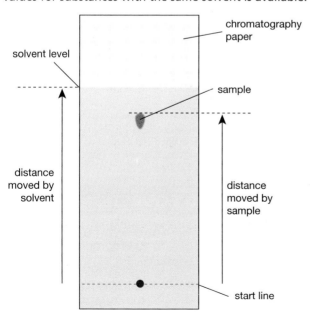

FIGURE 4: Measuring the R_f value of a sample.

QUESTIONS

5 Look at Figure 4. Measure the distances moved by the solvent and the sample and calculate the R_f value of the sample.

6 Five groups of students did a paper chromatogram on a dye and measured the R_f value. Their results were:
0.74, 0.76, 0.88, 0.72, 0.73

a Why is it a good idea to make several measurements of a result?

b Which of the measurements is an outlier? What should be done about it?

c Estimate the true value of the R_f value and the range of the values measured.

Gas chromatography

We are learning to:
> recall how gas chromatography is used
> understand the term 'retention time'
> interpret data on retention time and peak heights in gas chromatography

Can gas chromatography detect life on Mars?

Since the *Viking* landers of the 1970s, Mars space probes have carried miniature gas chromatography equipment. Their purpose is to test whether the Martian soil contains substances produced by living organisms. Early results have been uncertain but later probes may provide an answer.

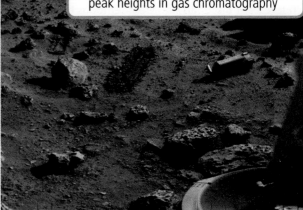

FIGURE 1: Martian soil has been analysed for signs of life.

Using gas chromatography

Gas chromatography is used to analyse many different types of mixture. It is used at airports to test for explosives or drugs. It can be used to find all the substances that make up a sample of a fuel. The substance being tested must be able to form a gas at a temperature below about 400 °C.

In gas chromatography the mobile phase is a gas. Gases such as argon, helium and nitrogen are used because they are unreactive. The gas carries the samples through a long column, which is actually a coiled tube. The tube has a lining of a solid that acts as the stationary phase. The tube is enclosed in an oven so that the temperature can be changed.

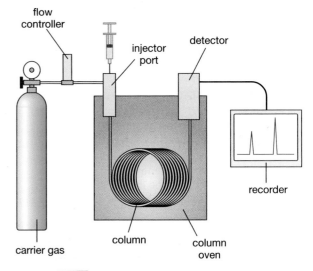

FIGURE 2: The arrangement of parts of a gas chromatography machine.

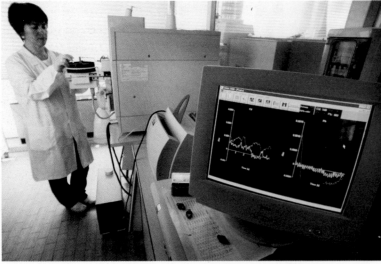

FIGURE 3: An analyst using a gas chromatograph to test the aroma of coffee.

QUESTIONS

1 Why must the gas used in gas chromatography be unreactive?

2 Why is it necessary to heat the chromatography tube for some samples?

Q gas chromatography GCSE

Retention time

As the gas flows through the tube (Figure 2), the different substances in the sample stick to the lining for different lengths of time. The substances are spread out through the tube. At the end of the tube the gas passes through a detector. Each of the substances is detected as it comes out of the tube and is recorded as a peak on the screen.

Timing starts the moment the sample is injected into the carrier gas. The time taken for a substance to pass through the gas chromatograph is called the retention time. The **retention time** for each substance in the sample depends on the length and lining of the chromatography tube, the speed of flow and type of gas and the temperature.

Watch out!

Not all substances in a mixture will appear on the gas chromatogram. They have to be volatile and registered by the detector.

 QUESTIONS

3 Explain why the components of a sample reach the end of the chromatography tubes at different times.

4 Look at Figure 4. What is the retention time for the ethane gas in the sample?

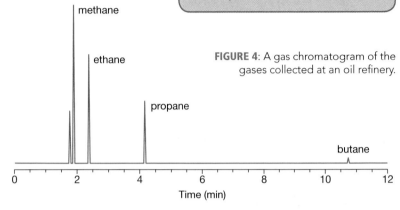

FIGURE 4: A gas chromatogram of the gases collected at an oil refinery.

Interpreting gas chromatograms

The amount of a substance in a sample affects the size of its peak in the gas chromatogram.

The pattern of peaks in the chromatogram are a bit like a fingerprint, as they can indicate to the analyst the source of the sample. For example, a gas chromatogram of a heroin sample can indicate from where the drug was obtained.

A **mass spectrometer** is often attached to the detector. This instrument is able to identify the substances as they pass through the detector.

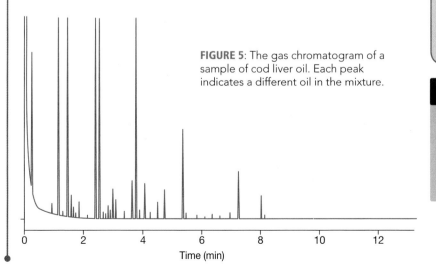

FIGURE 5: The gas chromatogram of a sample of cod liver oil. Each peak indicates a different oil in the mixture.

QUESTIONS

5 Look at Figure 4. Explain how the retention time varies with the size of the hydrocarbon molecule.

6 Look at Figure 5. What could you do to prove that this sample of cod liver oil came from the stock of a particular supplier?

Did you know?

Gas chromatography can detect drugs such as Ecstasy in hair. The point in the hair where the drug is found indicates the time when the drug was taken. Employers may use this test to see if workers are using drugs.

Quantitative analysis

We are learning to:

> understand how to carry out quantitative analysis

> recall how to make up a solution with a concentration in g/dm³

> (Higher) carry out calculations on the concentration of solutions

Why should drivers worry about concentration?

It is illegal in the UK to drive with more than 80 mg of alcohol to 100 ml of blood. In normal concentration units this is 0.8 g/dm³. This quantity needs to be measured accurately as it is evidence that may be used in court to decide whether a driver is guilty of driving when drunk.

FIGURE 1: Police use the alcohol breath-test to give a rough indication of whether the driver is above the legal limit.

Making up solutions

A **standard solution** is a solution with a known amount of a solute dissolved in a fixed volume of the solution. Standard solutions are very important in quantitative analysis so they must be prepared carefully.

> Measure out the mass of the solute you want to dissolve and put it in a clean beaker. Solids should be crushed to a powder.

> Add a little distilled water and stir.

> If not all the solute dissolves, add a little more water until it does.

> Pour the solution carefully into a **volumetric flask**.

> Add a little more water to the beaker, swirl it around to remove any traces of the solution from the sides of the beaker. Pour this into the volumetric flask.

> Very carefully, add distilled water up to the mark on the neck of the flask.

> Put the stopper on the flask and give it a shake.

FIGURE 2: The apparatus needed to make up a standard solution.

FIGURE 3: When a volumetric flask is filled up to the line it contains an accurately measured volume of liquid.

QUESTION

1 Explain why:

a distilled water is used to make up a standard solution

b a volumetric flask instead of an ordinary beaker is used to make up a standard solution

c the flask is shaken when the solution has been made up.

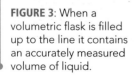
Q standard solutions

Solutions in quantitative analysis

The concentration of a solution is the number of grams of solute in a litre (1 dm³) of the solution. The unit is written as g/dm³.

To measure a property of a solution quantitatively, you first need to measure the mass or the volume of the solute and then the volume of solution when it has been made up. You should take measurements on a number of samples in case you make any errors.

The **mean** of the results gives the **best estimate** of the **true value** of the quantity.

The **range** of the results gives an idea of **uncertainty** in the **accuracy** of the results.

Outliers are measurements that do not seem to fit the pattern of the results. If you show them to be incorrect outliers you can discard them, but otherwise you should include them in the calculation of the mean.

Watch out!

One measurement of any quantity could be wrong for a variety of reasons, so you should always repeat all measurements.

FIGURE 4: The intensity of the colour of these solutions of cobalt chloride depends on their concentration.

Did you know?

A 250 cm³ volumetric flask, when filled to the line, will contain a volume of solution between 249.9 and 250.1 cm³. This is an uncertainty of 0.4 cm³ in 1000 cm³ or 0.04%.

QUESTIONS

2 A bottle of sodium hydroxide is labelled 'concentration 80 g/dm³'. What does this mean?

3 A bottle of hydrochloric acid said it had a concentration of 36 g/dm³. Four 20 cm³ samples of the acid were taken and the pH of each was measured with a pH meter. The results were 0.9, 1.1, 1.8, 1.0. What was the mean and range of the pH of the acid? Comment on your answer.

Calculating concentration (Higher tier only)

$$\text{concentration of solution (g/dm}^3) = \frac{\text{mass of solute (g)}}{\text{volume of solution (dm}^3)}$$

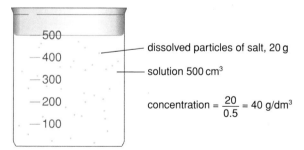

dissolved particles of salt, 20 g

solution 500 cm³

$$\text{concentration} = \frac{20}{0.5} = 40 \text{ g/dm}^3$$

FIGURE 5: Calculating the concentration.

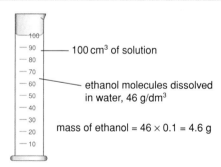

100 cm³ of solution

ethanol molecules dissolved in water, 46 g/dm³

mass of ethanol = 46 × 0.1 = 4.6 g

FIGURE 6: Calculating the mass of solute.

1 dm³ is 1000 cm³ so a volume measured in cm³ must be divided by 1000 to give a volume in dm³. 1 dm³ is the same volume as 1 litre (1000 millilitres).

The formula can be rearranged to calculate the mass of a solute in a particular solution.

mass of solute (g) = concentration (g/dm³) × volume (dm³)

QUESTIONS

4 What is the concentration of a solution of sodium carbonate containing 10.6 g dissolved in 200 cm³ of the solution?

5 What mass of sulfuric acid is there in 50 cm³ of a solution of concentration 100 g/dm³?

Acid–base titration

We are learning to:

> recall how to carry out a titration

> interpret titration results and assess their accuracy

> (Higher) use equations and formula masses to interpret titration results

What's the best indigestion remedy?

Indigestion is caused by excess acid in the stomach. There are many indigestion remedies that contain a base that neutralises the acid. The best remedy will be the one that reacts with the most acid without harmful side effects. The most accurate way to find which remedy is best is to use quantitative analysis.

FIGURE 1: Indigestion can be painful.

Doing titrations

An acid–base titration measures how much of an acid is needed to neutralise a base. First, the sample may have to be dissolved in water. A pipette filler and pipette can be used to put an accurate volume of the sample solution into a conical flask. Then follow this method carefully, to get accurate results.

1 Add a few drops of an indicator to the conical flask.
2 Fill a burette with the standard solution. Run the solution through the burette to fill the jet at the bottom. Record the reading on the burette.
3 Slowly, add the solution from the burette to the conical flask. Swirl the conical flask to mix the solutions.
4 When the indicator is about to change colour, add the solution from the burette one drop at a time.
5 When the indicator changes colour permanently, record the reading on the burette.
6 Wash out the conical flask and repeat the titration.

QUESTIONS

1 What apparatus would you use to do each task?

a Measure 20 cm³ of an alkaline solution accurately.

b Find out, accurately, what volume of an acid will react with 20 cm³ of an alkali.

2 How can you tell when just enough hydrochloric acid has been added to neutralise a solution of sodium hydroxide?

Interpreting results

There are plenty of reasons why titration results can vary – the pipette may not be filled correctly, solutions are splashed or spilled, the colour change is missed, burette readings are not read carefully. It is usual to do a rough titration to get an idea of the volume of the burette solution that will be required. For the next titration the solution can be added very slowly close to the end-point when the colour changes. At least three results, with a variation of no more than 0.1 cm³, are required. If the results vary by no more than 0.1 cm³ then the uncertainty in the data is very small.

The mean of the results can be used in a formula for working out the quantity required.

Example 1

A drain cleaner contains sodium hydroxide (NaOH) solution. A chemist reacts 20 cm³ samples of the drain cleaner with a hydrochloric acid (HCl) solution of concentration 75 g/dm³. A mean volume of 19.5 cm³ of hydrochloric acid is needed to neutralise the solution. What is the concentration of the sodium hydroxide in the drain cleaner?

The formula given is:

$$\text{concentration of sodium hydroxide} = \frac{75 \times \text{volume of HCl} \times \text{RFM NaOH}}{36.5 \times 20}$$

The RFM of sodium hydroxide, NaOH is 23 + 16 + 1 = 40

$$\text{Concentration of sodium hydroxide} = \frac{75 \times 19.5 \times 40}{36.5 \times 20} = 80.1 \, \text{g/dm}^3$$

RAM = relative atomic mass
RFM = relative formula mass

Hint: Use the Periodic Table to find the RAMs.

Hint: So with the titration result of 19.5 cm³ the calculation becomes:

Hint: Don't forget the units.

🔍 analysis of indigestion remedies

Did you know?

Titration is still an important technique in many analytical laboratories, but now it has been automated. A pH meter will send data to a computer, which operates the tap of the burette and stops the titration when the mixture is neutral.

Watch out!

Remember to look out for the units of quantities, particularly volume, which could be in cm^3 or dm^3.

 **QUESTION**

3 In a test on a different drain cleaner than the one in Example 1, but using the same hydrochloric acid, the chemist gets the following results.

$20.2\,cm^3$, $20.1\,cm^3$, $20.0\,cm^3$, $20.1\,cm^3$

a What is the mean of the results?

b Use the formula given in Example 1 to calculate the concentration of sodium hydroxide in the second sample of drain cleaner.

c Use the titration results to assess the uncertainty in your answer to part **b**.

 ## Using equations (Higher tier only)

The steps in interpreting the results of qualitative analysis, using the equation for the reaction and the RFM of the reactants, are shown in Example 2.

Example 2

A chemist is investigating the mass of sodium carbonate in a sample of washing powder. The chemist dissolves 5 g of the washing powder in water and reacts it with a solution of hydrochloric acid of concentration $50\,g/dm^3$. A mean of $22.7\,cm^3$ of hydrochloric acid was needed to neutralise the washing powder. The RFM of hydrochloric acid is 36.5. The equation for the reaction is:

$$Na_2CO_3(aq) + 2HCl(aq \rightarrow 2NaCl(aq) + H_2O(l) + CO_2(g)$$

What is the mass of sodium carbonate in the sample?

Hint: Use the Periodic Table to find the RAMs.

Step 1: The RFM of sodium carbonate = $23 \times 2 + 12 + 16 \times 3 = 106$

Step 2: Calculate the mass of hydrochloric acid in the volume of acid used in the titration.

Mass of HCl used = $50 \times \dfrac{22.7}{1000} = 1.135\,g$

Hint: Mass = concentration (g/dm^3) × volume (dm^3)

Step 3: The equation shows that 2 formula units of HCl reacts with 1 formula unit of Na_2CO_3

$2 \times 36.5 =$ **73** g of HCl reacts with **106** g of Na_2CO_3

So: **1.135** g of HCl reacts with $1.135 \times \dfrac{106}{73}$

$= 1.65\,g$ of Na_2CO_3

So the 5 g sample of washing powder contains 1.65 g of sodium carbonate.

Hint: Use the equation to find how much sodium carbonate this mass of hydrochloric acid reacts with. Put the substance you know first and the substance you are investigating last.

Hint: Note where the numbers go.

 **QUESTION**

4 An archaeologist investigated how much calcium hydroxide was used in the mortar between the bricks of an old house. Crushed samples of the mortar weighing 5 g were reacted with hydrochloric acid of concentration $80\,g/dm^3$.

The equation for this reaction is: $Ca(OH)_2(aq) + 2HCl(aq) \rightarrow CaCl_2(aq) + 2H_2O(l)$

The titration results were $20.9\,cm^3$, $21.0\,cm^3$, $21.0\,cm^3$, $20.9\,cm^3$.

What mass of calcium hydroxide is in the samples? Assess the uncertainty of your answer.

🔍 acid base titration GCSE

Preparing for assessment: Analysing, evaluating and reviewing

To achieve a good grade in science you will need to be able to use your skills and understanding to understand how scientists plan, run and evaluate investigations.

These skills will be assessed in your exams and in Controlled Assessments. This activity supports you in developing the skills of analysing data to support a conclusion and evaluating the accuracy and repeatability of the data.

✳ Balancing acids and alkalis

Matt and Cheryl's class were investigating the neutralisation of alkalis by acids. They wanted to find out how the amount of an acid needed to produce a neutral solution varied with the concentration of the alkali used. Different groups in the class used different solutions of sodium hydroxide but they all used the same volume of sodium hydroxide, the same indicator and the same solution of hydrochloric acid with a concentration of 3.65 g/dm³.

Matt and Cheryl carried out a titration, using a sodium hydroxide solution with a concentration of 4.00 g/dm³. They used a pipette to measure out 20.0 cm³ of the sodium hydroxide into a conical flask and added a few drops of an indicator. They titrated this solution with the hydrochloric acid. They did a trial measurement then repeated the titration another four times. Their results are shown in the first table below.

Matt and Cheryl's data.

Titration number	1	2	3	4	5
Reading on burette at start of titration (cm³)	0.00	10.00	0.00	5.00	4.50
Reading on burette at end of titration (cm³)	20.80	30.10	19.90	25.05	24.45

The other groups in the class displayed their results.

The equation for the reaction is:

sodium hydroxide + hydrochloric acid → sodium chloride + water

NaOH(aq) + HCl(aq) → NaCl(aq) + H₂O(l)

(RAMs: H = 1, O = 16, Na = 23, Cl = 35.5)

Class data.

Group	Concentration of sodium hydroxide used (g/dm³)	Mean volume of acid needed for neutralisation (cm³)	Range of results	Number of results
A	1.00	5.10	4.90 – 5.20	4
B	2.00	10.05	9.7 – 10.35	3
C	3.00	15.80	15.00 – 16.6	2
D	5.00	24.95	24.90 – 25.10	4
E	6.00	30.10	–	1

Task 1

> Calculate the volume of hydrochloric acid used in each of Matt and Cheryl's titrations.
> Which of Matt and Cheryl's results should be used to calculate the mean volume of acid that they used?

Task 2

> Explain why Matt and Cheryl's trial run should not be used in calculating their mean.
> Calculate the mean value of Matt and Cheryl's results.
> Are there any outliers in Matt and Cheryl's results? Explain your answer.
> Draw a table of the class data, including Matt and Cheryl's result.

Task 3

> Draw a best-fit line graph of the class results.
> Show that there is a mathematical relationship between the concentration of the sodium hydroxide solution and the volume of acid needed, for example, when one quantity is doubled the other doubles too.
> What was the range of Matt and Cheryl's results? Do you think that their results were accurate and repeatable enough to draw a conclusion from this investigation?

Task 4

> Add the ranges of the class results to the points on your graph.
> Calculate the mass of sodium hydroxide and the mass of hydrochloric acid used at the neutralisation point for each of the results obtained by the class.
> Do the masses of sodium hydroxide and hydrochloric acid agree with the masses predicted by the equation for the reaction?
> Discuss whether the class data shows sufficient repeatability and suggest reasons for any outliers.

Maximise your grade

Use these suggestions to improve your work and be more successful.

E
To be on target for grade E you need to:
> display your results in simple graphs or charts, or carry out simple calculations such as working out the mean of several repeated readings
> identify the results which are outliers in a set of data or explain why a set of data does not have outliers.

To be on target for a grade D or C, you also need to:
> draw a best-fit line graph, with the correct scales and axes, or a similar complex chart or diagram, or compare your results mathematically

C
> look at the pattern of a set of results or the scatter of points in a graph to assess the accuracy and repeatability of the data and explain your assessment.

To be on target for a grade B or A, you also need to:
> draw graphs that show the range of the data or which have a number of sets of data on one set of axes, or look for patterns in data, using mathematical formulae or gradients of graphs

A
> be critical of the repeatability of the data and suggest explanations for outliers.

C7 Checklist

To achieve your forecast grade in the exam you'll need to revise

Use this checklist to see what you can do now. Refer back to pages 66–115 if you're not sure. Look across the rows to see how you could progress – *bold italic* means Higher tier only.

Remember, you'll need to be able to use these ideas in various ways, such as:
> interpreting pictures, diagrams and graphs
> applying ideas to new situations
> explaining ethical implications
> suggesting some benefits and risks to society
> drawing conclusions from evidence you've been given.

Look at pages 206–212 for more information about exams and how you'll be assessed.

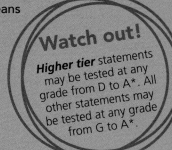

Watch out!

Higher tier statements may be tested at any grade from D to A*. All other statements may be tested at any grade from G to A*.

To aim for a grade E	To aim for a grade C	To aim for a grade A
understand that the chemical industry produces 'bulk' and 'fine' chemicals and recall examples of each; understand that developing new products requires people doing a variety of jobs		understand that there are laws which ensure that new chemical processes protect the health of people and do not harm the environment
understand that there are several stages in the manufacture of a product	understand how a process can be made more sustainable	understand how improving the atom economy of a process improves its sustainability
understand the terms exothermic and endothermic and draw energy diagrams for reactions	understand that energy is used to break bonds, and that energy is given out when bonds are made; understand that this is shown by the activation energy in more detailed energy diagrams	
understand that catalysts and enzymes are used in industry to speed up reactions	understand that catalysts provide an alternative route for a reaction with a lower activation energy; understand that enzymes work best under certain conditions; *use data on the energy required to break covalent bonds to calculate the energy changes in reactions*	
use the Periodic Table to obtain relative atomic masses	calculate relative formula masses of molecules and compounds; *calculate the masses of reactants and products using balanced equations*	

To aim for a grade E

recall that alkanes are a family of hydrocarbons, and recall the names and formulae of some alkanes; recall that alkanes burn

write word equations for reactions

recall the names, formulae and uses of methanol and ethanol; recognise that alcohols have an –OH group

understand that ethanol is made by the fermentation of sugars with yeast, and that the ethanol solution must be distilled to concentrate it

recall that ethanol can be made from ethane found in crude oil, and that ways of using bacteria to turn biomass into ethanol are being investigated

recall the names, formulae and properties of carboxylic acids

recall that vinegar is a weak solution of ethanoic acid, which is a carboxylic acid

recall that esters have pleasant smells and are found in fruits; recall that esters are used as food flavourings, solvents and plasticisers

To aim for a grade C

use structural and 3D formulae to represent alkanes; understand that alkanes are unreactive because of their strong covalent bonds

interpret *and write* balanced symbol equations

compare the properties of alcohols with water and alkanes; understand the combustion of alcohols; *recall and compare the reaction of sodium with alcohols and with water and alkanes*

understand that fermentation takes place under optimum conditions of temperature and pH

compare the conditions required and the sustainability of the various processes for making ethanol and interpret data provided on the processes

recall the structural formulae of carboxylic acids and understand that the properties are due to the –COOH group; understand that carboxylic acids react as typical acids with metals, alkalis and carbonates

understand that carboxylic acids are classed as weak acids because their reactions are less vigorous than those of strong acids

recall that esters are formed by the reaction of a carboxylic acid with an alcohol in the presence of an acid catalyst; *understand the procedure and techniques for making and purifying an ester*

To aim for a grade A

understand that alkanes are 'saturated', and that 'unsaturated' hydrocarbons have a C=C double bond

understand why there is a limit to the concentration of ethanol that can be achieved by fermentation

understand that solutions of weak acids have a higher pH value than similar solutions of strong acids

C7 Checklist

To aim for a grade E	To aim for a grade C	To aim for a grade A

understand that animals and plants produce fats and oils largely as a store of energy

recall that fats and oils are esters of glycerol and fatty acids

recall that fat molecules are largely saturated while oil molecules are unsaturated

understand that many reactions are reversible and that the ⇌ symbol in an equation shows this

understand that a reversible reaction can reach equilibrium where the amounts of reactants and products stay the same; *understand that a chemical equilibrium is dynamic, meaning the forward and backward reactions continue to take place*

understand why nitrogen fertiliser is needed; recall that ammonia for making fertiliser is produced by the Haber process, using air, natural gas and steam

recall that the Haber process reaction is reversible; understand how recycling reactants and the choice of temperature and pressure improve the yield of the Haber process, and that the choice of catalyst increases the rate and improves the economy of the reaction; *explain how the choice of conditions in the Haber process is a compromise to give the most economical process*

understand the environmental effects of manufacturing ammonia and of the use of fertilisers

understand how bacterial enzymes fix nitrogen from the air and how these are now being developed to produce fertilisers

interpret and evaluate data comparing the sustainability of ways of producing fertilisers

understand the difference between qualitative and quantitative analysis; understand that analysis should be carried out on a sample that represents the bulk of the material; understand the special procedures used to prepare, collect and store samples; recall that analysis is often carried out on solutions

understand that in chromatography, samples are separated by a mobile phase moving through a stationary phase; understand the difference between aqueous and non-aqueous solvents; describe and compare paper and thin-layer chromatography

understand that in chromatography the components of the sample become distributed between the stationary and mobile phases by a dynamic equilibrium; understand the use of reference materials and locating agents in chromatography

understand that the components are separated because they have a different pattern of distribution; use a formula to calculate R_f values and understand how R_f values are used

To aim for a grade E

To aim for a grade C

To aim for a grade A

recall the procedure for analysing mixtures using gas chromatography; understand the term 'retention time'

use retention times and peak heights to interpret gas chromatograms

recall how to make up a standard solution, and that the unit for concentration is g/dm^3

use a formula to calculate the concentration of a solution or the mass of solute dissolved in a volume of the solution

recall the procedure for carrying out an acid–base titration

understand the stages in quantitative analysis, such as titration, to ensure the accuracy and repeatability of data; assess the uncertainty in a set of results; use a given formula to interpret titration results; *use balanced equations and RFMs to interpret titration results*

Exam-style questions

Foundation

1 Methyl ethyl ketone (MEK) is a useful solvent for inks and polymers. It is used as 'polystyrene cement' for sticking polystyrene parts together. Over a million tonnes of MEK is produced every year. MEK is not considered to be a very hazardous chemical.

$$
\begin{array}{ccccc}
 & H & O & H & H \\
 & | & \| & | & | \\
H- & C- & C- & C- & C-H \\
 & | & & | & | \\
 & H & & H & H
\end{array}
$$

AO1 **a** Explain whether MEK is a bulk or fine chemical. [1]

b Here are five statements about making MEK. Which two statements, when put together, suggest that the production of MEK may not be sustainable? [2]

A: Making MEK uses catalysts

B: Making MEK uses hydrocarbons from crude oil

C: MEK has to be separated from other products

D: Crude oil will run out one day

E: Some of the other products formed when MEK is produced are poisonous

AO2 **c** One stage of the production of MEK uses an alcohol called butan-2-ol. On this drawing of the structure of butan-2-ol, circle the part of the molecule that is responsible for the characteristic properties of alcohols. [1]

$$
\begin{array}{ccccc}
 & & & H & \\
 & & & / & \\
H & O & H & H & \\
| & | & | & | & \\
H-C-C-C-C-H \\
| & | & | & | & \\
H & H & H & H &
\end{array}
$$

AO2
AO3 **d** Some trees produce MEK naturally in small quantities in their nuts and some bacteria can produce MEK from cellulose in plants. What are the advantages and disadvantages of obtaining MEK from plant material? Suggest whether you think this source of MEK is a better or worse alternative to the present source.
The quality of written communication will be assessed in your answer to this question. [6]

AO2 **e** Explain why the government has strict regulations on the transport and storage of the substances used in the manufacture of MEK. [2]
[Total 12]

2 In the Haber process, nitrogen reacts with hydrogen to make ammonia. The equation for the reaction is:
$$N_2(g) + 3H_2(g) \rightleftharpoons 2NH_3(g)$$

AO1 **a** What does the $\rightleftharpoons$ sign show? [1]

AO1 **b** In the reaction only 20% of the reactants are made into ammonia. What is done to increase the overall yield of ammonia in the Haber process? [1]

AO2
AO3 **c** The Haber process uses an iron catalyst. How does the catalyst speed up the reaction? [1]

d A new factory producing ammonia is using a new catalyst that works better than the traditional iron catalyst used in the Haber process. This means that the plant can run at a temperature of about 200 °C instead of 450 °C. The plant also uses a higher pressure than usual. Describe and explain how the conditions in the new plant will affect the yield of ammonia. Give your assessment of how this will affect the costs of the process.
The quality of written communication will be assessed in your answer to this question. [6]

AO2 **e** Some bacteria are able to use nitrogen from the air to produce fertilisers for plants. Why are scientists studying these bacteria? [1]
[Total 10]

3 A forensic scientist was asked to analyse three samples of a drug labelled A, B and C, found on a suspected illegal drug dealer. The scientist decided to use paper chromatography for the analysis. She placed a spot of each sample of the drugs on a line close to the bottom of the sheet of paper. She also put on a spot of the pure drug that the samples were thought to contain as a reference. She prepared the chromatogram shown below.

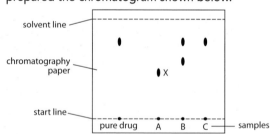

AO3 **a** Look at the chromatogram. What conclusions can the scientist make about the three samples found on the suspect? [3]

AO1 **b** Explain why some substances have travelled further up the chromatogram than others. [2]

c The R_f value of the reference material is 0.8.
$$R_f = \frac{\text{distance travelled by solute}}{\text{distance travelled by solvent}}$$

AO2 What is the R_f value of the substance that makes the spot marked X? [2]
[Total 7]

AO1 recall the science   AO2 apply your knowledge   AO3 evaluate and analyse the evidence

Worked example

Foundation

Scalegon is used to remove limescale from baths and toilets. It contains methanoic acid.

AO2 a Methanoic acid reacts with limescale because it is weak acid. Why might it be safer to use methanoic acid to remove limescale rather than a strong acid such as sulfuric acid? [1]

methanoic acid is not as dangerous as sulfuric acid. ✗

AO1 b A scientist working for *Scalegon* has to check that the concentration of methanoic acid in the product is correct. What are the units of concentration? [1]

g.dm³ ✗

AO1 c The scientist decides to carry out a quantitative analysis of a sample of *Scalegon* by titrating it with a standard solution containing 160 g of sodium hydroxide in 1 dm³ of solution . He measures out 10.0 cm³ of *Scalegon* into a conical flask. Which of the following apparatus is best for measuring the *Scalegon*? [1]
A: a 100 cm³ beaker   B: a 100 cm³ measuring cylinder
C: a 10 cm³ measuring cylinder   D: a 10.0 cm³ pipette

C ✗

AO1 d The scientist fills a burette with the sodium hydroxide solution and adds a few drops of an indicator to the conical flask. How does he find out how much sodium hydroxide solution is needed to react with the methanoic acid in the *Scalegon* sample? [2]

He opens the tap on the burette and lets the sodium hydroxide run

into the conical flask. He shakes the flask. ✔ *When the indicator*

changes colour, he closes the tap and reads off the burette. ✔

AO2 e The scientist got a mean value of 22.5 cm³ in the titration.
  i Calculate the relative formula mass of methanoic acid, HCOOH. (RAMs: H = 1, C = 12, O = 16) [1]

  1 + 12 + 16 + 1 = 30 ✗

  ii Use the formula given below to work out the concentration of the methanoic acid in the *Scalegon*. [2]

$$\text{Concentration of methanoic acid} = \begin{array}{c}\text{mean volume of} \\ \text{sodium hydroxide} \\ \text{used}\end{array} \times \begin{array}{c}\text{RFM of} \\ \text{methanoic} \\ \text{acid}\end{array} \times 0.4$$

  = 22.5 x 30 x 0.4

  = 270 ✔✔   [Total 8]

How to raise your grade

Take note of the comments from examiners – these will help you to improve your grade.

No marks. The answer is insufficient and merely restates the question. Weak acids do not react as violently as strong acids because they have a higher pH.

Incorrect. The correct unit is g/dm³ which means grams per cubic decimetre.

Incorrect. The correct answer is D. A pipette can measure out to an accuracy of 0.05 cm³ while a measuring cylinder can only be read to about 0.2 cm³.

2 marks. The answer correctly states how the acid and alkali are mixed and when to stop and read the volume of alkali used.

No marks. The correct answer is 46 because there are two oxygen atoms in the molecule, and 1 + 12 + 16 + 16 + 1 = 46.

2 marks. The correct answer should be 414 g/dm³ but the marks are awarded because the incorrect answer from part **i** has been correctly put in the formula and the calculation carried out correctly. This is an example of an error carried forward. There are no marks awarded here for the units, but check the question – if the units are asked for then there may be a mark for giving them.

Exam-style questions

Higher

4 The reaction between hydrogen gas and chlorine gas is explosive in the light. The reaction is *exothermic* with a low *activation energy*.

AO1 **a** Explain the terms in italics. [2]

AO1 **b** Draw an energy profile for the reaction, labelling the overall energy change for the reaction. [2]

c The equation for the reaction is:

$H_2(g) + Cl_2(g) \rightarrow 2HCl(g)$

The table shows the energy involved in making or breaking some bonds.

Bond	Energy (kJ/mol)
H–H	436
Cl–Cl	243
H–Cl	432

AO1 **i** Calculate the energy change involved in breaking bonds in this reaction. [1]

AO1 **ii** Calculate the energy change involved in making bonds in this reaction. [1]

AO2 **iii** Calculate the overall energy change for the reaction. [1]

[Total 7]

5 Biodiesel is a renewable fuel made by reacting vegetable oils with methanol. The reaction is catalysed by sodium methoxide, which is made by reacting sodium with methanol. The equation for the reaction is:

$2CH_3OH(l) + 2Na(s) \rightarrow 2CH_3ONa(s) + H_2(g)$

AO1 **a** How does this reaction resemble the reaction of sodium with water? [1]

AO2 **b** How does the behaviour of sodium with methanol, water and an alkane such as paraffin oil differ? [2]

AO2 **c** What mass of methanol would completely react with 2.3 g of sodium? Use the Periodic Table on page 215 to help you. [3]

[Total 6]

AO2 **6** Ammonia gas (NH_3), produced by the Haber process, is reacted with nitric acid solution (HNO_3) to make the fertiliser, ammonium nitrate solution (NH_4NO_3).

a Write a balanced equation for the reaction, with state symbols. [1]

b The ammonium nitrate solution has a concentration of 800 g/dm³. What is the mass of ammonium nitrate in 100 cm³ of the solution? [1]

To check that the nitric acid is the correct concentration for the reaction with the ammonia, diluted samples of the acid are analysed by titration with a standard solution of sodium hydroxide with a concentration of 20 g/dm³. The equation for the reaction is:

$NaOH(aq) + HNO_3(aq) \rightarrow NaNO_3(aq) + H_2O(l)$

10.0 cm³ of the diluted acid is titrated with the sodium hydroxide solution. The test was done four times and the results obtained were as shown in the table.

Test	1	2	3	4
Volume of sodium hydroxide solution used (cm³)	19.80	19.95	20.20	20.05

c Calculate the concentration of the diluted nitric acid. Use the Periodic Table on page 215 for relative atomic masses. Show your working. [6]

[Total 8]

7 This question is about the production of ethanol.

AO1 **a** There are a number of ways of producing ethanol for use as a fuel, including:
A: from ethane using catalysts
B: fermentation using yeast
C: using genetically modified *E. coli* bacteria.

i Match the processes A, B and C to the raw materials given below.
1: Cellulose from wood and waste plant matter
2: crude oil
3: sugars from plants such as sugar cane and corn. [1]

ii Match the processes A, B and C to the following figures for world production of ethanol as a fuel in 2010. (Figures are approximate.)
1: 87 billion litres
2: 4 billion litres
3: 0 litres [1]

AO1 **b** Describe, with equations, the steps in the production of ethanol from ethane. [2]

AO1

AO3 **c** Ethanol obtained from sugar cane and corn is in solution in water and must be distilled. The remaining woody parts of sugar cane called bargasse can be used as the fuel for this. Corn ethanol must be heated by other sources. Ethanol produced by bacteria will require less separation and ethanol obtained from ethane is pure. Discuss the costs and benefits of the three processes for producing ethanol fuel suggesting which may be the most sustainable source of fuel for the future. The quality of written communication will be assessed in your answer to this question. [6]

[Total 10]

AO1 recall the science   AO2 apply your knowledge   AO3 evaluate and analyse the evidence

✳ Worked example

Higher

How to raise your grade

Take note of the comments from examiners – these will help you to improve your grade.

AO2 **a** Many fruits contain esters. Which of the following is a possible reason for this?

A: As a store of energy for the seeds.

B: To attract animals with their smell and flavour to disperse the seeds.

C: To attract insects by their bright colours.

D: To collect sunlight in photosynthesis. [1]

B ✔

Correct. Esters are volatile and have distinctive smells and flavours.

b The equation for the formation of an ester is shown below

$$CH_3COOH(l) + CH_3OH(l) \rightleftharpoons CH_3COOCH_3 (l) + H_2O(l)$$

AO2 **(i)** Name the two reactants and the ester that is formed. [3]

reactants: ethanoic acid, methanol, ✔✔

ester: ethyl methanoate ✘

2 marks only. The names of the reactants are correct but the name of the ester has been written the wrong way round – the alcohol should come first i.e. methyl ethanoate.

AO1 **(ii)** What further substance is required to speed up the reaction? [1]

sulfuric acid ✔

1 mark. Any strong acid will catalyse the reaction.

AO2 **(iii)** The reactants are *heated under reflux* to decrease the time taken to reach an equilibrium in the reaction. What does *heated under reflux* mean? [1]

The mixture is heated for a long time. ✘

AO1

No mark awarded. Heating under reflux involves heating the reaction mixture so that any vapours formed are condensed and returned to the reaction container.

AO2 **d** Describe the procedures for separating and purifying the product. Explain what happens in each stage and name the apparatus required.
The quality of written communication will be assessed in your answer to this question. [6]

The mixture is heated in a flask. The gases given off are collected and pass through a condensor which turns the gases back to a liquid which is collected. This is called distilation. The ester has the lowest boiling point of the substances in the mixture so boils off first.

A drying agent is added to the distilate to remove water that is given off with the ester.

Then the product is distiled again and only the gas collected at the boiling point of the ester is condensed and collected. ✔✔✔

[Total 12]

This answer gains 4 marks. Many of the points have been covered in the answer, it is well structured and uses technical terms appropriately, but there are a few spelling errors (condenser, distillation, distillate, distilled). To achieve full marks you need to cover all the parts of the separation, including the use of a tap funnel to remove acid and alcohol impurities. (See the example banded mark scheme for QWC questions on page 211.)

What you should already know...

The Earth is in orbit around the Sun

Our solar system has eight planets, many of which have moons in orbit about them. The Earth has a single moon.

Our Sun is a typical star in a huge galaxy of stars, and the Universe has thousands of millions of galaxies.

The stars are vast distances from us, and these distances can be measured in light-years.

 What shape is our galaxy, and what is it called?

Light is a wave

Light waves are part of the electromagnetic spectrum. They are described by wavelength, frequency and speed, and they travel through empty space at a constant speed.

Light travels in straight lines but may be refracted when it passes from one medium to another.

 How is energy transferred by light?

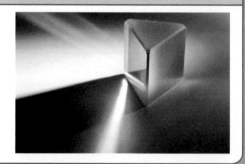

We use different methods to measure the distance of a star

The brightness of a star depends on the amount of light it emits and on its distance from us.

The effect of parallax on the apparent position of a star as the Earth moves around the Sun can be used to measure the distance of a 'nearby' star.

We know from the light detected that all distant galaxies are moving away from us, and this led to the Big Bang theory of the beginning of the Universe.

 What other evidence has been found for the Big Bang?

A star's energy comes from nuclear fusion

In a star the temperature and density are so great that nuclear fusion occurs, transforming hydrogen to helium and giving out a lot of energy. As stars get older, different fusion reactions occur, producing other elements.

The energy generated from fusion is radiated from the star's surface. The radiation that we receive from stars gives us information about it.

 What types of radiation, other than visible light, can we detect from stars?

In P7 you will find out about...

> the apparent motion of the Sun, Moon, stars and planets across the sky

> the leap of imagination needed for astronomers to explain the odd paths of planets against the background of stars

> how the phases of the Moon, and solar and lunar eclipses occur

> how refraction of light leads to the formation of an image by a convex lens

> the construction of a simple optical telescope and how it forms a magnified image

> the use of reflecting astronomical telescopes with curved mirrors

> the effect of diffraction of light on astronomical images

> measuring distance to stars, using the parallax angle

> Cepheid variable stars, and how these can be used as distance indicators

> the historical debate about the size of the Universe and the nature of spiral nebulae

> Hubble's discovery of the *Andromeda* galaxy and the development of his relationship between galactic recessional velocity and distance

> the radiation emitted from stars and its dependence on surface temperature

> the formation of spectra and their importance in astronomical observations

> the relationships between pressure, volume and temperature of a gas

> what is meant by the absolute zero of temperature

> how stars are born in giant molecular clouds of gas

> the nuclear fusion reactions that power stars

> the collapse of a star when its nuclear fuel runs out

> the final stages of a star's life, ending as a white dwarf or a neutron star or a black hole

> the different types of telescopes used today, and the factors that are important in the choice of their location

> the particular advantages and disadvantages of orbiting telescopes

> how astronomers collaborate in their research

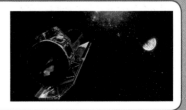

The solar day

We are learning to:
> explain the daily motion of the Sun, Moon and stars
> (Higher) explain the difference between a sidereal day and a solar day

How can we explain the movement of the Sun?

The movement of the Sun, Moon and stars across the sky has fascinated people since ancient times. Some pictured the Sun as a god in a chariot, being chased across the sky. Even now it is easy to imagine the Sun travelling across the sky each day from east to west.

FIGURE 1: Druids say certain stones at Stonehenge mark sunrise on the longest day of the year.

Measuring a day

The earliest clocks were made by the Egyptians 3500 years ago. They marked the position of the shadow cast by a vertical post. When the post's shadow next fell at the same point, they knew that the Sun was again in the same position in the sky, so one day had passed. The Egyptians divided the daylight period into 10 equal periods plus two more of twilight. The night was divided into 12 equal periods. This led to the 24-hour day.

A **solar day** is the time that passes between the Sun appearing at its highest point in the sky on two successive days. A sundial measures this.

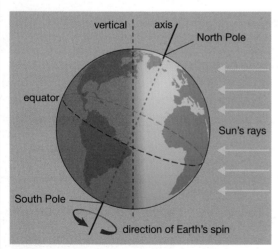

FIGURE 3: The Earth spins on its axis so that the Sun appears to rise in the east and set in the west.

FIGURE 2: Sundials measure the passage of the Sun across the sky.

QUESTIONS

1 In a survey, about one-third of the people asked thought that the Sun went round the Earth.

  a Suggest why they might think this.

  b How would you persuade them it was the other way round?

2 What is the problem with the Egyptian way of defining the hour?

Q solar day

The motion of the Moon and stars

The Earth's daily rotation also makes the Moon appear to travel across the sky from east to west – but the Moon is also orbiting the Earth. This orbital motion means that the Moon takes longer than 24 hours to return to the same position in the sky. On average, the Moon rises about 50 minutes later each day than on the previous day.

The stars also appear to move across the sky. If you point a camera at a region of the night sky and leave the shutter open for a few hours, the rotation of the Earth blurs the images of stars into arcs. In Figure 4 the camera is pointing towards the Pole star, which is above the Earth's North Pole. All the other stars, and any visible planets, seem to rotate around it as the Earth spins.

The stars take a little less than 24 hours to return to the same position in the night sky.

QUESTIONS

3 Suppose the Moon rose at 5.00 am this morning. Explain why it will be about 29 days before it will rise at this time again.

4 The times for the stars, Sun and Moon to cross the sky are all different. Which of these times is closest to the time it takes the Earth to rotate once? Explain your reasoning.

FIGURE 4: A long exposure photograph of the night sky. The red arrow shows the direction of rotation of the stars.

Sidereal days (Higher tier only)

Why is the time taken for a star to be seen in the same position slightly less than 24 hours? This is because in fact it takes 23 hours 56 minutes 4.09 seconds for the Earth to rotate through 360°. This is known as a **sidereal day**. It is different from a solar day because of the Earth's orbit around the Sun. By the time the Earth has turned through one complete revolution, it has also moved relative to the Sun, as shown in Figure 5.

FIGURE 5: After one full rotation of the Earth, the Sun is not quite overhead again.

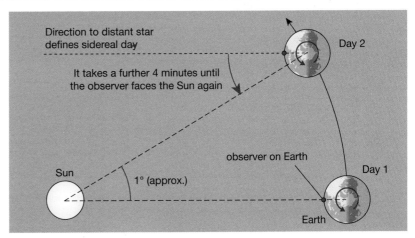

QUESTION

5 The gravitational pull of the Moon is gradually slowing down the Earth's rotation. How will this affect the length of the day? What will happen to the number of days in the year?

Did you know?

The length of a sidereal day varies slightly throughout the year, because the Earth's speed around the Sun varies. We now use radio waves from distant objects called quasars to measure the day.

The Moon

We are learning to:
> explain the phases of the Moon
> explain eclipses of the Sun and of the Moon

Should we go back to the Moon?

Men last walked on the Moon in December 1972. Now scientists are planning to go back. Unmanned spacecraft, such as the *Lunar Crater Observation and Sensing Satellite* (LCROSS), have been probing the Moon's secrets. LCROSS sent a 2300 kg impactor crashing into the Moon. Debris was thrown 50 km above the lunar surface, where it was analysed. The results showed that there is frozen water below the Moon's surface: water that might be useful to a future Moon base.

FIGURE 1: LCROSS fired a van-sized projectile at the Moon at over 5600 mph to make a crater as big as a tennis court.

The phases of the Moon

The Moon is our nearest astronomical neighbour. It orbits the Earth at an average distance of 384 000 km. It does not give off any light of its own. We see it because it reflects the Sun's light. As the Moon moves it reflects more, or less, light towards the Earth. We see the sunlit part of the Moon change shape from a full circle to a crescent and back again. These shapes are known as the **phases of the Moon** (Figure 2).

The Moon takes 27.3 days to orbit the Earth. But because the Earth is moving around the Sun, it takes the Moon a bit longer to get back to the same position relative to the Sun. In fact there are 29.5 days between two full Moons. This is known as a **lunar month**.

> ## QUESTIONS
>
> **1** How many days are there between a full moon and a new moon?
>
> **2** How many full moons are there in a year?

sunlight

new Moon

full Moon

dark side

far side

how the Moon appears from Earth

FIGURE 2: One side of the Moon is lit by the Sun. As the Moon orbits the Earth, we see the 'phases' of the Moon.

Did you know?

The Moon is a rocky, dense body with virtually no atmosphere. The surface temperature varies from −200 °C in the lunar night to 27 °C in the sunlight.

Eclipses

The diameter of the Moon is about $\frac{1}{8}$ that of the Earth. This is an unusually large moon for a planet the size of Earth. The Sun's diameter is about 400 times bigger than that of the Moon, but the Sun is also 400 times further away from Earth. This coincidence means that the Sun and Moon both appear to be the same size from Earth.

As the Moon orbits, it sometimes passes between the Sun and the Earth, casting a shadow on the Earth. This is called a **solar eclipse** (Figures 3 and 4).

When the Moon travels into the Earth's shadow, it can no longer reflect the Sun's light and observers on Earth see a **lunar eclipse** (Figures 5 and 6).

🔍 lunar month   eclipse

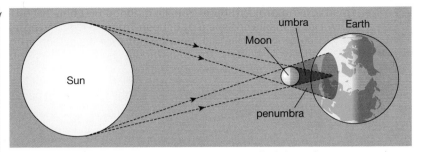

FIGURE 3: Observers In the area of total shadow, called the umbra, see a total eclipse. In an area of partial shadow, the penumbra, there is a partial eclipse.

FIGURE 4: A solar eclipse: at 'totality' the Moon exactly blocks the Sun and the corona becomes visible.

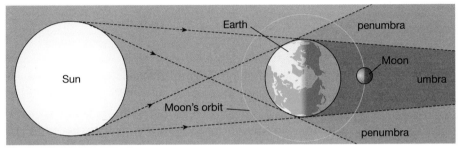

FIGURE 5: A lunar eclipse occurs when the Moon is in the Earth's shadow.

FIGURE 6: A total lunar eclipse.

QUESTIONS

3 A lunar eclipse always occurs at the same phase of the Moon. Explain which phase this is.

4 Which do you think lasts longer, a lunar eclipse or a solar eclipse? Explain your answer.

Did you know?

A total lunar eclipse turns the Moon orange-red. Sunlight is bent (refracted) around the Earth by the atmosphere. (See pages 136–137, Refraction of light.)

The Moon's orbit

As the Moon orbits the Earth once a month, you might think that there should be a lunar eclipse and a solar eclipse every month. But the orbit of the Moon is not in the same plane as the Earth's orbit around the Sun (Figure 7). We only get an eclipse when the Sun, Moon and Earth all line up. That happens less frequently, only two or three times a year on average.

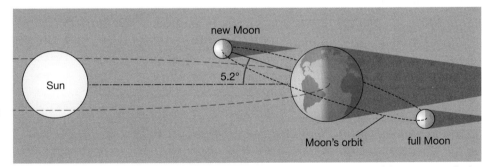

FIGURE 7: The Moon's orbit is inclined at an angle to the Earth's orbit around the Sun. Usually the Moon's shadow passes above – or below – the Earth. Similarly, the full Moon is not usually in the Earth's shadow.

QUESTION

5 The Moon's orbit is not circular. The Moon's distance from the Earth changes as it orbits. Suppose there is a solar eclipse when the Moon is at its furthest distance from Earth. What difference would an observer notice?

The problem of the planets

We are learning to:

> recall the names of the naked-eye planets

> describe the motion of the planets

> realise how explanations of the solar system have been developed using evidence and creative thought

Who says the Earth moves?

The ancient Greeks believed that the Earth was stationary, at the centre of the Universe, and that the Sun, Moon, planets and stars revolved around it. This view survived until 1542, when a Polish monk, Copernicus, published a book describing a solar system with the Sun at the centre. Copernicus used data recorded many years earlier by the Islamic astronomer, Al-Battani, to support his hypothesis.

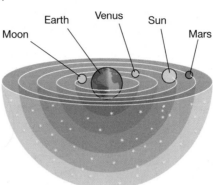

FIGURE 1: The Earth-centred (geocentric) model of the solar system.

The naked-eye planets

Humankind has known about Mercury, Venus, Mars, Jupiter and Saturn since ancient times. These planets reflect enough light towards Earth to be visible with the naked eye. The amount of light that a planet reflects to Earth depends on:

> how close the planet is to the Sun

> how close the planet is to Earth

> the size of the planet

> the nature of the planet's surface.

Did you know?

Venus sometimes passes directly between the Earth and the Sun. This 'transit of Venus' has been used to measure the distance from Earth to the Sun and the speed of light. The next one will be visible from Hawaii in 2012, but after that you'll need to wait until 2117!

FIGURE 2: Each planet orbits at a different speed so its distance from Earth, and its apparent brightness, changes.

QUESTIONS

1 Like the Moon, Mercury and Venus have phases. These can only be seen through a telescope, but it is impossible to see either planet when it is a 'full' disc. Explain why. (Figure 2 may help you with this.)

2 Explain why Mars, as seen from Earth, varies in brightness.

3 Venus and Jupiter are the brightest planets, but they are bright for different reasons. Explain why.

Q geocentric model

Wandering stars

Ancient astronomers observed the motion of the planets. They noticed that, as well as moving with the daily rotation of the sky, the planets moved across the sky relative to the fixed stars. The word 'planet' comes from the Greek for 'wandering'.

If you record the position of a planet at the same time every night, it traces an unusual path across the sky. Sometimes it even goes backwards. This is called **retrograde motion** and it was very difficult to explain, using an Earth-centred model.

The Earth-centred model could explain the daily motion of the Sun, Moon and stars across the sky. It also felt intuitively correct. However, this model of the solar system couldn't easily explain the motion of the planets, nor the way they varied in brightness. It took a leap of imagination to devise a new model of the solar system – one in which all the planets, including Earth, orbited the Sun.

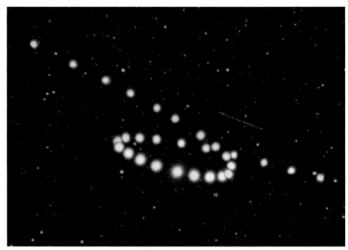

FIGURE 3: The path of Mars shown by superimposing 35 pictures taken at the same time of night, one week apart.

QUESTIONS

4 Figure 3 shows the motion of Mars, compared to the stars. Why are the photographs taken at the same time every night?

5 Why was it difficult for the Greeks to explain retrograde motion? (Look back at Figure 1.)

Explaining retrograde motion

Copernicus realised that the motion of the planets would be easy to explain if the Sun were at the centre and all the planets revolved around it. The planets closer to the Sun move faster in their orbits than the outer planets do. So Earth catches up with Mars and then goes past it. This makes it look as if Mars is moving backwards (Figure 4).

FIGURE 5: Al-Battani (AD858–929) made detailed observations that Copernicus used and that helped to change our view of the Universe.

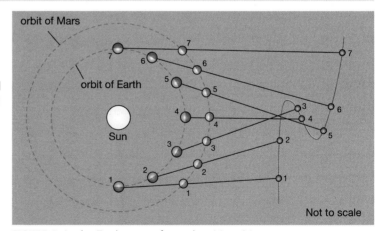

FIGURE 4: As the Earth moves faster than Mars, Mars appears to go backwards against the background of stars.

QUESTION

6 Copernicus's Sun-centred model caused uproar. Galileo supported it but the Roman Catholic Church insisted that the Earth was at the centre of the Universe. Suggest some scientific arguments for and against the Sun-centred (heliocentric) model.

Q heliocentric model

Navigating the sky

We are learning to:
> explain why the night sky changes with the seasons
> understand how stars can be located
> (Higher) understand what is meant by the celestial sphere

How do migrating birds navigate?

At least one species of bird, the Indigo Bunting, uses the stars to navigate. These small birds, which fly from North America to Mexico, seem to learn the patterns of the night sky while they are young. They can identify the Pole Star and fly away from it to the south. Young birds raised in a planetarium, where the stars were turned about a different star, called *Betelgeuse*, flew the wrong way when they were older.

FIGURE 1: Indigo Buntings recognise patterns in the stars.

Summer and winter stars

For centuries people have used the stars to navigate. They identified patterns in the stars. They called these patterns **constellations**. The patterns enabled them to make sense of the night sky. Figure 2 shows the constellation *Sagittarius*, in the summer sky in the northern hemisphere. But the winter sky looks different – the familiar summer constellations are missing.

We see different stars in the summer from the winter because the Earth has moved to the other side of its orbit around the Sun. At night we are looking away from the Sun, into the Universe (Figure 3).

The winter sky may seem more impressive because the nights are long and there are some very bright stars on show – but it is in the summer that we can see more stars. In the summer months our night skies aim towards the centre of the galaxy. That hazy look to a clear summer sky is the light from billions of stars in the central disc of our galaxy.

Did you know?

The *Milky Way* is a band of light stretching from the northeast to the southwest across the sky. Look for it in a dark summer sky, well away from light pollution. When we are looking at the *Milky Way*, we are looking towards the dense centre of the galaxy. In the winter we look away from this, to the edge of a spiral arm of our galaxy.

FIGURE 2: *Sagittarius* in the summer sky, against the background of the *Milky Way*.

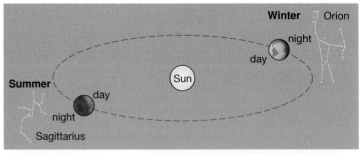

FIGURE 3: We view the night sky in summer in the opposite direction to the night sky in winter.

QUESTIONS

1 The Pole Star (*Polaris*) is visible all year round from the northern hemisphere. Suggest why.

2 There is no star above the South Pole. Explain why this could make navigation by the stars more difficult.

Finding a star

Suppose that you want to tell someone how to find a particular star. You need to give two pieces of information: which direction to face (e.g. how far west or east) and how high up to look.

The height of the star in the sky, above the equator, is given as an angle called the **declination** (dec). A negative declination means that the star is south of the equator.

A star that is directly above the equator has a declination of 0°. The Pole Star (*Polaris*) is almost directly above the North Pole and has a declination of 90°.

The angle that defines the direction (east–west) to look is called the **right ascension** (RA). These two angles form a coordinate system for locating or describing the location of a star.

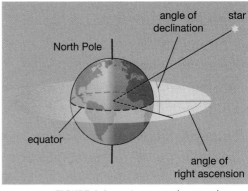

FIGURE 4: Locating a star by angular coordinates.

● QUESTIONS

3 Where would you look for a star that had a declination of 80°?

4 The declination of the Sun changes throughout the year. If the Sun's declination is a negative number, what does that tell you?

The celestial sphere (Higher tier only)

When you look at the night sky, imagine an invisible dome stretching over you. The light from every astronomical object is projected onto this dome. Together with the skies of the southern hemisphere, this forms the **celestial sphere**. The celestial sphere has a north pole directly over the Earth's North Pole and an equator over the Earth's equator (Figure 5). We use the celestial sphere as a reference for the coordinate system.

The declination is measured from the celestial equator, in degrees, minutes and seconds. One minute (1') is equal to $\frac{1}{60}$ degree. One second (1") is equal to $\frac{1}{60}$ minute.

The plane of the Earth's orbit, the **ecliptic**, is shown in Figure 5. Viewed from Earth, the ecliptic shows the path of the Sun during the year. The right ascension is measured from the point where the Sun moves to the northern hemisphere. This is the spring (or vernal) equinox and it happens around 21 March every year.

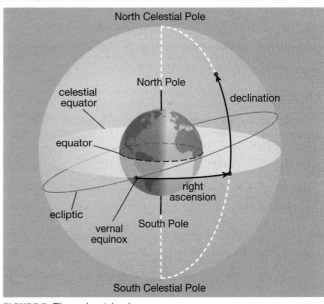

FIGURE 5: The celestial sphere.

Although it is an angle, the right ascension is measured in units of time: hours, minutes and seconds. The celestial sphere rotates with the Earth once every 24 hours, so 24 hours is equivalent to 360°. Therefore 1 hour is equivalent to 15°.

The coordinates of the star *Betelgeuse*, for example, are written:

RA = 05h 55m 10.3053s

dec = +07° 24' 25.426"

● QUESTION

5 a Why do the coordinates change for a planet and not for a star?

b Actually, over a long period of time, the coordinates for a star change slightly. Suggest why this might be.

Refraction of light

We are learning to:
> explain what is meant by refraction
> describe how a lens brings light to a focus

Why do stars twinkle?

Stars seen from the surface of the Moon don't twinkle at all. They shine steadily from a sky that is black, day and night. It is the Earth's atmosphere that makes the sky blue in the day and makes the stars twinkle at night. The twinkling effect of stars is caused by refraction of light in the Earth's atmosphere.

FIGURE 1: The Earth seen from the Moon – the Moon's sky is always black.

The speed of light

Light travels at about 300 million m/s through empty space. When it reaches the atmosphere it slows down a little. Light travels slightly more slowly in air than in a vacuum, and it travels much more slowly in water or in glass. The speed of light depends on the substance (medium) in which it is travelling.

This principle applies to all waves. The speed of any wave, such as sound or water waves, depends on the medium through which it travels. As the waves slow down, they get closer together. In other words, the wavelength decreases. This is called **refraction**.

Refraction does not change the frequency of the wave. To see why, look at Figure 2. The number of waves that leave the deep water every second must be the same as the number that enter the shallow water every second.

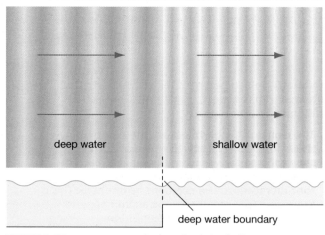

deep water   shallow water

deep water boundary

FIGURE 2: Water waves travel more slowly in shallow water, so they slow down and get closer together.

QUESTION

1 When sound waves pass from the air into water, they speed up.

 a What happens to their wavelength?

 b What happens to the frequency?

Q refraction GCSE

Changing direction

When a wave hits the boundary between two materials at an angle, refraction causes the wave to change direction (Figure 3). When travelling into a medium where the speed is lower, it is like a car driving into mud. The wheel that hits the mud first slows down first and the car changes direction.

If a light wave passes from air through a glass block, it will change direction as it enters the block and again when it leaves (Figure 4). This is because light travels more slowly in glass, or

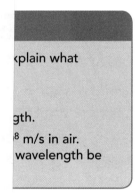

Medium 1: wave travels faster

Medium 2: wave travels slower

grass

fast

slow

mud

FIGURE 3: The part of the wave front [bo]undary first will [ ] first and this effect will [ ]ection of the wave.

[w]ave. This represents [blo]ck is called the [ ] towards the normal [a]s it leaves the block.

Angle of refraction < angle of incidence.

[ex]plain what

[ ]gth.

[ ]⁸ m/s in air. [ ] wavelength be

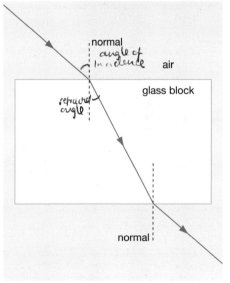

normal
angle of incidence
air
glass block
refraction angle
normal

FIGURE 4: Refraction of light as it passes through glass.

Bringing light to a focus

By shaping the glass block we can use refraction to bring light to a focus. A glass **convex lens**, which is thicker in the middle than at the edges, can refract light rays so that they come together or **converge**. Rays of light that strike the lens parallel to its axis will meet at the **focal point** or **focus**.

● QUESTION

4 A more powerful convex lens can converge light in a shorter distance. Sketch what Figure 5 would look like if a thicker, more powerful lens were used.

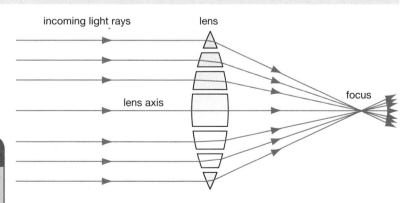

incoming light rays

lens

lens axis

focus

FIGURE 5: The light ray moves towards the normal as it hits the glass and away from the normal as it leaves. So shaping the glass to form a convex lens makes the light converge to a focus.

Forming an image

We are learning to:

> explain what is meant by the power of a lens

> explain how lenses form an image of astronomical objects

How can one pair of glasses suit all users?

In some countries it is difficult for people to get the right glasses to correct their eyesight. Now an Oxford professor has designed self-adjusting spectacles. The lenses are filled with fluid; more fluid is pumped in for users who need stronger glasses.

FIGURE 1: A billion people in the developing world have poor eyesight. Self-adjusting glasses can restore their vision.

The power of a lens

Convex lenses are used to bring light rays together. Parallel light rays that strike the lens are brought together at the **focal point** of the lens (Figure 2). The distance from the lens to the focal point is called the **focal length**. A lens is said to be more powerful if it can converge the light in a shorter distance. So a powerful lens has a short focal length.

The **power** of a lens is measured in **dioptres**, D. Power is calculated using this equation:

$$\text{power (dioptres, D)} = \frac{1}{\text{focal length (metres)}}$$

Making the faces of a lens more curved makes the lens more powerful.

Watch out!

A symmetrical lens has a focal point on either side of the lens, the same distance, f, from the centre of the lens.

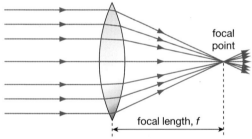

FIGURE 2: A more powerful lens has a shorter focal length.

QUESTIONS

1 A lens has a focal length of 2 m. What is its power?

2 Sketch a diagram to show what happens to parallel rays of light that hit a lens of power 2 dioptres. Mark in the focal length.

3 How does pumping more fluid into the glasses in Figure 1 make them more powerful?

Focusing light from the stars

The closest star to Earth, other than the Sun, is *Proxima Centauri*. Light from the star takes over four years to reach the Earth. At that distance, even in the largest telescope, the star just looks like a point of light. The rays of light reaching a lens on Earth are parallel (Figure 3) and so are brought to a focus at a single point (Figure 4). If the incoming light is not parallel to the **principal axis** through the centre of the lens, the focus will be away from this axis.

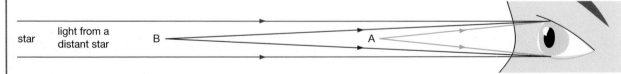

FIGURE 3: The light rays from a nearby object, A, form a large angle at the eye. The further away the object, B the smaller the angle. A star is so far away that the light rays from the star are parallel as they reach the eye.

Q focal length   power of a lens   dioptres

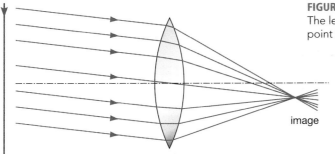

FIGURE 4: The light rays from a star are parallel. The lens brings the rays to a focus, forming a point image of the star.

image

◉ QUESTION

4 Some stars are much larger than our Sun. Why do they look like points of light?

Forming an image of the Moon (Higher tier only)

Objects that look larger than a point, such as the Sun, Moon or galaxies, are called **extended objects**. We can use a lens to make an image of an extended object on a screen. We can use a **ray diagram** to show how the image is formed (Figure 5).

We represent the object by an arrow and then follow what happens to rays of light leaving the tip of the arrow. We represent the lens by a vertical line. Although light leaves the arrow tip in every direction, there are three rays we can predict accurately.

Ray 1: Any ray that hits the lens parallel to the axis will be refracted through the focal point.

Ray 2: A ray that travels through the focal point will be refracted parallel to the axis (just the reverse of ray 1).

Ray 3: A ray that hits the centre of the lens will be undeviated.

The focused image of the arrow tip will be formed where the rays meet again (Figure 5).

Watch out!

Note that refraction actually takes place at the curved edges of the lens but, if the lens is thin, we can draw the diagram as if all the refraction occurs at the lens at the central plane.

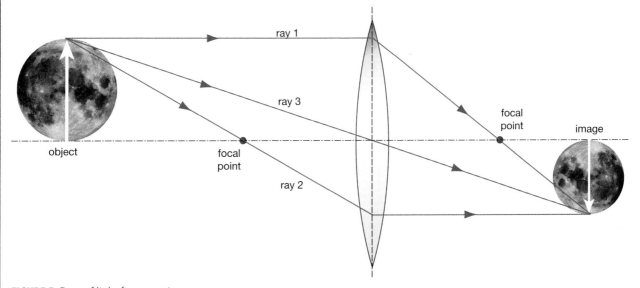

FIGURE 5: Rays of light from a point on the extended object (such as the Moon) are brought together again by the lens to form a focused image. This is not drawn to scale: the Moon is much further away and its image will be much smaller.

◉ QUESTION

5 How would Figure 5 look if a lens with a higher power were used? What effect would it have on the image of the Moon?

🔍 ray diagram   convex lens   real image

The telescope

We are learning to:
> describe how a simple telescope works
> explain how a telescope makes a magnified image
> (Higher) calculate the magnification of a telescope

Do other planets have moons?

All the planets in the solar system, apart from Mercury and Venus, have moons. Jupiter has over 60. Jupiter's four largest moons were first seen by Galileo in 1610 with his improved telescope. He observed that they changed position as they orbited Jupiter. The discovery showed that the Earth was not the centre about which everything else in the solar system orbited.

FIGURE 1: An image from the Hubble Space Telescope of Jupiter and one of its moons.

FIGURE 2: Through an ordinary telescope you can see the four largest of Jupiter's moons.

The simple telescope

A simple telescope can be made from two convex lenses: the **objective lens** and the **eyepiece**. The objective lens has a long focal length (low power) and the eyepiece has a short focal length (high power). The lenses are placed so that the length of the telescope is the sum of their focal lengths (Figure 3).

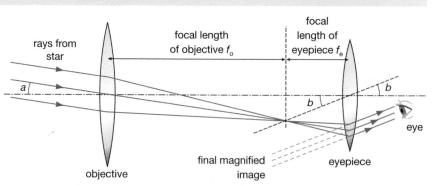

FIGURE 3: The arrangement of the objective lens and eyepiece lens in an astronomical telescope.

The objective lens has a larger diameter than the eyepiece. The objective needs to have a large area to collect more light and make a brighter image. The objective forms an image of the object at its focal point.

The eyepiece is smaller than the objective, but has a greater power. The eyepiece is used like a magnifying glass to look at the image formed by the objective. Your eye sees a magnified image.

Did you know?

A simple telescope produces an inverted (upside-down) image. For astronomical use, this doesn't usually matter.

QUESTION

1 A telescope is made from two convex lenses of power 2 D and 5 D.

   a Which is the objective and which is the eyepiece?

   b What other difference would there be between the two lenses?

🔍 refracting telescope

Magnification

When you look at a distant object, such as a star, your eye refracts the parallel rays of light to form an image on your retina at the back of your eye. We say your eye is focused on infinity, as the source of the parallel rays is effectively at an infinite distance from your eye. When you look at the same star through a telescope, parallel rays enter your eye so your eye is still focused on infinity (Figure 3).

The effect of the telescope is to increase the angle between the light rays and the axis of the telescope. Look at the angles in Figure 3 and notice that the angle marked *b* is bigger than the angle marked *a*. This increases the apparent separation between stars and makes extended objects, such as the Sun, Moon or planets, look bigger.

If the image of an extended object through the telescope appears twice as big as with the naked eye, we say the telescope has a **magnification** of 2.

The magnification is equal to the ratio of the angles, $\frac{b}{a}$.

QUESTIONS

2 Explain why the length of the telescope needs to be equal to the sum of the focal lengths of the two lenses.

3 Suppose you got the two lenses mixed up and you put your eye to the objective. What would you notice about the image?

Calculating the magnification (Higher tier only)

The magnification of a telescope depends on the ratio of the focal lengths of the lenses. Look again at Figure 3.
The magnification of the telescope is given by $\frac{b}{a}$.

$$\frac{b}{a} = \text{ratio of the focal lengths} = \frac{f_o}{f_e}$$

so: $\boxed{\text{magnification} = \dfrac{\text{focal length of objective}}{\text{focal length of eyepiece}}}$

Suppose that you made a telescope using a lens of power 2 D as the objective and one of power 10 D for the eyepiece. The focal lengths of these lenses would be:

objective lens, $f = \dfrac{1}{\text{power}} = \dfrac{1}{2} = 0.5\,\text{m}$

eyepiece lens, $f = \dfrac{1}{\text{power}} = \dfrac{1}{10} = 0.1\,\text{m}$

so the magnification would be $M = \dfrac{f_o}{f_e} = \dfrac{0.5}{0.1} = 5\times$.

FIGURE 4: You can buy a refracting telescope with a magnification of at least 100× quite cheaply, but if the objective lens is small, the image will not be very bright and it will lack detail.

QUESTIONS

4 You have three lenses. Their focal lengths are 10, 20 and 50 cm respectively. Which two lenses would you choose to make a telescope of the highest magnification?

5 A refracting telescope is made from two lenses, of power 1 D and 50 D.

a What will the magnification of the telescope be?

b How long will the telescope be?

Did you know?

Professional astronomers use reflecting, rather than refracting telescopes. These use mirrors to collect and focus the light, rather than lenses.

FIGURE 5: The Keck reflecting telescopes are housed in domes in Hawaii.

🔍 angular magnification

Preparing for assessment: Planning and collecting

To achieve a good grade in science you will need to be able to use your skills and understanding to understand how scientists plan, run and evaluate investigations. These skills will be assessed in your exams and in Controlled Assessments. This activity supports you in developing the skills of planning an investigation.

✺ I can see clearly now

Jane and Farouk are investigating how they can use a pair of converging lenses to work as an astronomical telescope. They will need two converging lenses which they can fix to the metre rule and test it out by looking through it at some distant object.

They have studied converging lenses in lessons and know that this kind of lens will make rays of light 'close in'. If the incoming rays are from a distant object they can be regarded as being parallel. The rays will then meet at a point called the focal point. They can find out what the focal length of each lens is by using it to focus an image of a distant object onto a white card and measuring the distance from the lens to the card.

They also know that for a telescope they need to have one lens as an objective lens and the other as

an eyepiece lens. The objective lens gathers light rays from a distant object and produces an image. This image is the object for the eyepiece lens. This means that the length of the telescope will be the focal length of the objective lens added to the focal length of the image lens.

They could use any two converging lenses; however, in order to get the best possible magnification, they need to choose carefully.

They have a selection of lenses, some more powerful than others. First they are going to test the various lenses and then select the most suitable pair to make a telescope that will magnify distant objects as much as possible.

Finally they'll test it. There's a row of trees at the edge of the playing fields that they might use.

✹ Task 1

> What materials will they need to test and select the lenses to use?

> Which material do you think they could use to make the telescope?

> What would the students need to be careful about when conducting the experiment?

✹ Task 2

> What do you think they will find out as they experiment with lenses of different powers?

> What kind of scientific terms should they use?

> What equipment might they find useful?

> What hazards would there be in their investigation?

✹ Task 3

> What variables are there in this investigation?

> Suggest a hypothesis they might make, which they could test, relating to the focal lengths of the lenses they should use

> Suggest a procedure they might adopt that would produce useful data; include safety precautions.

✹ Task 4

> Considering the hypothesis, what quantitative prediction might they make about the best combination of lenses and how they should be positioned?

> What equipment should they use to produce data that is precise and reliable?

> Suggest a suitable risk assessment.

✹ Maximise your grade

Use these suggestions to improve your work and be more successful.

E

To be on target for grade E you need to:
> suggest how the students should work safely

> offer a testable prediction for the students and justify it, using relevant scientific terms

> identify equipment the students could use to collect data and identify and comment on hazards.

C

To be on target for a grade D or C, you also need to:
> identify major factors and scientific knowledge the students should use to make a testable hypothesis about how one factor will affect the outcome

> suggest techniques and equipment the students should use which are appropriate for the range of data required

> identify any significant risks for the students and suggest some precautions.

A

To be on target for a grade B or A, you also need to:
> suggest one factor the students could investigate and propose a testable hypothesis and quantitative prediction

> suggest equipment and techniques the students should use to achieve precise and reliable data

> produce a full and appropriate risk assessment.

The reflecting telescope

We are learning to:

> explain why astronomers need large telescopes

> understand the advantages of reflecting telescopes

What happens when a space telescope goes wrong?

The Hubble Space Telescope is a reflecting telescope. It has a mirror, rather than a lens, for its objective. Hubble has produced amazing pictures but its first images were blurred. A measuring instrument used in making the mirror had a speck of paint on it. All the measurements were slightly out. The mirror was the wrong shape by $\frac{1}{50}$ of the width of a single hair. It took five spacewalks to fit corrective mirrors to repair the telescope.

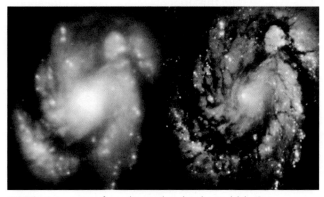

FIGURE 1: Images of a galaxy, taken by the Hubble Space Telescope (HST) before and after adjustments to its mirror.

 ## A light-bucket

Reflecting telescopes can look like elaborate dustbins. They are often described as light-buckets. The telescope is an open-topped cylinder with a highly polished mirror at the bottom. If you want to see a faint star, then the larger the hole (aperture) in the top of the cylinder, the better.

Just like the light from a torch, the light from a star spreads out and becomes fainter the further it travels. The light from a distant star has been spreading out in all directions for billions of kilometres by the time it reaches Earth. The light can be very faint when it finally gets here. A large aperture telescope is needed to collect enough light to produce an image.

FIGURE 2: An effective telescope needs to collect more light than your eye. The larger the mirror, the more light it can collect. This telescope's main mirror has a diameter of 6 metres.

QUESTION

1 Suppose the aperture of a telescope is 50 cm in diameter, and the pupil of your eye has a diameter of 0.5 cm. How much more light will the telescope collect than your eye? (**Hint**: Work out the area of each aperture. The area of a circle radius r is πr^2.)

Did you know?

The Keck telescope in Hawaii is currently the largest optical telescope in the world. Its mirror is 10 m across. Plans are being made for a much bigger telescope (pages 182–3).

🔍 reflecting telescope

The Newtonian reflecting telescope

Newton built a reflecting telescope, using a **concave mirror** to receive the light (Figure 3). A mirror reflects light, rather than refracting it. The concave mirror is the opposite shape to a convex lens – the mirror 'caves in' in the middle – but it has the same effect on the light as a convex lens. A concave mirror converges the parallel light towards a focal point. A secondary mirror reflects the light through an eyepiece lens.

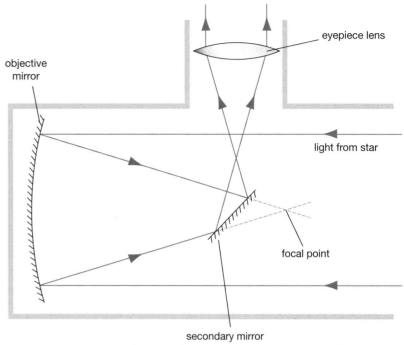

FIGURE 3: A Newtonian reflecting telescope produces an image at infinity.

QUESTIONS

2 The secondary mirror in a Newtonian telescope is quite small. Why is this a good idea?

3 The objective mirrors in some Newtonian telescopes have very long focal lengths, up to 10 m. Why could this have been awkward for astronomers in the past?

Solving the problems of refracting telescopes

A refracting (lens) telescope needs to have a large objective lens if it is to form a detailed image or show faint objects – but it is difficult to manufacture such large lenses. The two curved faces have to be perfectly shaped. Such a lens will be heavy, but it can only be supported around the edge. Newton observed another problem with lenses. Because glass refracts light of different wavelengths by different amounts, a refracting telescope produces an image with coloured edges. This effect is called **chromatic aberration**. Newton solved this problem in his reflecting telescope by using a mirror in place of a lens.

QUESTIONS

4 Suggest three reasons why it might be better to use a mirror than a lens in a large telescope.

5 You can create a spectrum by passing white light through a glass block. Explain why this happens.

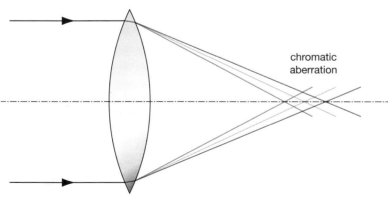

FIGURE 4: A lens has a different focal length for every colour of light, so a simple refracting telescope produces images with coloured fringes (right).

Diffraction

We are learning to:
> explain what is meant by the diffraction of light
> explain how diffraction affects the image we see through a telescope

What is the biggest telescope?

The largest telescopes in the world are radio telescopes. By the time it is completed in 2024 the Square Kilometre Array (SKA) will be the biggest telescope ever built. 3000 separate dish antennae will be linked together electronically, with a total area of 1 million square metres. It will be sensitive enough to detect an airport radar on a planet 50 light-years – that's 300 million million miles – away.

FIGURE 1: The proposed Square Kilometre Array (SKA).

Diffraction

Telescopes need to be large so that they can pick up enough energy to detect weak sources. Telescopes also need to be large if they are to produce detailed images. This is because of an effect called **diffraction**.

When waves pass through a gap or round an obstacle (Figure 2), they tend to spread out (diffract). Diffraction is greater when the gap, or the obstacle, is about the same size as the wavelength of the wave.

FIGURE 2: Waves passing through the gap, spread out in an effect known as diffraction.

We don't normally notice the diffraction of light, because the wavelength of light is much smaller than everyday objects – but if we shine light through a very small gap the effect can be seen. Figure 3 shows what happens when a narrow laser beam is shone through a very narrow slit. The laser beam spreads out to form a central bright area (central maximum) with bright **fringes** on either side. If the slit were made narrower, the central maximum would get wider.

FIGURE 3: The diffraction pattern caused by passing laser light through a small gap.

QUESTIONS

1 Look at a light source, such as a street lamp, and squeeze your eyelids quite tight so that you are squinting through a small gap. The image of the street lamp smears out into a large blur. Why does this happen?

2 If someone speaks to you from around the corner of a building you can hear them. Suggest why.

diffraction GCSE

Factors affecting diffraction

The diffraction of a wave through a gap, or around an obstacle, depends on:

> the wavelength of the wave

> the diameter of the gap or obstacle.

For a given gap or obstacle, waves with a longer wavelength diffract more. Suppose someone is speaking to you round the corner of a building. You can hear them but you cannot see them. The sound waves have a long wavelength (typically 10–100 cm) and so they diffract around the corner. Light waves have much shorter wavelength (about 5×10^{-7} m). They hardly diffract at all and so you can't see around corners.

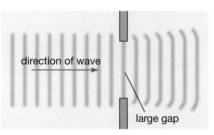
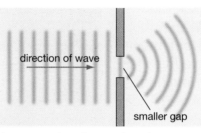

FIGURE 4: Diffraction is greater when the gap size approaches the wavelength.

QUESTIONS

3 Claire lives close to the foot of a steep hill. The transmitter for radio signals is on top of the hill. Claire can't see the transmitter but she can receive radio signals. Can you explain this?

4 Sound waves diffract as they leave a loudspeaker. Which notes will diffract the most? Why might there be a particular problem with small loudspeakers?

Diffraction and images

Light is diffracted as it passes through a gap, such as the pupil of your eye or the **aperture** of a telescope. The aperture is the objective lens or objective mirror. If you are looking at a point of light, such as a star, diffraction will spread the light and you will see a bright, central disc surrounded by circular fringes, instead of a sharp point (Figure 5).

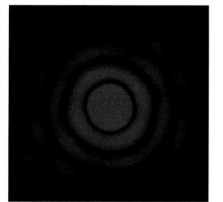

FIGURE 5: Diffraction through a circular aperture means that the image of a star will form a pattern like this.

Suppose two stars are close together in the sky. Diffraction will cause the two images to smear out into discs. If these discs overlap it will be difficult to decide if there are two stars or just one (Figure 6). If we can't tell the stars apart we say the image is 'not resolved'. To improve the **resolution** we need to reduce the diffraction and that means having a wider pupil or a telescope with a bigger diameter aperture.

The problem of diffraction is worse as wavelengths become longer.

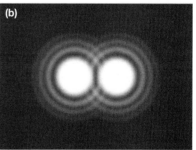

FIGURE 6: These pictures of a double star were taken with a large telescope, using apertures of different diameters. (a) uses the smallest aperture and (c) the largest aperture.

QUESTIONS

5 The diameter of the pupil in an eagle's eye is three or four times the diameter of a human pupil. Give two reasons why large pupils are an advantage to the eagle.

6 Explain why radio telescopes need to be so much bigger than optical telescopes.

Spectra

What is a quasar?

In 1963 radio astronomers discovered a powerful source of radio waves, which they named 3C 273C. The resolution of their telescope was not good enough to pinpoint the source but they had a stroke of luck. The object sometimes got blocked by the Moon, which helped them to show that the radio waves were coming from a faint blue star-like object – but was it a star? It was when astronomers examined the spectrum of 3C 273C that the real mystery became clear.

FIGURE 1: 3C 273C is the furthest object that can be seen with an amateur telescope.

Forming a spectrum

Stars and galaxies emit radiation at many wavelengths, from radio waves to gamma rays. A spectrum can help us to determine how much energy is emitted at each wavelength.

We can form a spectrum of the visible radiation that is emitted by passing the light through a glass prism. As the shorter wavelengths are refracted more than the longer wavelengths (pages 136–137), the different colours that are present in the light become visible.

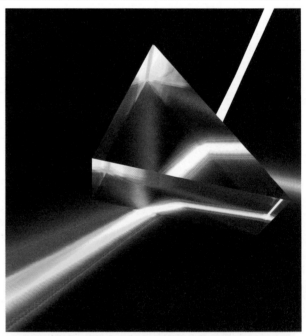

FIGURE 2: White light is separated into its component colours.

FIGURE 3: A rainbow is a spectrum of the Sun's light, created by raindrops acting as prisms.

The colours that can be seen in a spectrum depend on the temperature and chemical composition of the light source. A star's spectrum can tell you how hot it is and what it is made of.

QUESTIONS

1 Why does blue light change direction more than red light as it passes through a prism?

2 Light from the Sun produces a different spectrum than light from a fluorescent tube. Suggest why the spectra are different.

spectra   prism

Diffraction gratings

A prism is not the only way of producing a spectrum. Astronomers use **diffraction gratings** to produce spectra. A diffraction grating is made by drawing thousands of very closely spaced lines on a reflecting plate. Light then reflects from the plate and the different wavelengths are diffracted by different amounts. The result is that specific wavelengths are visible from certain angles, thus producing a spectrum.

Diffraction gratings produce a more evenly spread spectrum than a prism does and a reflective grating wastes very little light.

> ## QUESTIONS
>
> **3** Why does a prism waste more light than a reflective grating?
>
> **4** A DVD acts as a diffraction grating, but gives a different width spectrum compared to a CD. Suggest a reason why this is the case.

FIGURE 4: A CD acts as a reflective diffraction grating.

The quasar problem

The astronomical object labelled 3C 273 looked almost like a star, so it became known as a 'quasi-stellar-object', or **quasar** for short. When astronomers examined its spectrum, they got a shock. Compared to a star in our galaxy, the light from the quasar was highly shifted to the red end of the spectrum. A **redshift** (see *Science A* page 215) is caused by the object moving away from us. But this redshift was bigger than anything seen before. The object appeared to be moving away at 40 000 km/s.

According to theories of the expanding Universe, this speed of recession could only be possible if the object was a very long way from Earth. The quasar seemed to be 2.5 billion light-years away – the furthest object yet identified. But that led to another problem. How could we see something so far away? It must be giving off enormous amounts of energy. It would have to be several hundred times more powerful than an entire galaxy but only about the size of our solar system. Some scientists refused to accept this and suggested that the redshift was due to some other effect.

It wasn't until 20 years later, after many more quasars had been discovered, that an explanation was generally accepted. Quasars are now believed to be among the most distant objects in the Universe. They are also among the brightest, emitting enormous power despite being relatively small. The power is thought to come from matter as it falls into a supermassive black hole at the centre of a galaxy.

FIGURE 5: A quasar, showing jets of X-rays and high-energy electrons.

Did you know?

Some quasars emit powerful jets of X-rays and electrons that can extend for as much as a million light-years.

> ## QUESTIONS
>
> **5** Why did some scientists refuse to believe that quasars were so far away?
>
> **6** Why do you think that it took 20 years for scientist to come to an agreement?

The distance to the stars

We are learning to:
> explain how parallax is used to measure distances to the stars
> understand how the parsec is defined
> calculate distances in parsecs

Can we sail to the stars?

We shall need a new propulsion system to fly to the stars, preferably one that doesn't need fuel! The distances are enormous, the flight will take many years and there are no filling stations on the way. One possibility is to sail, using light from the Sun as the wind. The light exerts a small but continuous pressure on the sail, which could eventually reach high speeds.

FIGURE 1: Japan launched *Ikaros* in 2010. It used a solar sail to travel to Venus.

Parallax

It is difficult to tell how far away the stars are. We can't do it simply by using a star's brightness as a guide. Stars that look equally bright in the night sky could be faint stars that are nearby or bright giant stars that are far away.

One method of measuring the distance to a star is to use the apparent motion of the star as the Earth moves around the Sun. This is called the **parallax** method. Parallax is a familiar effect. As you travel in a car and look out of a side window, objects close to the road, such as lamp-posts, seem to race past. Objects that are a long way off, such as the Moon, don't seem to move at all. We see the same effect as we look at the night sky. As the Earth moves around the Sun, the nearby stars seem to move, compared to the background of distant stars – which appear to be fixed. The closer the star, the larger its apparent movement.

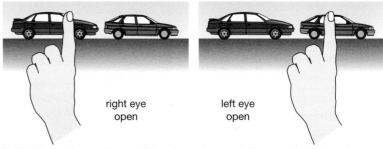

right eye open   left eye open

FIGURE 2: Look at a distant object through your right eye only. Point at it. Keep focused on the object but open your left eye instead. Your finger will appear to move.

QUESTION

1 Do the brief experiment described in Figure 2.

   a What happens if you keep your finger close to your eye?

   b What would you see if your arms were so long that your finger was close to the object?

   c What difference would it make if your eyes were much further apart?

Measuring the distances to the stars

To find the distance to a nearby star, you need two measurements. The position of the star compared to a distant star is measured twice; the readings are taken six months apart (Figure 3). The angle labelled p is called the parallax angle. The bigger the parallax angle, the closer the star is to Earth. In practice, the parallax angle is measured by comparing two photographs taken six months apart.

Parallax angles are measured in seconds of an arc ("). 1 second is $\frac{1}{60}$ of a minute, which is $\frac{1}{60}$ of a degree. Angular seconds are often referred to as arcseconds.

Watch out!
The method of parallax can only be used to measure the distance to nearby stars.

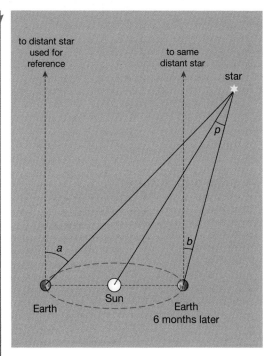

FIGURE 3: The reference star is so far away that its position in the sky doesn't change. The nearby star moves relative to the reference star, so angles *a* and *b* differ slightly (exaggerated here) and the parallax angle *p*, by geometry, is half of (*a* – *b*).

Did you know?

The Hipparcos satellite measured the distance to more than 100 000 stars, to an accuracy 200 times better than Earth-based measurements.

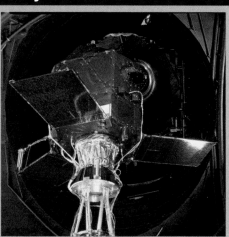

FIGURE 4: The Hipparcos satellite.

QUESTIONS

2 Suggest why the Hipparcos satellite was able to make measurements that were much more accurate than those based on Earth.

3 How many arcseconds are there in the angle at the centre of a whole circle?

The parsec

The **parsec** is a unit of length defined using the parallax shift of a star (Figure 5). When the parallax angle is 1 second of arc, the distance to the star is 1 parsec (1 pc):

$$\text{distance (parsecs)} = \frac{1}{\text{parallax angle (seconds)}}$$

The closest star to us is *Alpha Centauri*. This has the largest parallax angle of any star, at 0.79". Its distance from Earth is therefore $\frac{1}{0.79}$ = 1.27 pc.

Parallax angles are very small. Compare the parallax angle for *Alpha Centauri* (0.79") with the angular size of the full Moon (1800"). Parallax measurements don't work well when the angles get too small to measure. This is why the method of parallax can only be used for nearby stars. About 0.02" is the best that can be achieved with ground-based observations.

QUESTIONS

4 The brightest star in the sky is *Sirius*; it has a parallax angle of 0.38". How far away is it, in parsecs?

5 *Betelgeuse* is much further away, probably between 150 and 200 pc. Why is it difficult to be more precise?

6 Some stars really do move relative to Earth. This would affect the parallax measurement. How could you detect this 'proper motion'?

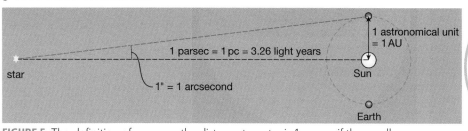

FIGURE 5: The definition of a parsec: the distance to a star is 1 parsec if the parallax angle is 1 second.

Watch out!

The distance from Earth to the Sun is known as 1 **astronomical unit** (1 AU).

What is the most distant object ever seen?

A burst of gamma rays from the catastrophic explosion of a giant star may be the most distant object yet seen. The star was so far away that its light took over 13 billion years to reach Earth.

FIGURE 1: The Swift gamma-ray telescope is designed to look for gamma-ray bursters.

We are learning to:

> understand the relative scale of interstellar and intergalactic space

> recall the factors affecting a star's luminosity

> understand what affects a star's brightness, as seen from Earth

Light-years, parsecs and megaparsecs

Light travels at a constant speed in space, so we can use the time taken for light to travel between two objects as a measure of the distance between them. 1 **light-year (ly)** is the distance travelled by light in one year.

The distance to the nearest star is 4.2 light-years, but it is 2.5 million light-years to our neighbouring galaxy, *Andromeda*.

Astronomers also measure distance in a unit called the **parsec (pc)**. This is defined using the parallax angle of a star (see pages 150–151).

    1 pc = 3.26 ly

The distances to stars are measured in parsecs but the distances between galaxies are measured in megaparsecs (Mpc), that is millions of parsecs.

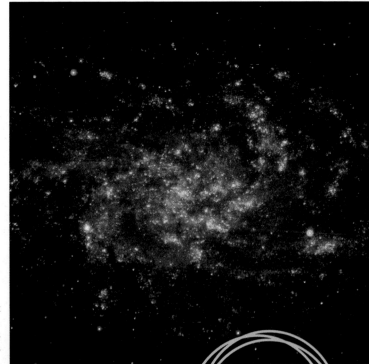

FIGURE 2: The *Triangulum* galaxy is the furthest object that can be seen with the naked eye, but it is very close in intergalactic terms. It is about 1 Mpc (3 million ly) away from us and is 15 300 pc (50 000 ly) across.

QUESTION

1 Which of these three distances is most likely to be the distance to the *Sagittarius* dwarf galaxy?

  A 1 pc **B** 1 ly **C** 1 Mpc

Watch out!

To convert megaparsecs to parsecs you have to multiply by 1 million, which is 10^6.

Luminosity

Stars are not all the same. They vary enormously in size, in surface temperature and in the power they emit.

The total power emitted by a star is called its **luminosity**. This is the total energy emitted by the star in one second across all wavelengths and in all directions. The luminosity depends on:

> radius – larger stars have a greater emitting area (surface area) and therefore emit more radiation

> surface temperature – the hotter the star, the more radiation it emits. The surface temperature also affects the colour of a star. Hotter stars burn blue-white, cooler stars look red.

Did you know?

Our Sun has a surface temperature of about 5500 °C and a radius of 700 000 000 m. Its power output is colossal, 3.9×10^{26} joules every second, but there are stars with luminosity thousands of times greater than this.

QUESTIONS

2 In Figure 3, which star has the higher surface temperature, *Rigel* or *Betelgeuse*? How do you know?

3 *Betelgeuse* is cooler than the Sun but its luminosity is 60 000 times greater. What does that tell you about *Betelgeuse*?

FIGURE 3: In the constellation of *Orion* there are two exceptionally bright stars – the red supergiant *Betelgeuse* (top left) and the blue giant star *Rigel* (bottom right).

Apparent brightness

From Earth, the star *Sirius* looks much brighter than the blue giant star *Rigel* but, in fact, *Rigel* emits much more energy. *Sirius* looks brighter because it is much nearer; *Sirius* is only 8.6 ly away compared to *Rigel*, which is 900 ly away. *Rigel* (Figure 3) is a colossal star, emitting enormous power.

The reason that *Rigel* looks fainter than *Sirius* is that its light spreads out further as it travels through space. The radiation from a star spreads out equally in all directions (Figure 4). The further away from the star you are, the more the radiation is spread out and the fainter the star looks.

Did you know?

If you go twice as far from a star, you only receive $\frac{1}{4}$ of the light. This reduction is known as the inverse square law and it applies to many things, for example, the gravitational force from a planet.

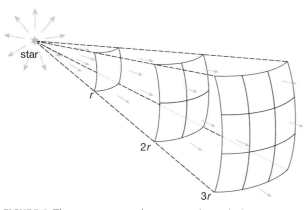

FIGURE 4: The same power that passes through the area at *r* passes through 4× the area at 2*r* and 9× the area at 3*r*.

QUESTIONS

4 Two stars A and B look equally bright in the night sky. Star A is found to be twice as far away.

a What can you say about the luminosity of the two stars?

b What could cause the two stars to have different luminosities?

5 To convert ly to metres you have to multiply the speed of light, 3×10^8 m/s, by the number of seconds in a year. *Rigel* is 900 ly away. How far is that in metres?

Cepheid variables

We are learning to:

> recall what Cepheid variable stars are

> realise that the same data can lead to quite different explanations

> understand how correlation between variables can lead to new discoveries

> (Higher) understand the importance of Cephid variable stars as a standard candle in the measurement of distance

Will the Sun flare up and affect the Earth?

The Sun's brightness varies, reaching a maximum about every 11 years. Its total power output only changes by 0.1% but the Sun being more active can have dramatic effects. The solar maximum of 1859 led to Northern Lights that were bright enough to read by and caused telegraph offices to catch fire. A similar event now could damage satellites and disrupt GPS and mobile phones. The next solar maximum is predicted for 2013.

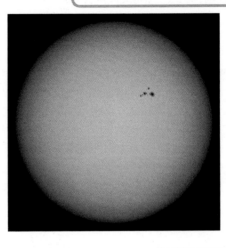

FIGURE 1: There is a correlation between the number of sunspots and the Sun's luminosity.

Variable stars

Some stars vary in brightness much more frequently and more dramatically than the Sun. Some **variable stars** flash like a lighthouse, changing their brightness every few minutes, while some take hours, days or months to change. The time taken to go through a complete cycle is called the **period** of the star.

The variable star *Mira* was the first to be observed. In 1638 its period was measured as 11 months. Another variable star, *Algol*, was discovered 30 years later. But *Algol* varies in a different way. Its brightness is usually constant but every three days the brightness dips for about 10 hours.

The accepted explanation for variable stars was that, like the Sun, stars had dark spots. As the star rotated, it showed a darker or brighter side to Earth. But why was the pattern so different for *Algol*?

In 1783, John Goodricke suggested that *Algol* was being orbited by a darker body that passed in front of the star, blocking some of the light. He was finally shown to be correct by astronomical observations 100 years later. *Algol* is actually a **binary star**. A bright star is orbited by a dimmer partner.

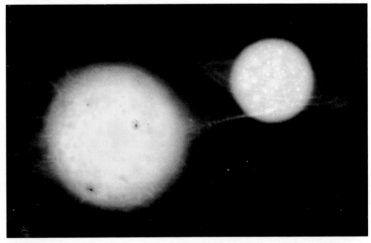

FIGURE 2: The binary star system *Algol*: a cool, orange star orbits and eclipses the hot, white star, causing the brightness seen from Earth to drop every three days.

QUESTIONS

1 By 1783 there were two explanations for variable stars. What were they?

2 Suggest how you might decide between them. Why do you think it took 100 years to find the right explanation for *Algol*?

3 Can you suggest any other explanations for variable stars?

Pulsating stars

In 1912, Henrietta Swan Leavitt was studying photographs of the *Magellenic clouds*, which are now known to be nearby galaxies. She made a study of 1777 variable stars. Forty-five of these were of a type known as **Cepheid variable stars**. These are large, pulsating stars with brightness that changes in a predictable way (Figure 3).

All the stars in her study came from the Magellenic cloud so Leavitt assumed they were all the same distance away. Their brightness could then be compared fairly. Leavitt noticed that the brighter the star, the longer it took to go through its brightness cycle. By plotting a graph, she found a **correlation** between the brightness and the period of a Cepheid variable star. (Figure 5).

Leavitt's discovery led to a new way of measuring distances in space.

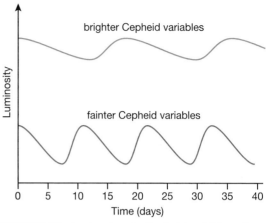

FIGURE 3: The luminosity of a Cepheid variable varies over a few days.

FIGURE 4: Henrietta Leavitt's work helped to explain the nature of galaxies.

QUESTIONS

4 Look at Figure 3.

a What is the period of the fainter star?

b What is the period of the brighter star?

5 All the stars in the study came from the same galaxy. Why was this important?

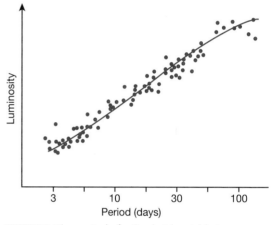

FIGURE 5: The period of a Cepheid variable is correlated with its luminosity.

Standard candles (Higher tier only)

If we know how much light an object emits, and how bright it seems from Earth, it is possible to work out how far away it is. An object of known brightness is called a **standard candle**.

A Cepheid variable star is a standard candle. If we measure its period, we can find its luminosity from Leavitt's graph (Figure 5). Then we measure the light that we receive on Earth. Comparing the two values will allow us to calculate how far away the star is.

QUESTION

6 A Cepheid variable star has a long period but looks faint from Earth. What can you deduce about its distance?

FIGURE 6: If we knew how much light each of the lanterns gives out, we could calculate how far away the faint ones are.

Galaxies

We are learning to:

> recall how the *Milky Way* and other galaxies were identified

> understand how Cepheid variables helped to reveal the nature of galaxies

> realise that the same data can lead to quite different explanations

How many galaxies are there?

The Hubble Ultra Deep Field image looks far out into space and time. Some of the light that formed this image had been travelling for 13 billion years. It shows galaxies just 400 million years after the Big Bang. The image is of a very small region of the sky, only 1% of the area of the full Moon, and yet it contains about 10 000 galaxies.

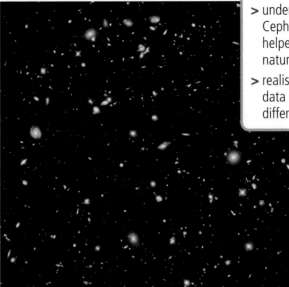

FIGURE 1: The Deep Field image is formed from 800 separate pictures taken over 400 orbits of the HST, equivalent to an exposure time of 1 million seconds.

The *Milky Way*

It is difficult to tell what the shape and size of our galaxy is from inside it. Astronomers looking at the Milky Way (Figure 2) through telescopes saw millions of stars. They realised that our Sun is just one of millions of stars in our galaxy, which is called the *Milky Way*. It is a spiral galaxy (Figure 3). However, a hundred years ago there was no agreement on the size of the galaxy.

One method of measuring the galaxy was developed by Harlow Shapley. He used Cepheid variable stars (pages 154–155) to measure the distances to groups of stars called **globular clusters** (Figure 3). He then made the assumption that all the globular clusters were the same brightness and size, so he could measure distances further away, where no Cepheid stars were visible. After years of painstaking work Shapley suggested that the diameter of the *Milky Way* might be as large as 300 000 light-years (ly). That was much bigger than many astronomers believed, and meant that our galaxy would be the biggest, and maybe the only, thing in the Universe.

FIGURE 2: The *Milky Way* appears as a band of light stretching from northeast to southwest across the sky. The stars are densely packed there because we are looking towards the centre of the galaxy.

globular clusters   galactic bulge

galactic disc

galactic centre

FIGURE 3: A spiral galaxy like our own. The globular clusters shown are concentrations of thousands of old stars that surround the galaxy.

QUESTIONS

1 Explain why we see more stars in some directions than others.

2 What was the weakness in Shapley's method?

Nebulae

There are patches of light in the sky that look like fuzzy, bright clouds rather than points of light. These are known as **nebulae**. By 1900, thousands of nebulae had been observed. Some of these were known as spiral nebulae, because of their shape, but there was disagreement about what they were.

Some astronomers suggested that spiral nebulae were new solar systems being formed – each being a spinning cloud of gas that would condense into a star and planets. Others felt that nebulae were actually distant galaxies, each one formed from billions of stars. Their nebulous appearance could be due to their enormous distance from Earth. This was known as the 'island universe' hypothesis.

Many astronomers found it hard to believe that there were thousands of island universes, each one like our own galaxy. There was other evidence that pointed to the nebulae being quite small. In 1883 the *Andromeda* nebula got much brighter for a time. If it was so far away, the change in brightness couldn't be explained. We now know that this was a supernova (pages 176–7) within *Andromeda*, and that *Andromeda* is a spiral galaxy very like our own *Milky Way*. At the time, the change in brightness observed was seen as strong evidence against the 'island universe' idea.

FIGURE 4: In the early 20th century it was not known what spiral nebulae like this were.

Watch out!

We now know that there are many different types of nebula. A nebula can be a cloud of gas, a cluster of stars, the remnants of an exploded star, a whole galaxy or even a cluster of galaxies.

QUESTIONS

3 Explain why the nature of the spiral nebulae was such an important question for astronomy.

4 Why did the supernova in *Andromeda* almost put scientists on the wrong track in the nebula debate?

The great debate

In 1920, in Washington, two astronomers debated the nature of the nebulae.

Heber Curtis argued for the island universe hypothesis. He said that the spiral nebulae were galaxies like our own. He believed that our galaxy was only 30 000 ly across and that our Sun was near the centre of it.

Harlow Shapley thought our galaxy was much bigger, 300 000 ly across, and that it formed the whole Universe. He believed that the Sun was not at the centre of the galaxy and that the spiral nebulae were just clouds of gas, relatively small and nearby.

Astronomers found it difficult to decide who made the stronger case. It would take a new approach and new data to resolve the issue.

QUESTION

5 What new data could help to decide which theory was right?

Q nebula   Curtis-Shapley

The expanding Universe

We are learning to:

> recall how Hubble measured the distance to the galaxies

> use the Hubble equation

> explain how Hubble's results were evidence for an expanding Universe

Is the Universe still expanding?

The Big Bang theory states that the Universe started from a massive explosion, about 14 billion years ago, and expanded from an extremely small point to its current size. Physicists expected gravity gradually to slow down the expansion – but separate recent observations agree that the Universe is expanding more quickly now than in the past. Physicists are puzzled. It may be that something called dark energy is pushing the galaxies apart. Dark energy could make up 75% of the Universe. But no-one knows what dark energy is.

FIGURE 1: The WiggleZ project at the Anglo-Australian telescope has found new evidence for the existence of dark energy.

Hubble and the *Andromeda* nebula

In 1925 Edwin Hubble finally showed that some nebulae were actually galaxies. He was studying photographs, taken over several years, of the *Andromeda* nebula when he noticed a star that varied in brightness. He had discovered a Cepheid variable star. Over the next few weeks Hubble measured the brightness of the star, which varied with a period of 31 days. Such a long period meant a very luminous star (pages 154–5), yet it appeared very faint here on Earth. Hubble realised that the star was very distant, at least one million light-years away. The star, and the nebula, were much too far away to be in our galaxy. The *Andromeda* nebula had to be a galaxy in its own right.

FIGURE 2: Hubble used images from the 100-inch reflector telescope on Mount Wilson in California to show that other galaxies existed.

QUESTIONS

1 How did Hubble know that the star in *Andromeda* was so far away?

2 Why do you think the star hadn't been noticed before?

Moving galaxies

By the time of Hubble's discovery, scientists already knew that the nebulae were moving. If the spectrum of light from a galaxy was compared to the spectra of stars in our own galaxy, there were similar patterns but the galactic spectra were shifted, almost always to the red end of the spectrum (Figure 3). This **redshift** suggested that most of the galaxies were moving away from us.

FIGURE 3: The dark lines in the spectrum from distant galaxies are shifted towards the red end of the spectrum. The bigger the shift, the faster the galaxies are moving apart.

Hubble was looking for a link between a galaxy's distance and the speed at which it moves away from us (its recessional velocity). He looked for Cepheid variable stars in other galaxies so that he could measure the distances. The further away the galaxy, the fainter the light and the more difficult it was to find a Cepheid star that could be observed. However, after several years Hubble had enough results to publish (Figure 4). He had found a correlation between a galaxy's distance and its recessional velocity. Hubble had discovered that the further away the galaxy, the faster it was moving away from us.

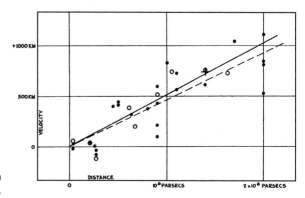

FIGURE 4: Hubble's original graph showing the link between recessional velocity (vertical axis) and distance (horizontal axis).

QUESTIONS

3 Look at Hubble's results (Figure 4). Why do you think he included a second, dotted, line?

4 Some results are below the axis, showing negative velocity. What could this mean?

Hubble's law

Hubble's results lie close to a straight line through the origin. This means the recessional velocity, v, of a galaxy is proportional to its distance, d, from Earth. In other words, the speed of recession is equal to the distance multiplied by a number, called the **Hubble constant** (H).

> speed of recession (km/s) = Hubble constant × distance (Mpc)

The Hubble constant is measured in units of km/s per Mpc. It tells us how quickly the galaxies appear to be moving away. The most recent data suggests that the Hubble constant, H, is equal to 75 km/s per Mpc.

Expanding space (Higher tier only)

The fact that almost all the galaxies are moving away from us suggests that either:

> we are at the centre of the Universe and the galaxies are being repelled from us

or

> every galaxy is moving away from every other galaxy.

The second explanation seems more likely. The Universe would look similar from every galaxy, so it must be space itself that is expanding.

The expansion suggests that the Universe was much smaller in the past, and is evidence for the Big Bang Theory.

QUESTIONS

5 Calculate the recessional velocity for a galaxy that is 10 Mpc away.

6 How does a value for H help us to calculate the age of the Universe?

FIGURE 5: The Hubble Telescope has been able to see Cepheid stars in very distant galaxies. This has given us the most precise measurements yet of the Hubble constant, $H = 74.2 \pm 3.6$ km/s per Mpc.

The radiation from stars

We are learning to:
> describe the radiation emitted by hot objects
> explain what the colour of starlight tells us about the star
> explain how energy is transported through a star

Do people emit radiation?

We all emit radiation because of our body temperature. Skin temperature is around 30°C, which means we emit infrared radiation. Thermal cameras can detect this radiation and use it to form an image that shows temperature differences. These thermographic images are used to diagnose medical conditions such as breast cancer or poor circulation and even to research heating effects due to the use of mobile phones.

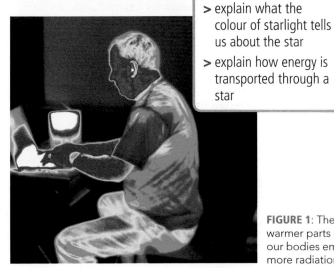

FIGURE 1: The warmer parts of our bodies emit more radiation.

Thermal radiation

Imagine heating a piece of metal in a flame. At first the warm piece of metal would give off infrared radiation; you couldn't see anything but you could feel it by placing your hand nearby. As the metal got hotter it would glow red, then yellow, then white.

All objects emit electromagnetic radiation across a range of wavelengths. The energy emitted at each wavelength depends on the temperature of the object. Hotter objects emit more energy at shorter wavelengths.

Stars behave in this way. The colour and luminosity of a star depend on its surface temperature. Hotter stars are more luminous and give off more shorter-wavelength radiation. A star that glows yellow, like the Sun, is hotter than a red star, such as *Betelgeuse*.

FIGURE 2: The hotter the object, the shorter the wavelength of the radiation emitted.

QUESTIONS

1 Look at Figure 2. Where is the hottest part of the metal? Where is the coolest part?

2 What is different about the motion of the particles in each case?

The radiation from stars

Figure 3 shows the radiation emitted from three different stars. The curves show how much energy (vertical axis) is emitted at each wavelength (horizontal axis). The area below each curve shows the total energy emitted.

A relatively cool star (curve A), with a surface temperature of 4200°C, is not very luminous. The total energy emitted is low, as shown by the small area under the curve. The peak of the graph lies towards the red end of the spectrum, so the star glows orange-red.

Q blackbody radiation

A much hotter star (curve C), with a surface temperature of 7200 °C, emits much more energy. The peak of the graph is in the violet part of the spectrum. Because the star is emitting strongly at all visible wavelengths, it will look blue-white.

The star represented by curve B peaks near the yellow part of the spectrum. This is similar to our Sun.

Did you know?

The Earth's atmosphere scatters the blue light from the Sun more than other colours. So the Sun looks yellower (less blue) than it would from space.

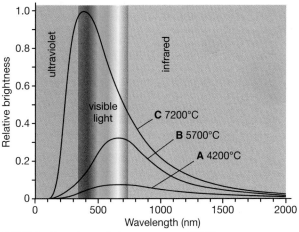

FIGURE 3: How the radiation emitted from a star depends on its surface temperature.

QUESTIONS

3 Look at Figure 3. What would the curve look like for a star with a surface temperature of 10 000 °C? What can you say about the star?

4 People have a skin temperature of 33 °C. Why don't they glow in the dark?

5 *Sirius B* has a surface temperature of 25 000 °C. What colour would you expect it to be? It looks quite faint from Earth, but is relatively close (9 ly). What does that tell you about the star?

Watch out!
The colour of an object does not necessarily tell you its temperature. A red book is *reflecting* red light. Thermal radiation is *emitted* by an object, not simply reflected from another source.

Energy transport in a star

The energy source that powers a star is nuclear fusion (pages 172–3). Nuclear fusion takes place deep within the star, in the core, where the temperature is around 16 million °C (for a star like our Sun). The nuclear reactions release photons of gamma radiation that travel outward through the star. These photons of gamma radiation interact with atoms throughout the **radiation zone** (Figure 4), losing energy as they go.

Further from the core, the star gets cooler. The cooler gas is more efficient at absorbing photons. The main energy transfer process in this region is **convection**. Regions of hot gas expand and rise towards the surface, where they lose energy, cool, contract and fall inwards again.

The surface of the star is called the **photosphere**. This is the part of the star that we can see. Energy is emitted into space, mainly in the form of electromagnetic radiation, of all wavelengths from radio to gamma rays. Because the surface temperature of the Sun is about 5500 °C , most radiation is emitted in the visible part of the spectrum (see Figure 3).

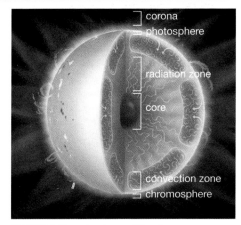

FIGURE 4: The structure of the Sun.

Did you know?

It takes about 1 million years for a photon of radiation emitted from the Sun's core to get to the surface. Although the photon travels at the speed of light, it has so many interactions on its way through the Sun that its progress is slow. If nuclear fusion in the Sun somehow switched off today, the Sun would keep shining for a long time.

QUESTION

6 Convection is important in energy transfer through the Earth as well as in the Sun. Explain what convection is and where convection happens in the Earth.

Analysing stellar spectra

We are learning to:
> understand the significance of spectral lines in the spectrum of a star
> explain how spectral lines are produced

What is the Sun made of?

In 1868 Pierre Jansen, a French astronomer, went to India to watch a total solar eclipse. As the Moon blocked out the Sun, Jansen viewed the Sun's corona through a spectroscope. The spectrum contained several coloured lines that he couldn't explain. Later that year Norman Lockyer repeated the experiment and realised he had discovered a new element. He called it helium, from the Greek word for Sun (*helios*), because it was first discovered on the Sun.

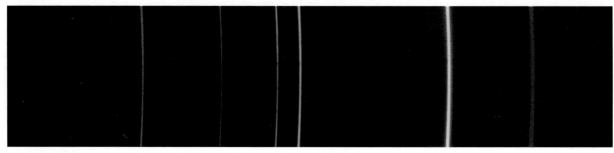

FIGURE 1: The emission spectrum of helium.

Line spectra

Robert Bunsen did more than just invent the famous gas burner. He used his burner to investigate the light emitted by different elements as they were placed in the flame. Bunsen, and his colleague Kirchhoff, looked at the light from the flaming substances through a prism. They saw that the spectrum wasn't continuous, like the colours in a rainbow. Instead, they saw a set of coloured lines that we call a **line spectrum**. Bunsen and Kirchhoff found that each element gave out its own, unique **emission spectrum**. They used this method to find new elements, such as caesium and rubidium.

Bunsen also discovered that if a bright, white light was shone through the vapour from the element, a spectrum was formed with dark lines on it. This is an **absorption spectrum**. Atoms of the element have absorbed some of the wavelengths from the white light. The position of the dark lines exactly matches the position of the bright lines of the emission spectrum (Figure 2).

QUESTIONS

1 'An emission spectrum is a fingerprint for the elements.' Explain what this means.

2 Bunsen and Kirchhoff discovered caesium in mineral water. How do you think they did it?

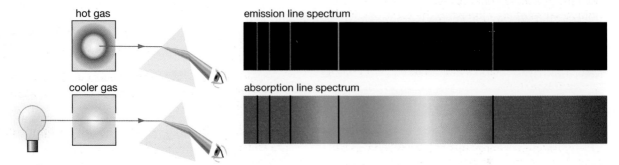

FIGURE 2: The black lines in an absorption spectrum exactly match the bright lines in an emission spectrum. These show the characteristic line spectra of hydrogen.

emission spectrum   absorption spectrum

Stellar spectra

Helium was discovered in the emission spectrum of the outer part of the Sun. This was during an eclipse, when the Moon blocked off the light from the rest of the Sun, otherwise the emission spectrum would have been difficult to see. The spectra from stars are usually absorption spectra.

A spectrum of the Sun's light has hundreds of dark lines on it (Figure 3). These are caused by elements in the Sun's cooler, outer atmosphere, which absorbs certain wavelengths of light. Every element has its own pattern of absorption lines so, by analysing a star's spectrum, we can say which elements are present in the star.

Spectra can also reveal the temperature of a star. When a photon of radiation is absorbed by an atom, the energy may be enough to knock one of the electrons out of orbit. This process is called **ionisation**. An atom that has lost an electron is known as an **ion**. The spectrum of an ion is different from the spectrum of the original atom, so astronomers can tell which atoms have been ionised. This gives a measure of temperature.

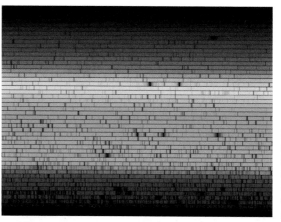

FIGURE 3: The spectrum of the Sun – by careful analysis of the lines we can tell which elements are present.

QUESTIONS

3 The spectral lines from other stars, and even from other galaxies, are similar to that from the Sun. What does that suggest about the elements throughout the Universe?

4 The spectrum from a hot blue star, such as *Sirius*, has some dark lines that are different from those for the Sun. Suggest why this might be.

Energy levels in atoms

Light is emitted from an atom when an electron loses energy. But the spectrum shows that only certain wavelengths (colours) of light are emitted. Since the colour of the light depends on its energy, this tells us something remarkable about electrons in atoms. Electrons can only lose energy in certain amounts.

This idea was first proposed by Nils Bohr, one of the founders of the theory of **quantum physics**. Bohr suggested that electrons in an atom only exist at certain **energy levels**. A photon of light is emitted when an electron drops from a higher energy level to a lower one. Atoms of a particular element have their own set of allowed energy levels, which lead to a unique set of energy jumps by the electrons. Therefore only photons of particular energies are emitted. The higher the energy of the photon, the higher the frequency – and the shorter the wavelength – of the light. This is why every element has its own unique emission spectrum.

An absorption spectrum can be explained by the same theory. The dark lines arise because light has been absorbed by electrons in the atom. Only when light of exactly the right energy hits the atom can this be absorbed and then an electron jumps to a higher energy level. That particular colour of light is removed, causing the dark lines in the spectrum.

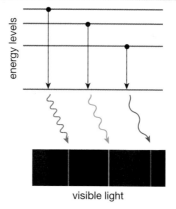

energy levels

visible light

FIGURE 4: As an electron jumps down between levels, it loses energy. This energy is emitted as a photon of light. Only certain energy levels are allowed, so only certain colours are emitted.

QUESTIONS

5 Nils Bohr said that the spectrum: 'was like a stained glass window into the heart of an atom.' What did he mean?

6 Look at Figure 4. There is no yellow light from this atom. Why is that?

7 How would you explain the emission of infrared or ultraviolet light from an atom?

Absolute zero

Where is the coolest place in the Universe?

The coldest place in the solar system is probably Triton, one of Neptune's moons. The surface of frozen methane is at a temperature of −235 °C. In interstellar space the temperature drops to −270 °C. The radiation left over from the Big Bang keeps the temperature three degrees above absolute zero. In 2010 the coldest thing in the Universe was a sample of rhodium metal in the physics labs of Helsinki University, which was cooled to 0.000 000 000 1 °C above absolute zero.

FIGURE 1: The coldest place on Earth is Ridge A, 14 000 m high on the Antarctic Plateau. It has an average winter temperature of −70 °C.

What do we mean by temperature?

Temperature isn't the same thing as energy. A burning match has a high temperature but not much energy. A bath of warm water has a lower temperature but more energy than the match. The idea of temperature is easier to understand if we think about the motion of molecules in a gas.

The air around you is made of molecules that are whizzing about at high speeds (hundreds of metres per second), in random directions. You can think of the molecules as tiny squash balls with perfect bounce that don't lose any energy when they collide with the walls. As the molecules hit the walls they bounce back, each one exerting a small force on the wall. The total force of all the billions of molecules on the whole area of the wall is what causes air pressure.

If you heated the air in the room, by turning on a radiator, for example, the molecules would move faster. The kinetic energy of the molecules would increase. The temperature of the air would also increase. The temperature of a gas depends on the average kinetic energy of its molecules. If we could find a way of continually cooling a gas down, the kinetic energy of the molecules would reduce. The molecules would move more and more slowly as the temperature dropped. Eventually the molecules would stop altogether. The temperature couldn't get any lower. We call this temperature **absolute zero**.

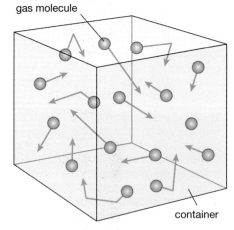

FIGURE 2: The molecules in a gas move in random directions at a range of speeds. The temperature depends on the average kinetic energy of the molecules.

QUESTIONS

1 Can anything be colder than absolute zero? Explain your answer.

2 You could increase the kinetic energy of the gas molecules by turning on an electric heater, or by turning on a fan. What's the difference?

Q absolute zero   absolute temperature GCSE   kinetic theory

Temperature and volume

Suppose a volume of gas is trapped in a cylinder by a piston (Figure 3). The piston is free to move; only air pressure from the atmosphere outside is holding it in place. As the gas is heated, its molecules will move faster. They will hit the piston harder and more often and push it upwards. The volume of the gas will increase. We could plot a graph to show how the volume of the gas increases with its temperature (Figure 4). The straight-line graph shows that there is a **linear relationship** between volume and temperature. The relationship is not directly proportional, because the line doesn't go through the origin – the volume of a gas doesn't fall to zero when the temperature drops to freezing point (0 °C).

Suppose we could keep cooling the gas: the volume would reduce further. Extrapolating the graph backwards (the dotted line in Figure 4a) shows that the volume of the gas would reach zero at −273 °C. This is absolute zero. It makes sense to redraw the vertical axis at this point and call it zero (Figure 4b). The horizontal axis now shows **absolute temperature** and is measured in units called **kelvin** (K).

To convert a temperature in Celsius (centigrade) to absolute temperature in kelvin, you need to add 273.

For example, 20 °C = 20 + 273 = 293 K

The volume, V, is **directly proportional** to the absolute temperature, T. Doubling the absolute temperature also doubles the volume. We write this as:

$$V \propto T \quad \text{or} \quad \frac{V}{T} = \text{constant}$$

This relationship only holds if the pressure of the gas is kept constant and the mass of gas stays fixed.

Watch out!

You must work in kelvin when you are solving problems involving gas volumes and temperature.

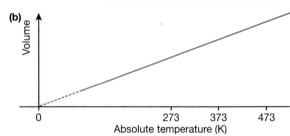

FIGURE 3   heat

QUESTIONS

3 2 m³ of air is trapped in a cylinder, like the one shown in Figure 3. The temperature of the gas is 20 °C. The gas is heated to a temperature of 60 °C. Calculate the new volume.

4 In reality, the volume of the gas cooled to 0 K wouldn't fall to zero. What might happen to the gas as it was cooled?

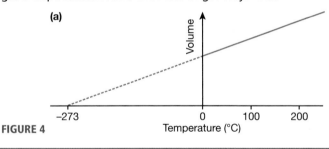

FIGURE 4

(a) Volume vs Temperature (°C): −273, 0, 100, 200

(b) Volume vs Absolute temperature (K): 0, 273, 373, 473

Temperature and pressure

We could carry out a similar experiment on a volume of gas trapped in a cylinder by a piston, heating the gas as before, but this time we could keep the piston fixed in place. The pressure of the gas would increase as the molecules move faster, hitting the walls of the container with greater force and colliding with the walls more often.

A graph of pressure against temperature shows that pressure is proportional to absolute temperature:

$$P \propto T \quad \text{or} \quad \frac{P}{T} = \text{constant}$$

This relationship only holds if the volume of the gas is kept constant and the mass of gas stays fixed.

Watch out!

You must work in kelvin when you are solving problems involving gas pressure and temperature.

QUESTIONS

5 The air in a car tyre is at a pressure of 200 kPa and a temperature of 7 °C. After a journey the temperature has risen to 27 °C. What is the new pressure?

6 What have you assumed in your answer to question **5**?

Q gas pressure   gas laws GCSE

The gas laws

Can liquid flow uphill?

Helium has the lowest boiling point of any element; it doesn't liquefy until −269 °C (4 K). When it is cooled further it behaves very strangely indeed. At 2 K, liquid helium will climb up the sides of its container and leak out. If you set some liquid helium spinning round in a cup and came back in a million years, the liquid would still be circulating. It has become a superfluid, a liquid with no resistance to motion.

FIGURE 1: Superfluid helium will creep up the sides of a container and escape.

Compressing a gas

When you put your finger over the end of a bicycle pump and push in the piston to reduce the volume, you can feel the pressure on your finger increase. The pressure is due to molecules of air colliding with your finger and the walls of the cylinder. As the piston is pushed in, the volume decreases and the molecules hit the walls more often.

Figure 3 shows an experiment to measure how gas pressure changes with volume. The pressure sensor and computer record the pressure as the volume is decreased. The pressure would increase if the temperature increased or if more gas molecules were added, so these variables must be controlled. Plotting the results shows that as the volume of a gas decreases its pressure increases, as shown in Figure 4.

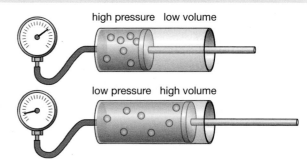

high pressure   low volume

low pressure   high volume

FIGURE 2: Compressing a gas in a piston

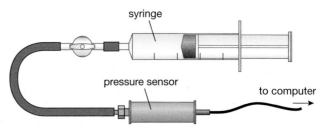

syringe

pressure sensor

to computer

FIGURE 3: Measuring the pressure as the volume of a gas is reduced. A pressure sensor can be linked to a computer to record the results. The compression is done slowly, to allow the temperature to stay constant.

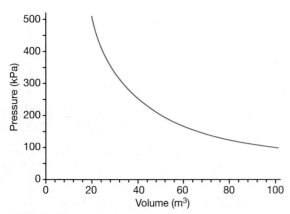

FIGURE 4: The graph shows how the pressure of a gas changes with its volume, if the temperature of the gas is kept constant and the mass of gas stays fixed.

QUESTIONS

1 Sarah says: 'Doubling the pressure of a gas halves its volume.' Use the graph in Figure 4 to check if she is right.

2 As you blow up a balloon the pressure and the volume both increase. This doesn't seem to fit the results shown above. Explain why.

Boyle's law

The scientist Robert Boyle was the first to investigate the relationship between the pressure and volume of a gas. He realised that for a fixed mass of gas at constant temperature, the pressure multiplied by the volume always gave the same answer.

> pressure × volume = constant

This is known as **Boyle's law**.

If the pressure increases, the volume must decrease by the same factor. If the volume increases, the pressure must decrease by the same factor.

Suppose that 20 cm³ of air at a pressure of 100 kPa is trapped in a syringe. If the syringe is pushed in to reduce the volume to 5 cm³, we can use Boyle's law to calculate the new pressure. The volume has decreased to $\frac{5}{20}$ or $\frac{1}{4}$ of its original value. The pressure will have increased by a factor of 4. So the new pressure is 400 kPa.

> ### Watch out!
> Pressure is measured in pascals, Pa. Volume is measured in cubic metres, m³. You can use other units in Boyle's law, such as cm³ provided that you are consistent.

⊙ QUESTIONS

3 Why do air bubbles get larger as they get closer to the surface of the water? (See Figure 5.)

4 A bubble of air grows in volume from 10 mm³ to 50 mm³. What will happen to the pressure of air inside the bubble?

FIGURE 5: Air bubbles get larger as they get closer to the surface of the water.

Pressure, volume and temperature

The state of a known mass of gas is described by the three quantities: Pressure, volume and absolute temperature. These quantities are linked by the three **gas laws**: the two laws presented on pages 164–165, and Boyle's law, above. These laws apply to a *fixed mass* of an **ideal gas**. An ideal gas has molecules that take up a very small fraction of the gas's volume and which are too far apart to affect each other. A gas that is well above its boiling point, and not under high pressure, will behave as an 'ideal gas'.

$$\frac{\text{pressure}}{\text{temperature}} = \text{constant} \quad \text{or} \quad P = \text{constant} \times T, \quad \text{at constant volume}$$

$$\frac{\text{volume}}{\text{temperature}} = \text{constant} \quad \text{or} \quad V = \text{constant} \times T, \quad \text{at constant pressure}$$

$$\text{pressure} \times \text{volume} = \text{constant} \quad \text{or} \quad P = \frac{\text{constant}}{V}, \quad \text{at constant temperature}$$

Direct and inverse proportionality (Higher tier only)

The first two laws are examples of **direct proportionality**: changing one of the variables means that the other one changes by the same factor. For example, doubling the absolute temperature of a gas would double its pressure.

The third law is an example of **inverse proportionality**: increasing one of the variables means that the other one decreases by the same factor. For example, doubling the volume of a gas would halve its pressure.

⊙ QUESTIONS

5 A quantity y is directly proportional to another quantity x. Explain what this means and sketch a graph to show how x and y are related.

6 A quantity y is inversely proportional to another quantity x. Explain what this means and sketch a graph to show how x and y are related.

🔍 inverse proportionality

Preparing for assessment: Analysing, evaluating and reviewing

To achieve a good grade in science you will need to be able to use your skills and understanding to understand how scientists plan, run and evaluate investigations. These skills will be assessed in your exams and in Controlled Assessments. This activity supports you in developing the skills of analysing, evaluating and reviewing an investigation.

✳ Under pressure

Ros and Matt are carrying out an experiment to investigate the relationship between the pressure of a fixed mass of gas and the volume it occupies. They are then going to relate this to a kinetic model, showing how this can explain the properties of a gas.

They think that if they apply more pressure to the gas it will be compressed into a smaller space. They predict that doubling the pressure would halve the volume. They know that temperature can also affect the gas and that this will have to be kept constant or it will affect the results. They also have some ideas about particle movement and think they might be able to use ideas about collisions in a set area to explain the changing results.

They use the foot pump to apply pressure to the column of air and record both pressure and volume.

Their results are shown in this table.

Pressure (kPa)	Volume (cm³)
100	50
110	45
120	42
130	39
140	37

After they had completed their experiment the apparatus was then used by other groups in the class. The data was shared, and Ros and Matt collected the results from three other groups. These are shown in the table below.

Group A		Group B		Group C	
Pressure (kPa)	Volume (cm³)	Pressure (kPa)	Volume (cm³)	Pressure (kPa)	Volume (cm³)
100	50	100	50	100	50
110	45	110	46	120	42
120	41	120	43	140	36
130	38	130	41	160	31
140	36	140	39	180	27
150	34	150	37		

The teacher then asked the students to process the data to explore the trend and see if their prediction was correct. Ros and Matt decided to plot all four sets of data in the same graph, using different colours.

Task 1

You will need produce a graph and then use it to explore these questions.

> Look at the data Ros and Matt have gathered and compare it with that from other groups. What's the same and what's different?

> Does the trend in the data overall support their hypothesis?

> What scientific terms is it important for them to use in their review of the investigation?

Task 2

> How well do the other group's results support Ros and Matt's data?

> How well does their hypothesis explain the pattern in the data?

> How could they use ideas about particles to improve their hypothesis?

> How should they structure their review of the conclusion?

Task 3

> How confident should they be about the data and why?

> What similarities or differences do you see as being important?

> What further data might they gather to make the conclusions more robust?

Maximise your grade

Use these suggestions to improve your work and be more successful.

E

To be on target for grade E you need to:

> compare the secondary data and primary data and spot similarities and differences

> comment on whether trends in the data support the hypothesis and use scientific ideas to suggest why

> use some relevant scientific terms correctly.

C

To be on target for a grade D or C, you also need to:

> explain how well the secondary data supports or undermines the primary data

> explain the extent to which the hypothesis can account for the pattern(s) shown in the data

> use scientific ideas to support or modify the hypothesis to account for the data

> organise your information effectively, with generally sound spelling, punctuation and grammar

> use specialist terms appropriately.

A

To be on target for a grade B or A, you also need to:

> assess and explain the levels of confidence that can be placed on the available data

> comment on the importance of any similarities or differences

> cive a detailed account of what extra data could be collected to increase confidence in the hypothesis

> ensure your report is comprehensive, relevant and logically sequenced, with full and effective use of relevant scientific terminology

> make few, if any, grammatical errors.

Star birth

Where are stars made?

The constellation of *Orion* is one of the easiest to find: look southeast in the winter months and *Orion* dominates the sky. Orion was a hunter; three bright stars represent his belt, from which a sword of bright stars hangs. See Figure 3 on page 153. If you look at the sword through a telescope, though, you will see that the brightest light is not a star at all. It is a **nebula**, an enormous cloud of hot gas and dust, where new stars are being born.

FIGURE 1: The nebula in *Orion's* sword.

Giant molecular clouds

The *Orion* nebula is part of an immense cloud of molecular gas. These giant molecular clouds (GMCs) are where stars begin their lives. They are mainly formed from hydrogen gas and interstellar dust, although there are small amounts of other particles such as helium and carbon and even water molecules.

Gravity is constantly acting to pull the molecules and dust together. As the cloud collapses, gravitational potential energy is transferred to kinetic energy. The particles move faster and the temperature of the cloud increases. The increase in temperature leads to an increase in pressure. Eventually the pressure of the gas pushing outwards is balanced by the force of gravity pulling inwards. The cloud is in equilibrium.

QUESTIONS

1 Where does the energy come from to heat up the giant molecular cloud?

2 Explain why the pressure of gas in the cloud increases as the cloud collapses.

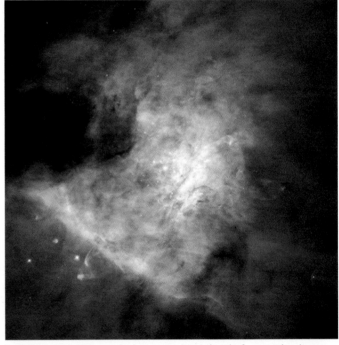

FIGURE 1: The *Orion* nebula is a massive cloud of gas with a large number of hot young stars.

Protostars

Giant molecular clouds are not uniform; there are regions of higher density. These are less stable than the rest of the cloud. It is these 'clumps' that collapse into denser regions that will eventually become stars.

The dense regions of gas and dust are only stable while the gas pressure balances the gravitational force. The explosion of a nearby star (a supernova), or a collision with another gas cloud can trigger a gravitational collapse. Once again, the gas becomes denser and hotter. The volume decreases and its temperature increases, causing the outward pressure to increase until it balances gravity once more. By now the dense region has become so hot, at 2000–3000 K, that it glows red. It is known as a **protostar**.

nebula   giant molecular cloud

The protostar's gravity attracts more gas and dust onto its surface. Over the course of a few million years the protostar becomes more massive. Eventually the core of the protostar becomes so hot and dense that nuclear fusion starts and a new star lights up.

FIGURE 3: A computer simulation of a protostar.

Did you know?

A protostar is formed from a mass of gas that is rotating. As the gas contracts, it rotates faster. Like an ice-skater who spins faster when she pulls her arms in, the protostar and the disc of material around it spin faster. This spinning disc of material may later form the planets of a solar system.

FIGURE 4: Contraction leads to faster spinning.

QUESTIONS

3 How does a protostar grow?

4 Why do protostars give out red light?

Powering the stars

Where does the Sun get its energy from? In the 18th century, scientists thought that the Sun might be powered by chemical reactions, burning like a fire. Knowing the mass of the Sun, and assuming that is made mostly of carbon, they calculated that it might burn for about 50 000 years. But geologists believed the Earth was at least 400 million years old. Surely the Earth couldn't be older than the Sun?

Lord Kelvin suggested that the Sun was powered by gravitational collapse, rather like protostars. That gave the Sun's age as 25 million years – but that was still not old enough for geological change or evolution to take place on Earth.

It wasn't until the early 20th century that the correct explanation was developed. It was based on the discovery of radioactivity (1898), the atomic nucleus (1911) and Einstein's theory of relativity (1905), which showed that mass could be converted to energy. In 1920 it was first suggested that the Sun's energy came from **nuclear fusion**. In the core of the Sun, hydrogen nuclei are pushed together to make helium. The reaction releases large amounts of energy, much more than any chemical reaction. This new theory put the age of the Sun at 4.5 billion years, with enough fuel left to keep the Sun shining for another 5 billion years or so.

QUESTIONS

5 What information would you need, to be able to work out how much longer the Sun will shine for?

6 Kelvin's calculation was widely accepted at the time and caused a vigorous scientific debate. Why was it so controversial?

Q protostar   age of the Sun

Nuclear fusion

We are learning to:

> explain the process of nuclear fusion
> use nuclear equations to describe fusion reactions
> understand the importance of scientists reviewing one another's work

Can we solve the world's energy problems?

Physicists have been trying to harness **nuclear fusion**, the energy that drives the Sun, since the 1950s. They have spent billions of pounds on massive experiments because fusion offers a clean, almost limitless energy source. So in 1989, when two scientists, Martin Fleischmann and Stanley Pons, announced they had achieved fusion using a table-top experiment built for less than $100 000, there was worldwide excitement. Unfortunately, no one has yet been able to repeat the experiment.

FIGURE 1: Fleischmann and Pons claimed to have been able to achieve fusion using quite simple equipment.

Fusion in the Sun

The innermost 10% of the Sun is called the core. Conditions are extreme, because of the enormous gravitational force. The density of the material in the core is 20 times greater than that of iron, yet it is still a gas due to the enormous temperature, around 15 million kelvin. At this temperature there are no atoms, just a **plasma** of electrons and nuclei. The Sun is 78% hydrogen, so most of the nuclei are just protons, whizzing round at high speed.

When two protons collide at such high speed they can fuse (join) together. They undergo a nuclear reaction to form a **deuterium** nucleus: this is a heavy type of hydrogen. The high speed is important. Every proton carries a positive charge so two protons will repel each other. It is only when they collide at high speed that they get close enough for the attractive **strong nuclear force** to overcome the electromagnetic repulsion.

Did you know?

Even with the high temperatures in the Sun's core, the fusion of two protons is so unlikely to occur that, on average, a proton will travel round in the Sun for a billion years before it fuses with another proton. Sunshine, and therefore all life on Earth, depends on this unlikely reaction.

QUESTIONS

1 Describe the conditions in the core of a star.

2 Why does nuclear fusion occur only in the core of a star?

Fusion reactions

The Sun is powered by the fusion of hydrogen into helium. This happens in a series of reactions called the **p–p cycle**, which starts with the fusion of two protons to make deuterium.

A nucleus of an element X can be written as $^A_Z X$ where A is the **mass number** (the total number of protons and neutrons) and Z is the **atomic number** (the number of protons). So $^{14}_6 C$ is a carbon nucleus with 6 protons and 8 neutrons. Elements in which the nuclei have the same number of protons but a different numbers of neutrons are called **isotopes**. There are several isotopes of carbon. There are three naturally occurring isotopes of hydrogen:

> $^1_1 H$ or hydrogen-1 (ordinary hydrogen) has just one proton

> $^2_1 H$ or hydrogen-2 (deuterium) has one proton and one neutron

> $^3_1 H$ or hydrogen-3 (**tritium**) has one proton and two neutrons.

Watch out!

Isotopes are chemically identical. For example, $^{14}_6 C$ and $^{12}_6 C$ both react with oxygen in the same way to form carbon dioxide.

Q nuclear fusion   p–p cycle

The reaction that fuses two protons to make deuterium can then be written:

$${}^1_1H + {}^1_1H \rightarrow {}^2_1H + {}^0_{+1}e + {}^0_0v$$ where: ${}^0_{+1}e$ is a **positron**, a positively charged electron (can be written β⁺)
${}^0_0v$ is a **neutrino**, a very low mass, neutral particle

Notice that the mass numbers (superscripts) balance on either side of the equation. The atomic number (subscripts) also balance, which shows that the charge is the same before and after the reaction. **Charge conservation** is ensured by the production of the positively charged positron. The positron is the **anti-matter** equivalent of the electron. A positron has exactly the same mass as an electron but it carries a positive charge.

Perhaps the surprising thing about this reaction is that mass is not conserved. The mass of two protons is more than the combined mass of the particles that are made in the reaction. Some mass has been lost in the reaction. The 'missing' mass has been turned into energy.

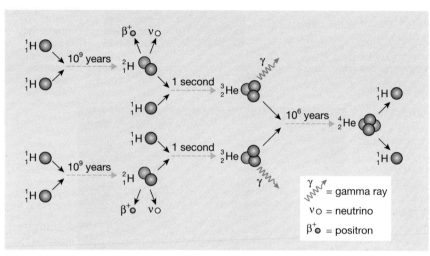

FIGURE 2: The p–p cycle is a chain of fusion reactions.

When Fleischmann and Pons announced to the world's press that they had achieved nuclear fusion with simple apparatus it seemed too good to be true, and perhaps it was. Their announcement came before the work had been checked by other scientists, in a process called 'peer review'. Since then, despite many attempts, other scientists have failed to replicate their results. Many scientists regard 'cold' fusion as a reminder of the importance of thorough peer review.

QUESTIONS

3 The second fusion reaction in the p–p cycle (see Figure 2) is a proton fusing with deuterium. Write down the equation that describes the reaction.

4 The final fusion reaction in this chain is the fusion of two helium-3 nuclei. What are the products of that reaction?

5 What are the possible consequences of announcing a new discovery before it has been reviewed by other scientists?

Einstein's energy equation (Higher tier only)

At each stage in the fusion process, mass is converted to energy. Although the amount of mass 'lost' is small for each reaction, there are an incredible number of reactions in the Sun, about 10^{38} per second. The Sun loses 6×10^{11} kg per second as it fuses hydrogen into helium. This mass is converted to energy, according to Einstein's equation:

$E = mc^2$ where: E = energy released (J)
m = mass (kg)
c = the speed of light (m/s)

The speed of light is 3×10^8 m/s, so squaring it gives a very large number, 9×10^{16}. Even a small amount of mass leads to an enormous release of energy. For example, if we could convert just 100 g of mass to energy, the energy released would be :

$E = mc^2 = 0.1 \times 9 \times 10^{16} = 9 \times 10^{15}$ J

This is enough to power the average UK household for about 15 years.

Did you know?

One way in which fusion has been achieved is by concentrating enormous laser power onto a pea-sized pellet of deuterium and tritium. 500 trillion watts of laser power compressed the pellet to 100 times the density of lead at a temperature of 100 million °C so that fusion could start.

QUESTION

6 Use the equation $E = mc^2$ to calculate how much energy the Sun emits per second.

Q peer review

The lives of stars

We are learning to:
> understand how different stars generate energy
> use the Hertzsprung–Russell (HR) diagram to identify stars of different types
> plot the path taken by a star on the HR diagram during its lifetime

Where were the elements made?

After the Big Bang the Universe was made almost entirely of hydrogen and a small amount of helium. All of the other elements were made much later, in stars.

Helium is made in the central core of stars. Stars much more massive than the Sun also make heavier elements. The heaviest elements of all are only made when massive stars explode at the ends of their lives.

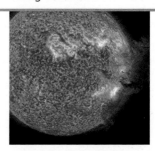

FIGURE 1: All of the elements in your body, apart from hydrogen, were made in stars.

Stars in the main sequence

Nuclear fusion of hydrogen to helium in the core of a star releases vast amounts of energy. This heats the gas in the core to extremely high temperatures. The enormous pressure from this gas, and from the radiation released from the core, pushes outwards. This pressure would blast the star apart but the star's mass is so large that gravity holds it together. The star is held in equilibrium – in a stable state – balanced between these huge forces (Figure 2).

The star is now said to be in the **main sequence**, the longest phase of its life. It will continue in this phase, fusing hydrogen into helium, for billions of years. Our Sun has been in the main sequence for about 5 billion years and has sufficient fuel to shine steadily for another 5 billion years.

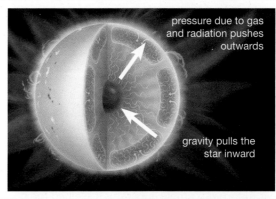

pressure due to gas and radiation pushes outwards

gravity pulls the star inward

FIGURE 2: A star in the main sequence is in equilibrium.

 QUESTION

1 What are the forces that act on a star?

Massive stars

Some stars are much more massive than our Sun. The gravitational force at the centre of these stars is immense. The temperature in the core is high enough to fuse larger nuclei together, despite the large repulsive forces. Helium nuclei are fused to make heavier nuclei such as beryllium, carbon and oxygen. If the temperature is high enough, the series of fusion reactions will continue until iron is formed.

The fusion of light nuclei releases energy but energy has to be supplied to form nuclei that are heavier than iron. Once the core stops releasing energy, the balance of forces keeping the star in equilibrium is lost and gravity will start to crush the star.

Did you know?

In 2010 scientists at the University of Sheffield discovered the largest star ever seen. Originally 320 times the mass of the Sun, the giant star is rapidly losing mass. Fusion is proceeding much faster than in the Sun. The star's life will be much shorter than the Sun's, measured in millions rather than billions of years. The star will die in a massive explosion, spreading heavy elements across space.

 QUESTIONS

2 Nuclear fusion of elements heavier than helium only occurs in massive stars. Explain why this is.

3 Elements heavier than iron cannot be made by fusion in the core of stars. Explain why this is.

Q main sequence   stellar nucleosynthesis

The Hertzsprung–Russell diagram

Stars vary enormously in size, luminosity and surface temperature. For example:

> *Rigel* in the constellation of *Orion* is a **supergiant**. It emits 85 000 times more energy per second than the Sun. Its surface is so hot (11 000 K) that it looks blue.

> *Arcturus* is a yellow **giant star**, slightly cooler than our Sun but over 200 times more luminous.

> *Sirius-B* is a **white dwarf**. Its surface temperature is 26 000 K so it emits much of its radiation in the ultraviolet (UV) part of the spectrum. It has almost the same mass as the Sun, but is only the size of the Earth.

The **Hertzsprung–Russell diagram** (HR diagram) shows the differences between stars (Figure 4). The luminosity of a star is plotted on the vertical axis, relative to the luminosity of the Sun. The surface temperature of a star is plotted on the horizontal axis, in kelvin. Because the surface temperature of a star determines its colour, the temperature axis also indicates the peak wavelength of light emitted by the star (see pages 160–161).

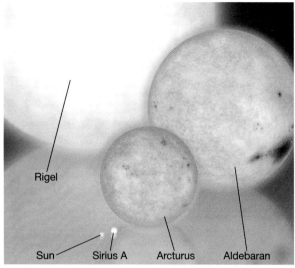

FIGURE 3: Relative sizes of different stars. On this scale *Sirius-B* would be a tiny dot.

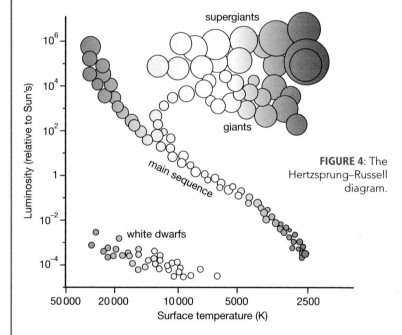

FIGURE 4: The Hertzsprung–Russell diagram.

When stars are plotted on the Hertzsprung–Russell diagram, they fall into three main groups.

> **Main sequence**: This diagonal line across the middle of the HR diagram contains stars in the stable part of their lives. All of these stars are fusing hydrogen into helium, but they cover a wide range of temperature and luminosity.

> **Supergiants** and **giant stars**: These groups contain stars that are much more massive than the Sun. Some are coming to the end of their lives (pages 176–7).

> **White dwarfs**: These are small hot stars where nuclear fusion has ceased. They will gradually cool and fade.

Watch out!

The axes on the HR diagram have non-linear scales. The luminosity axis goes up in multiples of 10^2. The temperature axis is also non-linear and goes backwards!

QUESTIONS

4 Make a sketch of the Hertzsprung–Russell diagram shown in Figure 4. Just draw a curve for the main sequence and sketch areas for the supergiants, giants and white dwarfs. Mark the positions of the following stars on the diagram:

a *Rigel* (mark it R)

b Sun (mark it S)

c *Arcturus* (mark it A)

d *Sirius B* (mark it B).

5 A star in the top right-hand corner of the Hertzsprung–Russell diagram is cool but very luminous. What does that tell you about the star?

The death of a star

We are learning to:

> understand what happens to a star as it runs out of fuel

> plot the path taken by a star on the HR diagram during its lifetime

> recall how white dwarfs, neutron stars and black holes are formed

What is a pulsar?

In 1967 Jocelyn Bell was analysing data from a radio telescope when she found a signal that repeated exactly every 1.3 seconds. This seemed too fast for a variable star. Neither was it a planet, as the source was outside the solar system. Perhaps it was a signal from a 'little green man', as Bell put it. But then she found a similar signal, repeating every 1.2 s. Jocelyn Bell had discovered **pulsars**, which are rapidly spinning **neutron stars** left behind by a supernova.

FIGURE 1: In 1967 Jocelyn Bell was a research student at Cambridge.

When the hydrogen runs out

When a star runs short of hydrogen in its core, fusion is reduced. Less energy is released and the pressure drops. Gravitational attraction is now larger than the outward pressure so the star contracts.

At this stage the core is mainly helium. It is surrounded by a shell of hydrogen. The gravitational collapse raises the temperature and hydrogen fusion begins in the shell. The energy released by this causes the outer layer of the star, the **photosphere**, to expand enormously. As the photosphere expands, its temperature drops and it shines red.

When the Sun reaches this stage it will expand to a hundred times its current size, swallowing up Mercury and Venus, becoming a **red giant** star.

A red giant star has a cool photosphere and a hot, dense helium core. It is tremendously bright because of its enormous size. The red giant phase of a star's life is much shorter than the main sequence. The hydrogen in the shell will begin to run out. What happens next depends on the star's mass.

QUESTIONS

1 Why does the photosphere cool as it expands?

2 Why will the Sun change colour when it becomes a red giant?

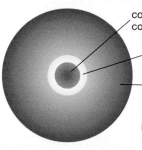

contracted helium core

hydrogen fusion in shell

expanded, cooled photosphere

FIGURE 2: Cross-section through a red giant.

The final fate of stars

Sun-sized stars

The hydrogen fusion in the shell of the red giant (Figure 2) produces more helium. This accumulates in the core, making it hotter and denser. When the temperature of the core reaches 100 million K, helium fusion begins. First beryllium and then carbon are formed:

$$^4_2\text{He} + {}^4_2\text{He} \rightarrow {}^8_4\text{Be} \qquad {}^8_4\text{Be} + {}^4_2\text{He} \rightarrow {}^{12}_6\text{C} + \gamma$$

and then further reactions produce larger nuclei such as nitrogen and oxygen.

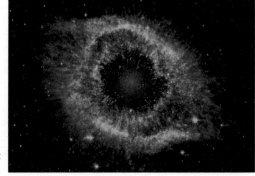

FIGURE 3: The *Helix* nebula. Radiation from the hot collapsed star at the centre lights up ejected material.

Q red giant   white dwarf

Stars with mass of up to eight times that of the Sun cannot create the necessary temperature for further fusion. When fusion stops, the core collapses and the outer layers are ejected into space in a shell of material known as a **planetary nebula** (Figure 3).

The exposed core is a hot sphere of carbon and oxygen, known as a white dwarf. Its density is enormous, about a million times greater than water. One teaspoonful would have a mass of several tonnes. No further nuclear fusion takes place. The white dwarf star takes billions of years to cool down but will eventually become a black dwarf, the cold remnant of a dead star.

Giant stars

Stars with mass more than eight times that of the Sun come to a more dramatic end. The extra gravitational force allows these supergiants to fuse heavier nuclei in their cores. Shells of carbon, oxygen and even heavier elements are formed. Eventually a core of iron and nickel is created.

Nuclear fusion of elements heavier than iron absorbs energy, rather than releasing it. The star cannot generate any more energy. There is nothing to oppose gravity and the star undergoes a catastrophic collapse, called a **supernova**. During the supernova, heavy elements such as lead, gold and even uranium are made. A massive shock wave rips the star apart, spreading the elements across space and leaving behind a dense core (Figure 5).

FIGURE 5: Jocelyn Bell's first pulsar was shown to be in the *Crab* nebula. Chinese astronomers recorded seeing a bright star flare up in the *Crab* in 1054. They had seen a supernova.

When the mass of the core is between about 1.4 and 4 solar masses, gravity is so strong that protons and electrons combine to form neutrons. The core has become a **neutron star**. A neutron star is typically only 20 km across. Imagine all the Sun's mass compressed to the size of a city; the star is so dense that a teaspoonful would have a mass of a billion tonnes.

If the mass of the core is greater than 4 solar masses then gravity is so strong that no force can resist it. The core collapses further, its density increases and gravity gets even stronger. Eventually, gravity is so strong that not even light can escape. A **black hole** has been formed. At the centre of the black hole, density and gravitational strength approach infinity. Nothing that enters the black hole can escape.

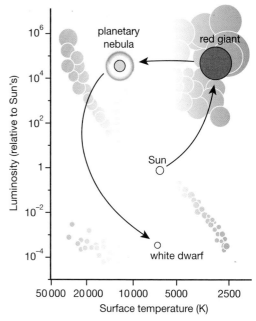

FIGURE 4: The path of a star such as the Sun passes through different phases after leaving the main sequence.

Did you know?

Gravity is so strong near the surface of a neutron star that an object dropped from a height of one metre would hit the surface at over a million kilometres per hour. Neutron stars can spin rapidly, beaming radio waves across the galaxy like a lighthouse. These are the pulsars discovered by Jocelyn Bell.

QUESTIONS

3 There probably aren't any black dwarf stars in the Universe. Why not?

4 Why can't small stars fuse heavier nuclei, such as carbon?

5 'Planetary nebula' is not an appropriate name. Why not?

6 Why is a star made entirely of neutrons so dense?

7 When Jocelyn Bell was trying to explain her observations, how could she rule out human-made signals? Or alien signals? How did pulsars become linked with supernovae?

8 Black holes are black. Space is mostly black. How might you set about observing a black hole?

The possibility of extraterrestrial life

Is there are anybody out there?

In 1960 Frank Drake was preparing for a meeting with astronomers, physicists and biologists to discuss the chances of finding intelligent life in the galaxy – other than on Earth. He came up with a list of factors that would determine the number of intelligent civilisations. The number of stars in the galaxy, about 2×10^{11}, was quite well known, but other factors, such as the fraction of stars with planets, were broad estimates. The meeting estimated that there may be only 10 advanced civilisations in the galaxy.

FIGURE 1: Drake's equation is an attempt to work out how many alien civilisations (N) may be trying to communicate.

$$N = N_s \times f_s \times f_p \times n_e \times f_l \times f_i \times f_c \times F_L$$

where: N_s is the number of stars in the galaxy
f_s is the fraction of stars suitable for life
f_p is the fraction of those stars with planets
n_e is the number of habitable planets or moons per system
f_l is the fraction of those on which life develops
f_i is the fraction of those on which intelligence develops
f_c is the fraction of those who try to communicate
F_L is the fraction of star's life for which civilisation lasts

Extrasolar planets

Searching for planets orbiting a distant star is a difficult task. At that distance, planets are too small for us to see them directly. They don't emit light of their own and the light they reflect gets lost in the glare of the star. Astronomers have to find other ways of detecting them.

They do this by studying the star. As the planet orbits, its gravity makes the star wobble. Astronomers look for tiny changes in the star's position, or small changes in the colour of the star's light, caused by the Doppler effect. Another way is to look for the small dip in light from a star as the planet moves between us and the star (Figure 2).

Using these methods, as at June 2011, astronomers have found over 500 planets around other stars. Most of these have been massive planets, such as Jupiter. So far no one has detected an Earth-like planet orbiting a star similar to the Sun.

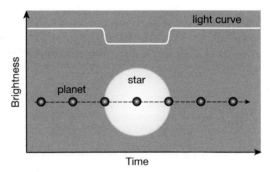

FIGURE 2: The transit method – light from the star dips in a regular way as the planet passes in front of it.

QUESTIONS

1 The first planet outside the solar system wasn't discovered until 1995. Why did it take so long?

2 Why might it be particularly difficult to detect Earth-like planets?

🔍 Planetquest   Planethunter   Exosolar

The Goldilocks zone

Many of the planets discovered so far are unlikely homes for life as we know it. Massive planets that orbit close to stars would be too hot and bathed in damaging radiation. A planet that is distant from the star is likely to be too cold. The **Goldilocks zone**, or habitable zone, is a region around a star where the temperature is just right. Here, water may exist as a liquid, something that is vital to life on Earth.

Detecting signs of life on distant planet is very challenging. NASA has proposed a project, called Terrestrial Planet Finding, which would look for signs of oxygen in the atmosphere of these planets. To do this, scientists would need to study the dim light reflected from the planet. This would require a space telescope of diameter four times that of Hubble and 100 times more precise. Originally planned to launch in 2014, the project has been delayed and may be cancelled due to lack of funding.

Despite the difficulties in detecting smaller planets, or finding evidence of life, scientists are optimistic that life exists on other planets. If only 10% of stars have planets, and only 0.1% of those are in the habitable zone, there would still be 20 million such planets in the galaxy. Life started quite early in the history of Earth and manages to survive in very harsh environments, so it seems reasonable to assume that some form of life does exist elsewhere in the galaxy.

FIGURE 3: A hydrothermal deep-sea vent.

QUESTIONS

3 Would you go ahead with a mission such as Terrestrial Planet Finder? Give your reasons.

3 Scientists believe that life will readily occur on the right sort of planet. What evidence is there for this?

Still waiting...

There is no generally accepted evidence of life anywhere other than on Earth.

In our solar system, Mars is perhaps the most likely place to have supported life in the past. There is evidence that liquid water used to exist there and some NASA scientists believe they have discovered fossil evidence of bacterial life in rocks. This is still not generally accepted.

Europa, one of Jupiter's moons, has a frozen surface but liquid water oceans may exist below. There is a possibility of life there – but no evidence yet.

Further afield the SETI (Search for ExtraTerrestrial Intelligence) project is listening for radio signals from advanced civilisations but, so far, has found nothing.

QUESTIONS

5 Look at the Drake equation shown in Figure 1. Which factors can be measured or accurately estimated? Which factors are very difficult to determine?

6 Why do you think that liquid water is seen as being important for life?

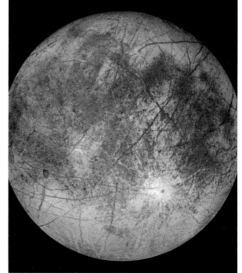

FIGURE 4: *Europa*, one of Jupiter's moons, is a candidate for life in the solar system. Some scientists believe that there are liquid oceans beneath its solid surface.

Q SETI

Observing the Universe

We are learning to:

> compare the advantages of space telescopes and ground-based telescopes

> recall and explain the location of the major ground-based telescopes.

> discuss the advantages of computer control of telescopes

How far back in time can we see?

In 2018 NASA will launch the James Webb Space Telescope (JWST). It will have a mirror 6.5 m in diameter and a sunshield as big as a tennis court. Its infrared capability will allow it to 'see' through the discs of dust that surround protostars to watch the formation of new planets. The Webb telescope will collect light from the earliest galaxies, formed over 13 billion years ago.

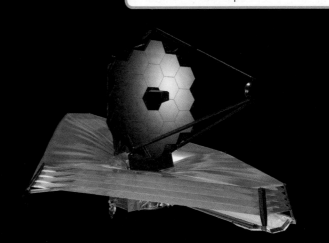

FIGURE 1: A full scale model of the JWST. The mirror and sunshield will be folded up for the launch and unfurled in space.

A new space telescope

Some people question the need to build a new space telescope, such as the JWST. The next generation of ground-based telescopes will be huge. Their mirrors, 30 m in diameter, will dwarf the JWST's 6.5 m mirror, giving a more detailed image. A space telescope is very expensive to launch and maintenance relies on space-walking astronauts. Now that the space shuttle has been retired, maintenance trips may be difficult to organise.

Supporters of the JWST point out the advantages of a telescope in space. The Earth's atmosphere absorbs some of the light before it reaches telescopes on the ground. It also causes unwanted refraction effects. Other wavelengths, such as X-rays, ultraviolet and infrared, are absorbed strongly by the atmosphere. Telescopes that observe the Universe at other wavelengths have to go into space (Figure 2). The JWST will be able to detect infrared radiation that would be blocked by the Earth's atmosphere.

FIGURE 2: XMM *Newton*, the European Space Agency's X-ray telescope, has to be in orbit above the Earth because it detects X-rays that would be blocked by the Earth's atmosphere.

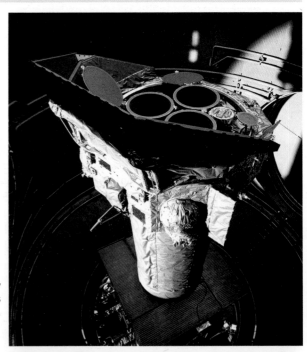

QUESTIONS

1 What are the main advantages of a telescope in space?

2 What are the main problems of a telescope in space?

Did you know?

Large modern telescopes have flexible mirrors that can change shape. 'Adaptive optics' eliminates the blurring effect of the atmosphere and improves the image quality.

space telescope   James Webb telescope   Keck telescope

Ground-based telescopes

Observing the stars from the surface of the Earth involves peering through the atmosphere. Refraction distorts the image so that stars appear to twinkle. Light pollution from streetlights or nearby towns reduces visibility and bad weather can prevent observations altogether.

To overcome these problems, the large telescopes used by professional astronomers are located in remote places, as high above sea level as possible. Astronomers need sites with as many cloudless nights per year as possible. The air has to be dry and free from pollution, because water vapour and particles will scatter the light. The table lists some of the more important telescopes in the world.

FIGURE 3: Ground-based telescopes need to be at high altitude, where there are dry, cloudless nights, the air is free from particulate pollution and there is no light pollution.

Some of the most important telescopes in the world

Telescope	Location	Altitude (m)	Size of telescope
Gran Telescopio Canarias	La Palma, Canary Islands, Spain	2400	10.4 m mirror
Keck	Mauna Kea, Hawaii	4123	10 m mirror
VLT Interferometer	Cerro Paranal, Chile	2635	four 8.2 m mirrors
Anglo-Australian	Coonabarabran, NSW, Australia	1742	3.9 m mirror

QUESTIONS

3 The telescopes on Mauna Kea are over 4000 m above sea level. What are the advantages and disadvantages of this location?

4 The European Southern Observatory at Cerro Paranal, Chile, is in the middle of the Atacama desert, the driest place on Earth. Why was it put there?

Computer control

Despite the exciting locations of many telescopes, professional astronomers often work from their own offices. Telescopes can be controlled by computer from a remote location. The telescope will be steered and locked on to the object of interest, continuously tracking it across the sky as the Earth rotates. The images are captured digitally by a charge coupled device (CCD), similar to those in digital cameras. The digitised images can be studied in real time or they can be enhanced and analysed by computer before being sent to the astronomer. Digital images and data are easily shared among astronomers.

Remote access offers enormous benefits to astronomers who can book time on telescopes in different time zones, and look at northern or southern skies. Astronomers can have access to the best telescopes in the world without the need to travel to remote mountain-tops. Sharing expensive facilities among astronomers from across the world is a cost-effective strategy.

It is now possible for amateur astronomers to rent time on telescopes via internet sites such as Global Rent A Scope (GRAS). Amateurs have access to better telescopes than they could afford to buy, in better locations and without the time-consuming set-up procedure.

FIGURE 4: Researchers working inside the control room for the Very Large Telescope (VLT) in Chile – the telescope mirrors are flexible and are constantly adjusted by the computers to compensate for errors.

QUESTION

5 Even small amateur telescopes can be controlled from a computer. What are the advantages of this?

Q space telescope   James Webb telescope   Keck telescope

International astronomy

We are learning to:
> explain why modern astronomy needs international collaboration
> understand the practical issues involved in building an observatory

Can amateur astronomers make important discoveries?

The last person to record a supernova in our galaxy was Johannes Kepler in 1604. He reported a 'new star' that flared as brightly as Venus. Astronomers are waiting for another supernova in our galaxy. One is long overdue. The first sign will be a flood of neutrinos. Neutrino observatories will detect this, but they won't be able to locate the supernova. Instead, they will send an alert to amateur astronomers all over the world who will scour the skies, trying to be the first to find the supernova.

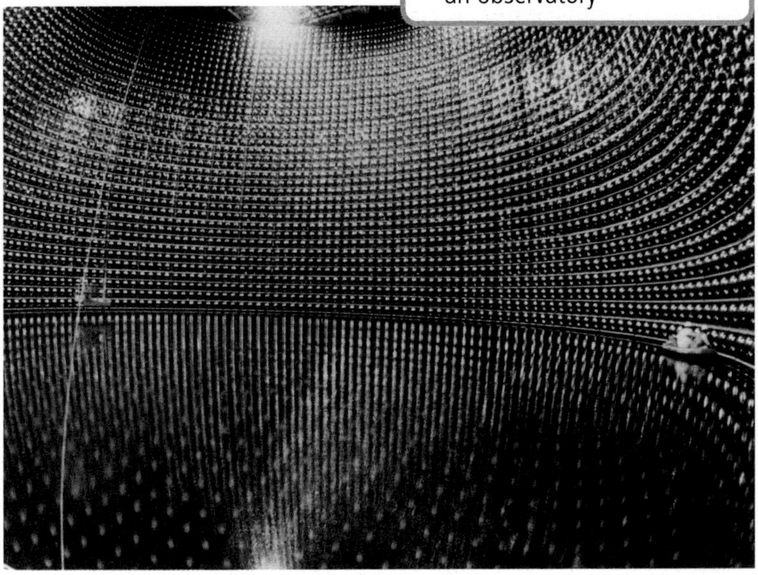

FIGURE 1: This neutrino telescope, located half a mile underground in a Japanese mine, is made from 12 million gallons of pure water. 12 000 detectors are looking for a flash of light caused by a neutrino.

Building a new telescope

European astronomers are planning the largest telescope ever built. The Extremely Large Telescope (ELT) will have a mirror that is 42 m across. It will cost over €1 billion to build and about €50 million every year to run. It should make its first observations in 2020.

The telescope is being built by the European Southern Observatory, an organisation of 15 countries, who will share the high costs. Each country will contribute specialist knowledge and skills. Partners in the UK include Oxford and Durham universities and British companies are building detectors and segments of the mirror.

The telescope has to be well away from the light of towns, in a dry climate and at high altitude, so the ELT will be built on a mountain in Chile's Atacama desert. The remote site is ideal for observing and will mean there is very limited social impact, but it will bring its own problems. The workforce to build and run the telescope will need to be brought to the site; accommodation and road links will have to be built. The site will also need 10 MW of electrical power.

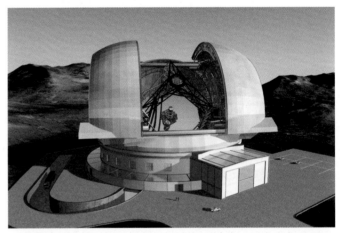

FIGURE 2: An artist's impression of the Extremely Large Telescope.

QUESTIONS

1 Why is a European telescope being built in Chile?

2 What are the advantages of a group of 15 nations cooperating to build the ELT?

Q observing supernovae   Swift telescope

Gamma-ray bursters

No one is exactly sure what causes bursts of gamma radiation from space. The bursts last from between fractions of a second to several minutes. Following the burst, there may be an afterglow of X-rays, ultraviolet and visible light. The bursts happen randomly, from any part of the sky, so observing them can be tricky.

An international project is using satellites to detect the bursters. One of the satellites, called *Swift* (see pages 152–3), is designed to detect the burst and then quickly spin round to point at the source. *Swift* sends the coordinates of the burster to observatories all around the world. Some of the telescopes may be aimed at the right area of sky to study the afterglow.

In March 2011, the *Swift* satellite detected a flash of gamma rays that lasted longer than normal. A team of astronomers led by the University of California suggested that it may have been caused by a star being torn apart as it fell into a massive black hole.

Did you know?

Enormous bursts of gamma rays from space were discovered accidentally in the 1960s by satellites belonging to the United States air force. The satellites were actually looking for evidence of nuclear weapons being tested.

QUESTIONS

3 The study of gamma-ray bursters needs international cooperation. Explain why.

4 Why does the gamma-ray telescope have to be in space? How can it detect the gamma rays even if it is pointing the wrong way?

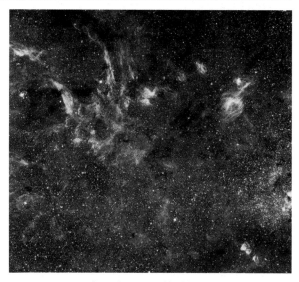

FIGURE 3: A map of gamma ray bursts from the *Swift* gamma-ray satellite.

Online research

Astronomical telescopes and satellites now produce millions of digital images. Analysing them is a time-consuming task. Computers can do some of the analysis, but the human eye is better. Websites such as Zooniverse encourage the public to help in the analysis of images. Projects include looking for exoplanets, hunting for supernovae and mapping the *Milky Way*.

The Milky Way Project is looking for bubbles. The Spitzer infrared space telescope has taken thousands of images of the *Milky Way* (Figure 4). The bubbles indicate areas of active star formation. By putting the images online and providing some simple software tools, researchers are getting the public to help them map the *Milky Way* and learn more about the origin of stars.

QUESTION

5 What are the advantages of asking the public to get involved with scientific research?

FIGURE 4: Infrared image of bubbles in the *Milky Way*, taken by the Spitzer telescope.

P7 Checklist

To achieve your forecast grade in the exam you'll need to revise

To achieve your forecast grade in the exam you'll need to revise.

Use this checklist to see what you can do now. Refer back to pages 128–183 if you're not sure. Look across the rows to see how you could progress – **bold italic** means Higher tier only.

Remember, you'll need to be able to use these ideas in various ways, such as:
> interpreting pictures, diagrams and graphs
> applying ideas to new situations
> explaining ethical implications
> suggesting some benefits and risks to society
> drawing conclusions from evidence you've been given.

Look at pages 206–212 for more information about exams and how you'll be assessed.

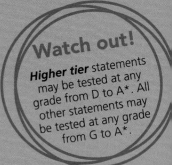

Watch out!

Higher tier statements may be tested at any grade from D to A*. All other statements may be tested at any grade from G to A*.

To aim for a grade E	To aim for a grade C	To aim for a grade A
recall and explain the apparent daily motion of the Sun, the Moon and the stars from east to west	*explain the difference between a sidereal day and a solar day*	
understand that some planets can be seen with the naked eye, and that all planets appear to move with the stars across the sky during the night	*understand that* over weeks and months the planets move relative to the fixed stars, sometimes with retrograde motion, *and explain this motion in terms of the orbits of the planets*	
explain the phases of the Moon and eclipses		*explain the low frequency of eclipses*
explain why different stars are seen at different times of the year		
understand that the positions of astronomical objects are described in terms of right ascension and declination	*understand how right ascension and declination relate to the celestial sphere*	
recall that the speed of waves is affected by the medium and that it will change if a wave moves from one medium into another; understand that a change in wave speed causes a change in wavelength and may cause a change in direction, which is called refraction		explain the refraction of light waves by the change in speed when they pass into a different medium
describe how refraction leads to the formation of an image by a convex (converging) lens; understand that a lens with a more curved surface is more powerful and calculate its power in dioptres		

To aim for a grade E	To aim for a grade C	To aim for a grade A

understand and draw diagrams to show how lenses focus light; interpret ray diagrams for lenses gathering light from stars

interpret and draw ray diagrams for convex lenses gathering light from extended sources

understand that astronomical objects are so distant that light from them reaches the Earth as effectively parallel rays

recall that a simple optical telescope has two converging lenses of different powers

understand the function of the two optical elements of a telescope *calculate the angular magnification of a telescope from the powers (or focal lengths) of the two lenses*

understand how concave mirrors bring a parallel beam of light to a focus

explain why most astronomical telescopes have concave mirrors as their objectives

explain why large telescopes are needed to collect the weak radiation from faint sources

recall that waves spread out from a narrow gap and that this is diffraction

draw and interpret diagrams showing wave diffraction through gaps of different size relative to the wavelength

recall that light can be diffracted, and that the effect is most noticeable when the gap is comparable to the wavelength

understand that radiation is diffracted by the aperture of a telescope, and that the aperture must be very much larger than the wavelength of the radiation detected by the telescope to produce sharp images

recall that a spectrum can be produced by a prism and by a diffraction grating

understand how parallax makes closer stars seem to move relative to more distant ones, and that a smaller parallax angle means that the star is further away

understand how the parallax angle of a star is measured

recall that the parsec is a unit of astronomical distance; recall that typical interstellar distances are a few parsecs, and intergalactic distances are measured in megaparsecs

recall that a parsec is similar in magnitude to a light-year

define the parsec in terms of parallax angle; calculate distances in parsecs for parallax angles expressed as fractions of a second of arc

recall that the luminosity of a star depends on its temperature and its size; explain qualitatively why the observed intensity of light from a star depends on the star's luminosity and on its distance from Earth

To aim for a grade E	To aim for a grade C	To aim for a grade A
recall that Cepheid variable stars pulse in brightness, with a period related to their luminosity; recall that this relationship enables the distance to Cepheid variable stars to be estimated	*explain qualitatively how the relationship between Cepheid period and luminosity enables astronomers to estimate the distance to these stars*	
recall that observations led to the realisation that the Sun was a star in the *Milky Way* galaxy, and revealed the existence of nebulae which were later shown to be galaxies	recall the main issue in the Curtis-Shapley debate: whether spiral nebulae were objects within the Milky Way or separate galaxies outside it; understand the role of observations of globular clusters in establishing the scale of the Milky Way, and of Cepheid variables in establishing the scale of the Universe and the nature of most spiral nebulae as distant galaxies	
recall that almost all galaxies are moving away from us	*understand that the recessional speed of galaxies gives their light a redshift, and that Hubble discovered that the greater the redshift, the further away the galaxy*	calculate the speed of recession of a distant galaxy *using the Hubble law: speed of recession (km/s) = Hubble constant × distance (Mpc);* recall that data on Cepheid variable stars has given better values of the Hubble constant; *understand how the motions of galaxies suggests that space itself is expanding*
recall that scientists believe the Universe began with a 'big bang' about 14 thousand million years ago		
recall that all hot objects emit electromagnetic radiation, and that the amount of radiation emitted at a particular wavelength (and hence the colour of the object) depends on the temperature of the object; recall that energy is radiated into space from the star's surface	understand that energy is transported from a star's core, where nuclear fusion takes place, to the surface by photons of radiation and by convection, and is radiated from the surface (photosphere)	
recall that specific spectral lines in the spectrum of a star provide evidence of the chemical elements present in it	use data on the spectrum of a star to identify elements present in it; *explain how electron energy levels within atoms give rise to line spectra*	

To aim for a grade E	To aim for a grade C	To aim for a grade A
understand a simple molecular model of the temperature and pressure of a gas; recall that −273 °C is the absolute zero of temperature, 0 kelvin (K), and convert absolute temperature in K to temperature in °C	understand that both the pressure and the volume of a gas are proportional to the absolute temperature	
recall that as the volume of a gas decreases, its pressure increases (at constant temperature)	recall Boyle's law: pressure × volume = constant (at constant temperature)	understand that the volume of a gas is inversely proportional to its pressure at a constant temperature and explain this using a molecular model

use the gas law equations

understand that in the Sun's core hydrogen nuclei fuse into helium nuclei, releasing energy; understand that energy is liberated when light nuclei fuse to make heavier nuclei	explain the formation and nature of a protostar *understand that Einstein's equation $E = mc^2$ is used to calculate the energy released during nuclear fusion and fission*; complete and interpret nuclear equations relating to fusion in stars, including the emission of positrons to conserve charge	
recall that hydrogen fusion keeps a star in the main sequence, the longest phase of its life	recall the conditions at the core of a star and that the more massive the star, the hotter its core and the heavier the nuclei it can create through fusion	recall that the Hertzsprung–Russell (HR) diagram is a plot of luminosity and temperature for stars, and identify regions on the graph where supergiants, giants, main sequence and white dwarf stars are located
recall the cause of a star leaving the main sequence and becoming a red giant		recall the reaction products in a red giant or supergiant star, and the final fate of a low-mass star and a high-mass star

understand that astronomers have found convincing evidence of planets around hundreds of nearby stars; understand that many scientists think that it is likely that life exists elsewhere in the Universe but that no evidence of extraterrestrial life has so far been detected

recall the locations of major observatories and describe factors that influence the choice of site; explain the advantages and disadvantages of computer control of telescopes and of telescopes outside the Earth's atmosphere; understand the reasons for collaboration in astronomical research

Exam-style questions

Foundation

AO1 **1** This diagram shows light entering and then leaving a rectangular block of glass.

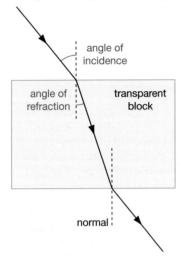

a When the light ray enters the block, what happens to:
i the direction of the ray [1]
ii the speed of the ray [1]
iii the wavelength of the ray? [1]

b Explain what happens when the ray leaves the block. [2]
[Total: 5]

AO1 **2** Absolute zero is –273.15°C, or 0 K.

a What does the K stand for? [1]

b What is the difference between a temperature rise of one K and one of one Celsius degree? [1]

c Explain absolute zero in terms of particle activity. [1]

AO2 **d** Why is it considered impossible to achieve temperatures lower than this? [1]
[Total: 4]

AO1 **3** Brian and Corinne are looking at the night sky. Brian says that the stars look as if they're bright spots in a dark dome. Corinne says that it might look like that at first glance but that, in fact, some of the stars are closer and if you study them over a period of time you can work out how far away they are.
Explain, with the aid of diagrams, why Corinne is right and how the distance to nearer stars can be calculated through observation.
The quality of written communication will be assessed in your answer. [6]
[Total: 6]

AO1
AO2 **4** Jo is investigating converging lenses of different strengths. She looks at the edges of them and sees that they look like this.

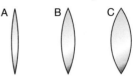

a Which of these lenses is the most powerful? [1]

b Explain how you could demonstrate which one was the most powerful. [2]

c Describe how you could measure the focal length of one of these lenses. [2]

d Draw and label a diagram to show how two of the lenses could be used to make a telescope. Indicate clearly which of the lenses you would use as the eyepiece and which as the objective, to get the maximum possible magnification. [3]
[Total: 8]

AO3 **5** In recent years a number of new telescopes have been planned and built. Some of these are located on Earth and some in space. You have been asked to comment on the desirability of locating an optical telescope on a small island in the South Pacific. The island is remote and has a large, central lowlying plateau.

a Suggest the positive features of such a location. [2]

b Suggest aspects that might be a disadvantage. [2]

c What aspects of the island might you want to find out more about before making a report? [2]
[Total: 6]

AO2 **6** This is a Hertzsprung–Russell diagram, relating the luminosity of a star to its temperature.

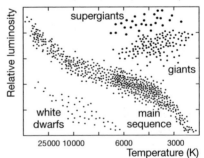

Describe how the location of an average star, such as our Sun, will vary on such a diagram during the course of its lifetime. [4]
[Total: 4]

AO1 recall the science   AO2 apply your knowledge   AO3 evaluate and analyse the evidence

✳ Worked example

Foundation

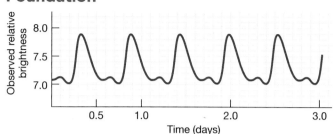

The graph shows how the observed brightness of a Cepheid variable star, X, varies over a number of days.

AO2 a What is the range of the relative brightness of star X over the period observed? [1]

The range is from 7.0 to 7.9. ✔

AO2 b What is the period of the variation of the brightness? [1]

The period is 1.4 – 0.7 = 0.7 days. ✗

The graph below shows the correlation between the period of variable stars and their luminosity.

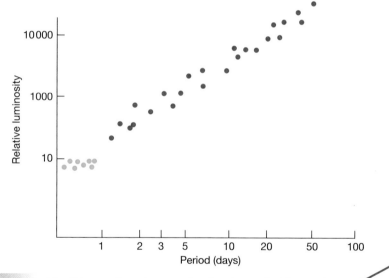

AO3 c Use this graph and your value for the period in part **b** to estimate the relative luminosity of star X. [1]

The relative luminosity is 9. ✔

AO1 d Suggest why Cepheid variable stars are useful to astronomers. [1]

We know how far away they are.

This is correct and gets 1 mark. Both upper and lower values have been read to within one decimal place, appropriate for the calibration on the graph.

This isn't correct – the student has used the time interval between the second and third peaks, but the second peak is nearer 0.9 than 0.7. On a graph like this it is reasonable to read to within 0.1.

This is correct. The graph is not easy to read as the points do not fall on a single line but this is a good estimate. Note that even though the wrong answer was given in part **b** and used in part **c**, as long as the graph is correctly used a mark is gained in part **c**.

This is true but doesn't explain why they are useful and so doesn't get the mark. It's because we know how far away they are that they provide us with a scale for the distance of objects in the Universe.

Exam-style questions

Higher

AO2
AO3 **7** A steel syringe plunger is drawn out to pull air into the syringe and the nozzle is then sealed up so that the air is trapped inside. The volume is recorded. A force is now applied to the plunger to compress the air. This is repeated with different amounts of force.

a Sketch a graph to show the relationship between the force applied and the volume of the air. [2]

b Explain, in terms of particle behaviour, what is happening as the force is increased. [2]

c When Tamsin carries out this experiment she notices that after she has increased the force the new volume reading changes a little. If she measures it straight away, the reading is a slightly different than if she lets it stand for a couple of minutes. Suggest why this should be. [2]

d Compressing the air with the plunger gives a springy sensation. Suggest whether this could be used as the basis for a car suspension system, instead of coil springs. [2]

[Total: 8]

AO1 **8** Emma and Jake are talking about the night sky. Jake says that, night after night, as long as it's clear, you can see the same constellations. Emma says that this can't be true and that in winter you see different constellations. With the aid of a diagram, explain who is right, and why. [3]

[Total: 3]

AO1
AO2 **9** The bulb has blown in the projector in Sam's teacher's room and she's had to borrow a portable one that stands on the bench top. So that the image fills the screen, the projector has to be moved further from the screen, but the image is then fainter. The teacher points this out to the class and asks them what they think the relationship is between the distance from the screen and the intensity of the light on the screen. Sam thinks: 'Surely if it's twice as far away the image will be half as bright?'
With the aid of a diagram, explain why Sam is wrong and what happens to the intensity if the distance is doubled. [3]

[Total: 3]

AO1 **10** Explain how redshift is used as evidence of an expanding Universe. The quality of written communication will be assessed in your answer. [6]

[Total: 6]

AO1
AO2 **11** This diagram shows how a converging lens forms an image of an object.

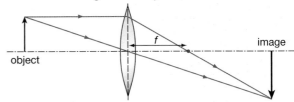

a Is the image enlarged, reduced or the same size? [1]

b Is the image the right way up or inverted? [1]

c If the object was moved further away from the lens, would the image be larger, smaller or the same size? [1]

[Total: 3]

AO2 **12** This table shows the parallax angle of some nearby stars.

Star	Parallax angle (arcseconds)
Proxima centauri	0.77
Barnard's Star	0.55
Sirius	0.38
Procyon	0.29

a Which star is the furthest away from Earth? [1]

b Calculate the distance of Sirius from Earth. [2]

c Which star is approximately 1.8 parsecs from Earth? [1]

[Total: 4]

AO3 **13** This is a news report about the discovery of planets in other solar systems.

> A red dwarf star 20 light-years away is again providing hints that it hosts the first definitively habitable planet outside our Solar System. The planet *Gliese 581d* is at the colder outer edge of the 'Goldilocks zone', in which liquid water can be sustained. It was discovered, along with the planet *Gliese 581c*, in 2007, occupying the outer and inner edges of the Goldilocks zone, respectively.
>
> *Gliese 581c* was soon determined to be too close to its host star to sustain water, with a surface temperature exceeding 1000°C. Conversely, the outlying planet 581d – with a mass about six times that of the Earth and twice its size – was initially taken to be too cold to have liquid water.
>
> BBC News 17 May 2011

a What is meant by the 'Goldilocks Zone'? [1]

b Why is this a critical consideration for this study? [2]

c Why is the distance to the host star important? [1]

[Total: 4]

AO1 recall the science   AO2 apply your knowledge   AO3 evaluate and analyse the evidence

Worked example

Higher

AO1 **a** Explain, with the aid of a diagram, how the movement of the Sun, Earth and Moon may cause a lunar eclipse. [3]

Sun *Earth* *Moon*

A lunar eclipse happens when the Sun, Earth and Moon are lined up in a row. ✔✔

AO1 **b** Explain why, even though the Moon orbits the Earth once every 28 days, we don't get a lunar eclipse every 28 days. [1]

We don't get a lunar eclipse every 28 days because the plane of the Moon's orbit around the Earth is not the same as the plane of the Earth's orbit around the Sun. ✔

AO2 **c** The Moon rotates on its axis once every 28 days. It also takes 28 days for the Moon to orbit the Earth. Due the direction of the rotation, this means that the same side of the Moon is always facing towards the Earth.

On the Earth we refer to the Sun rising and setting. Explain whether an astronaut on the surface of the Moon would see:

i   the Earth rise and set [2]

Yes, an astronaut on the surface of the Moon would see the Earth rise and set. This is because the Earth is rotating upon its axis. As it turns, other objects in the sky seem to rise and fall in the sky. ✘

ii   the Sun rise and set. [3]

Yes, an observer on the Moon would see the Sun rise and set. The Moon is rotating and this will cause the Sun to appear to move across the sky. ✔✔

The diagram correctly shows the alignment of the Sun, Earth and Moon necessary for a lunar eclipse; it also shows that the Moon is smaller than the Earth and the Sun is larger. It gets 2 out of the 3 marks. To improve the answer an indication of the orbits of the Moon and the Earth would need to be drawn in and an explanation given of how the alignment would cause an eclipse.

This is correct and gets the mark. The correct use of scientific term 'plane' supports the answer. Be prepared to draw a sketch if requested.

This is incorrect. As the same side of the Moon is always facing the Earth, the Earth doesn't move across the sky from the perspective of a viewer on the Moon. If you're on the side of the Moon facing the Earth, the Earth is always present in the sky.

This correctly explains why the Sun would rise and set and so gets 2 marks. The answer makes clear both what the effect is and why it happens. However, as it takes 28 days for a full cycle, it is quite conceivable that an astronaut could arrive in the lunar night and therefore not see any apparent motion of the Sun. The third mark would be allocated for indicating the length of a lunar day and its implications for an observer.

Carrying out practical work in GCSE Separate Sciences

Introduction

As part of your GCSE Separate Sciences course, you will develop practical skills and will carry out investigative work in science.

Investigative work can be divided into several parts:

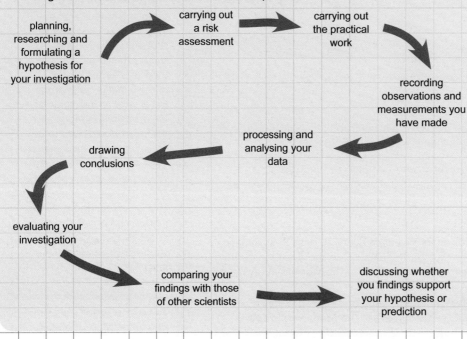

planning, researching and formulating a hypothesis for your investigation → carrying out a risk assessment → carrying out the practical work → recording observations and measurements you have made → processing and analysing your data → drawing conclusions → evaluating your investigation → comparing your findings with those of other scientists → discussing whether you findings support your hypothesis or prediction

✳ Planning and researching your investigation

A scientific investigation usually begins with you considering an idea, answering a question, or trying to solve a problem.

Researching what other people know about the idea or problem should suggest some variables that have an effect on the problem.

From this you should develop, or 'formulate', a hypothesis. For example you might notice that plants grow faster in a heated greenhouse than an unheated greenhouse.

Your hypothesis would be that 'the rate of photosynthesis is affected by the temperature of the environment of the plant'.

You would then plan how to carry out an investigation to test this hypothesis.

To formulate a hypothesis you may have to research some of the background science.

First of all, use your lesson notes and your textbook. The topic you've been given to investigate will relate to the science you've learnt in class.

Definition

A **hypothesis** is a possible explanation that someone suggests to explain some scientific observations.

Tip

When formulating a hypothesis, it's important that it's testable. In other words, you must be able to test the hypothesis in the school lab.

Also make use of the internet, but make sure that your internet search is closely focused on the topic you're investigating.

✔ The search terms you use on the internet are very important. 'Investigating temperature and photosynthesis' is a better search term than just 'photosynthesis', as it's more likely to provide links to websites that are more relevant to your investigation.

✔ The information on websites also varies in its reliability. Free encyclopaedias often contain information that hasn't been written by experts. Some question-and-answer websites might appear to give the exact answer to your question, but be aware that they may sometimes be incorrect.

✔ Most GCSE Science websites are more reliable but, if in doubt, use other information sources to verify the information.

As a result of your research, you may be able to extend your hypothesis and make a prediction that's based on science.

Example 1

Investigation: Plan and research an investigation into the effect of pH on the fermentation of sugars.

Your hypothesis might be 'I predict that yeast will produce more carbon dioxide per minute at pH7 than at any other pH'.

You should be able to justify your hypothesis with some scientific ideas. For example, 'yeast contains enzymes and I know that most enzymes work best in neutral pH solutions'.

> **Tip**
>
> You need to use your research to explain why you made your hypothesis.

✳ Choosing a method and suitable apparatus

As part of your planning, you must choose a suitable way of carrying out the investigation.

You will have to choose suitable techniques, equipment and technology, if this is appropriate. How do you make this choice?

For most of the practical work you are likely to do, there will be a choice of techniques available. You must select the technique:

✔ that is most appropriate to the context of your investigation, and

✔ that will enable you to collect valid data, for example, if you are measuring the effects of light intensity on photosynthesis, you may decide to use an LED (light-emitting diode) at different distances from the plant, rather than a light bulb. The light bulb produces more heat, and temperature is another independent variable in photosynthesis.

Your choice of equipment, too, will be influenced by measurements you need to make. For example:

✔ you might use a one-mark or graduated pipette to measure the volume of liquid for a titration, but

✔ you may use a measuring cylinder or beaker when adding a volume of acid to a reaction mixture, so that the volume of acid is in excess to that required to dissolve, for example, the calcium carbonate.

> **Tip**
>
> Technology, such as data-logging and other measuring and monitoring techniques, for example, temperature sensors, may help you to carry out your experiment.

> **Tip**
>
> Carrying out a preliminary investigation, along with the necessary research, may help you to select the appropriate technique to use.

Variables

In your investigation, you will work with factors which may affect an outcome.

The factors you choose (or are given), and of which you are asked to investigate the effect, are called input variables or **independent variables**.

What you choose to measure, as affected by the independent variable, is called the outcome variable or **dependent variable**.

Independent variables

In your practical work, you will be provided with an independent variable to test, or you may have to choose one – or more – of these to test. Some examples are given in the table.

Investigation	Possible independent variables to test
activity of amylase enzyme	> temperature > sugar concentration
rate of a chemical reaction	> temperature > concentration of reactants
stopping distance of a moving object	> speed of the object > the surface on which it's moving

Independent variables can be **discrete** or **continuous**.

> When you are testing the effect of different disinfectants on bacteria you are investigating discrete variables.

> When you are testing the effect of a range of concentrations of the same disinfectant on the growth of bacteria you are investigating continuous variables.

Range

When working with an independent variable, you need to choose an appropriate **range** over which to investigate the variable.

You need to decide:

✔ which variables you will test

✔ the upper and lower limits of the independent variable to investigate.

Once you have defined the range to be tested, you also need to decide the appropriate intervals at which you will make measurements.

The range you need to test depends on:

✔ the nature of the test

✔ the context in which it is set

✔ practical considerations

✔ common sense.

Definition

Variables that fall into a range of separate types are called **discrete variables**.

Definition

Variables that have a continuous range, or are numeric, are called **continuous variables**.

Definition

The **range** defines the extent of the independent variables being tested, for example from 15 cm to 35 cm.

Example 2

1 Investigation: Investigating the energy changes that occur when different fuels are burnt.

You may decide which fuels to test based on a range that you have been given. You may wish to test only a liquid or you may choose to test both solid and liquid fuels. You won't test certain fuels, such as pressurised gas, for safety reasons.

2 Investigation: Comparing the focal lengths of a number of lenses.

The range of lenses you use will depend on availability; comparing several converging lenses with different powers would be appropriate.

Temperature as an independent variable

You might be trying to find out the best temperature for growing tomatoes.

The 'best' temperature will differ, depending on the value of a number of other variables that, taken together, would produce tomatoes as fast as possible whilst not being too costly.

You should limit your investigation to just one variable, temperature, and then consider other variables such as fuel cost later.

✸ Dependent variables

The dependent variable may be clear from the problem you're investigating, for example the stopping distance of moving objects. But you may have to make a choice.

Example 3

1 Investigating the amount of sodium hydroxide needed to neutralise 25 cm^3 of hydrochloric acid.

There is more than one way of controlling the amount of chemical added:

> using a burette to carry out a titration reaction

> using a dropper pipette to count the number of drops of sodium hydroxide added.

There is also more than one way of detecting the end point:

> using a pH probe to measure the pH of the resulting solution

> using an indicator such as methyl orange.

Tip

The value of the *depend*ent variable is likely to *depend* on the value of the independent variable. This is a good way of remembering the definition of a dependent variable.

2 Investigation: Measuring the rate of a chemical reaction

You could measure the rate of a chemical reaction in the following ways:

> the rate of formation of a product

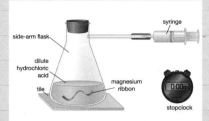

> the rate at which the reactant disappears

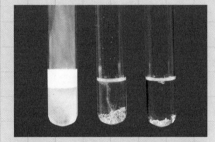

> a colour change

> a pH change.

✸ Control variables

The validity of your measurements depends on you measuring what you're supposed to be measuring.

Other variables that you're not investigating may also have an influence on your measurements. In most investigations, it's important that you investigate just one variable at a time. For a 'fair test', other variables, apart from the one you're testing at the time, must be kept constant. These are called **control variables**.

Some of these variables may be difficult to control. For example, in an ecology investigation in the field, factors such as varying weather conditions are impossible to control.

Experimental controls

Experimental controls are often very important, particularly in biological investigations where you're testing the effect of a treatment.

Definition

An **experimental control** is used to find out whether the effect you obtain is from the treatment, or whether you get the same result in the absence of the treatment.

Example 4

Investigation: Comparing the rates of reaction of ethanoic acid and hydrochloric acid with marble chips.

There are many factors that can affect the rate of a chemical reaction so it is important that you control all of the variables you are not investigating. You need to control the volume of acid used, e.g. 25 cm^3, and the strength of the acids, e.g. 1 mol/dm^3. You also need to control the amount of marble chips, e.g. 5 g, and the amount of time you are measuring the rate of reaction, e.g. the amount of gas produced in one minute.

✳ Identifying hazards and managing risk

Before you begin any practical work, you must assess and minimise the possible risks involved.

Before you carry out an investigation, you must identify the possible **hazards**. These can be grouped into biological hazards, chemical hazards and physical hazards.

Biological hazards include:

> microorganisms
> body fluids
> animals and plants.

Chemical hazards can be grouped into:

> irritant and harmful substances
> toxic
> flammable substances
> oxidising agents
> corrosive
> harmful to the environment.

Physical hazards include:

> equipment
> objects
> radiation.

Definition

A **hazard** is something that has the potential to cause harm. Even substances, organisms and equipment that we think of as being harmless, used in the wrong way may be hazardous.

Hazard symbols are used on chemical bottles so that hazards can be identified.

Scientists use an international series of symbols so that investigators can identify hazards.

Hazards pose **risks** to the person carrying out the investigation.

A risk posed by chlorine gas produced in the electrolysis of sodium chloride, for example, will be reduced if you increase the ventilation of the process, or devise a method to remove the gas so that workers cannot inhale it.

When you use hazardous materials, chemicals or equipment in the laboratory, you must use them in such a way as to keep the risks to an absolute minimum. For example, one way of reducing risks is to wear eye protection when using hydrochloric acid.

Definition

The **risk** is the likelihood of a hazard to cause harm in the circumstances of its use.

Risk assessment

Before you begin an investigation, you must carry out a risk assessment. Your risk assessment must include:

✔ all relevant hazards (use the correct terms to describe each hazard, and make sure you include them all, even if you think they will pose minimal risk)

✔ risks associated with these hazards

✔ ways in which the risks can be minimised

✔ whether or not it is appropriate to proceed with the investigation as planned, bearing in mind the hazards, the risks and the necessary management procedures

✔ results of research into emergency procedures that you may have to take if something goes wrong.

You should also consider what to do at the end of the practical. For example, used agar plates should be left for a technician to sterilise; solutions of heavy metals should be collected in a bottle and disposed of safely.

Tip

To make sure that your risk assessment is full and appropriate:

> remember that for a chemical reaction, the risk assessment should be carried out for the products and the reactants

> when using chemicals, make sure the hazard and ways of minimising risk match the concentration of the chemical you're using; many acids, for instance, while being corrosive in higher concentrations, are harmful or irritant at low concentrations.

Collecting primary data

✔ You should make sure that observations, if appropriate, are recorded in detail. For example, it is worth recording the colour of your precipitate when making an insoluble salt, in addition to any other measurements you make.

✔ Measurement should be recorded in tables. Have one ready so that you can record your readings as you carry out the practical work.

✔ Think about the dependent variable and define this carefully in your column headings.

✔ You should make sure that the table headings describe properly the types of measurement you've made, for example, 'time taken for magnesium ribbon to dissolve'.

✔ It's also essential that you include units – your results are meaningless without them.

✔ The units should appear in the column head, and not be repeated in each row of the table.

Definition

When you carry out an investigation, the data you collect are called **primary data.** The term 'data' is normally used to include your observations as well as measurements you might make.

Repeatability and reproducibility of results

When making measurements, in most instances, it's essential that you carry out repeats.

	Test 1	Test 2	Test 3

These repeats are one way of checking your results. One set of results from your investigation may not reflect what truly happens. Carrying out repeats enables you to identify any results that don't fit.

Results will not be repeatable of course, if you allow the conditions under which the investigation is carried out to change.

Definition

A reading that is very different from the rest, is called an anomalous result, or **outlier**.

Definition

If, when you carry out the same experiment several times, and get the same, or very similar results, you say the results are **repeatable**.

You need to make sure that you carry out sufficient repeats, but not too many. In a titration, for example, if you obtain two values that are within 0.1 cm³ of each other, carrying out any more will not improve the reliability of your results.

Reproducibility is particularly important when scientists are carrying out scientific research and make new discoveries.

> **Definition**
>
> The **reproducibility** of data is the ability of the results of an investigation to be reproduced by someone else, who may be in a different lab, carrying out the same work.

✳ Processing data

Calculating the mean

Using your repeat measurements you can calculate the arithmetic mean (or just 'mean') of these data. We often refer to the mean as the 'average'.

You may also be required to use formulae when processing data.

> **Definition**
>
> The **mean** is calculated by adding together all the measurements, and dividing by the number of measurements.

Significant figures

When calculating the mean, you should be aware of significant figures.

For example, look at the set of data below:

18	13	17	15	14	16	15	14	13	18

The total for the data set is 153, and ten measurements have been made. However, the mean should be given as 15, and not 15.3.

This is because each of the recorded values has two significant figures. The answer must therefore have two significant figures. An answer cannot have more significant figures than the number being multiplied or divided.

> **Definition**
>
> **Significant figures** are the number of digits in a number based on the precision of your measurements.

Using your data

When calculating means (and displaying data), you should be careful to look out for any data that don't fit in with the general pattern.

An outlier might be the consequence of an error made in measurement, but sometimes outliers are genuine results. If you think an outlier has been introduced by careless practical work, you should ignore it when calculating the mean. But you should examine possible reasons carefully before just leaving it out.

> ### Example 5
>
> Here are the results of an investigation into the energy requirements of two different mp3 players. The students measured the energy using a joulemeter for ten seconds.
>
> | mp3 player | Energy used in joules (J) | | | | | | |
> |------------|---------|---------|---------|---------|---------|---------|------|
> | | Trial 1 | Trial 2 | Trial 3 | Trial 4 | Trial 2 | Trial 6 | Mean |
> | Anglo | 5.5 | 5.3 | 5.7 | 5.4 | 5.5 | 5.4 | 5.5 |
> | Saxon | 4.5 | 4.6 | 4.9 | 3.2 | 4.5 | 4.7 | 4.6 |
>
> Note that one result (3.2) has been excluded from the mean calculation for the Saxon mp3 player because it was more than 10% lower than the other values, and so considered an outlier.

Displaying your data

Displaying your data – usually the mean values – makes it easy to pick out and show any patterns. And it also helps you to pick out any anomalous data.

It is likely that you will have recorded your results in tables, and you could also use additional tables to summarise your results. The most usual way of displaying data is to use graphs. The table will help you decide which type to use.

Type of graph	When you would use the graph	Example
Bar chart or bar graph	Where one of the variables is discrete	'The energy requirements of different mp3 players'
Line graph	Where independent and dependent variables are both continuous	'The volume of carbon dioxide produced by a range of different concentrations of hydrochloric acid'
Scatter graph	To show an association between two (or more) variables	'The association between length and breadth of a number of privet leaves' In scatter graphs, the points are plotted, but not usually joined

It should be possible from the data to join the points of a line graph using a single straight line or using a curve. In this way, graphs can also help you to understand the relationship between the independent variable and the dependent variable.

Tip

Remember when drawing graphs, plot the independent variable on the horizontal axis, and the dependent variable on the vertical axis.

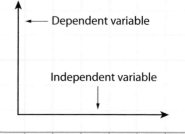

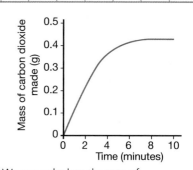

We can calculate the rate of production of carbon dioxide from the gradient of the graph.

✳ Variation in data

Plotting a graph of just the means doesn't tell you anything about the spread of data that has been used to calculate the mean.

You can show the spread or range of the data on your graphs using error bars or range bars.

Range bars are very useful, but they don't show how the data are spread between the extreme values. It is important to have information about this range. It may affect the analysis you do of the data, and the conclusions you draw.

Scientists use a number of techniques to look at the spread of data. You could refer to the work that you've done in Maths to look at some of these techniques.

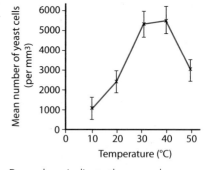

Range bars indicate the spread or range of values.

Conclusions from differences in data sets

When comparing two (or more) sets of data, we often compare the values of two sets of means.

Example 6

Investigation: Two groups of students measured the amount of sweat they produced after exercising for one hour. Their results are shown in the table below.

Student	Amount of sweat produced (ml)					Mean (ml)
	1	2	3	4	5	
Group 1	15	12	17	20	12	15
Group 2	11	9	12	13	10	11

When the means are compared, it appears that Group 1 produced more sweat than Group 2. The difference may be due to the amount and type of exercise each group did, or it may be purely by chance.

Scientists use statistics to find the probability of any differences having occurred by chance. The lower this probability is, which is found out by statistical calculations, the more likely it is, for example, that tyre A is better at stopping a vehicle than tyre B.

Statistical analysis can help to increase the confidence you have in your conclusions.

Tip

You have learnt about probability in your Maths lessons.

Drawing conclusions

Observing trends in data or graphs will help you to draw conclusions. You may obtain a linear relationship between two sets of variables, or the relationship might be more complex.

Example 7

Conclusion 1: As the temperature of the gas increased, its pressure also increased.

Conclusion 2: Increasing the temperature increased the energy of the gas particles causing them to move around faster. This means that there were more collisions between the gas particles and the sides of the container so therefore the pressure increased.

Definition

If there is a relationship between dependent and independent variables that can be defined, we say there is a **correlation** between the variables.

When drawing conclusions, you should try to relate your findings to the science involved.

> In making the first conclusion in Example 7, your discussion should focus on describing what your results show, including any patterns or trends between them.

> In making the second conclusion, there is a clear scientific mechanism to link the increase in temperature to an increase in gas pressure.

Sometimes there is a correlation between data, even if the independent variable is not necessarily the cause of the trend in the data.

✺ Evaluating your investigation

Your conclusion will be based on your findings, but must take into consideration any uncertainty in these introduced by any possible sources of error. You should discuss where these have come from in your evaluation.

The two types of errors are:

✔ random error   ✔ systematic error.

Errors can occur when the instrument you're using to measure lacks sufficient sensitivity to indicate differences in readings. They can also occur when it's difficult to make a measurement. If two investigators measure the height of a plant, for example, they might choose different points on the compost, and the tip of the growing point to make their measurements.

Measurements can also be either consistently too high or too low. One reason could be down to the way you are making a reading, for example taking a burette reading at the wrong point on the meniscus. Another could be the result of an instrument being incorrectly calibrated, or not being calibrated.

The volume of liquid in a burette must be read to the bottom of the meniscus.

Definition

Error is a difference between a measurement you make, and its true value.

Definition

With **random error**, measurements vary in an unpredictable way, for example when measuring the length of an object that is moving.

Definition

With **systematic error**, readings vary in a controlled way, for example, measuring the length of something with a ruler that was incorrectly calibrated.

Tip

What you shouldn't discuss in your evaluation are problems introduced by using faulty equipment, or by you using the equipment inappropriately. These errors can, or could have been, eliminated, by:

> the checking of equipment

> practising techniques beforehand

> taking care and being patient when carrying out the practical.

✺ Accuracy and repeatability

When evaluating your investigation, you might refer to accuracy and repeatability. But if you use these terms it's important that you understand what they mean, and that you use them correctly. The terms accuracy and repeatability can be illustrated by thinking about shots fired at a target.

Repeatable but not accurate

Repeatable and accurate

Unrepeatable and inaccurate

Definition

When making measurements:
> the **accuracy** of the measurement is how close it is to the true value

> **repeatability** is how close together readings of the same measurement are

✺ Improving your investigation

When evaluating your investigation, you should discuss how your investigation could be improved. This could be by improving:

✔ the reliability of your data. For example, you could make more repeats, or more frequent readings, or 'fine-tune' the range you investigate, or refine your technique in some other way

✔ the accuracy and repeatability of your data, by using more suitable measuring equipment.

In science, the measurements you make as part of your investigation should be as accurate as you can, or need to, make them. To achieve this, you should use:

✔ the most appropriate measuring instrument
✔ the measuring instrument with the most appropriate scale.

The smaller the scale divisions you work with, the more accurate your measurements. For example:

✔ in an investigation on how your heart rate is affected by exercise, you might decide to investigate this after a 100 m run. You might measure out the 100 m distance using a trundle wheel, which is sufficiently precise for your investigation
✔ in an investigation on how light intensity is affected by distance, you would make your measurements of distance using a metre rule with millimetre divisions; clearly a trundle wheel would not be accurate
✔ in an investigation on plant growth, in which you measure the thickness of a plant stem, you would use a micrometer or Vernier callipers. A metre rule would not be accurate.

✹ Using secondary data

Another method of evaluation is to compare your data – primary data – with **secondary data**. One of the simplest ways of doing this is to compare your data with data from other members of your class who have carried out an identical practical investigation. In your controlled assessment you will be provided with a data sheet of relevant secondary data.

You should also, if possible, search through the scientific literature – in textbooks, the internet, and databases – to find data from similar or identical practical investigations so that you can compare the data with yours.

Ideally, you should use secondary data from a number of sources, carry out a full analysis of the data you have collected, and compare the findings with your own. You should critically analyse any evidence that conflicts with yours, and suggest what further data might help to make your conclusions more secure.

You should review secondary data and evaluate it. Scientific studies are sometimes influenced by the **bias** of the experimenter.

✔ One kind of bias is having a strong opinion related to the investigation, and perhaps selecting only the results that fit with a hypothesis or prediction.
✔ Or the bias could be unintentional. In fields of science that are not yet fully understood, experimenters may try to fit their findings to current knowledge and thinking.

In other instances the 'findings' of experimenters have been influenced by organisations that supplied funding for the research.

You must reference secondary data you have used (see page 204).

Definition

Secondary data are measurements or observations made by anyone other than you.

Referencing methods

The two main conventions for writing a reference are the:

✔ Harvard system

✔ Vancouver system.

In your text, the Harvard system refers to the authors of the reference, for example 'Smith and Jones (1978)'.

The Vancouver system refers to the number of the numbered reference in your text, for example '... the reason for this hypothesis is unknown[5]'.

Though the Harvard system is usually preferred by scientists, it is more straightforward for you to use the Vancouver system.

Harvard system

In your references list, a book reference should be written:

> Author(s) (year of publication). *Title of Book*, publisher, publisher location.

The references are listed in alphabetical order according to the authors.

Vancouver system

In your references list a book reference should be written:

> 1 Author(s). *Title of Book*. Publisher, publisher location: year of publication.

The references are numbered in the order in which they are cited in the text.

Tip

Remember to write out the URL of a website in full. You should also quote the date when you looked at the website.

 ## Does the data support your hypothesis?

You need to discuss, in detail, whether all (or which) of your primary data, and the secondary data you have collected, support your original hypothesis. They may, or may not.

If your data does not completely match your hypothesis, it may be possible to modify the hypothesis or suggest an alternative one. You should suggest any further investigations that can be carried out to support your original hypothesis or the modified version.

It is important to remember, however, that if your investigation does support your hypothesis, it can improve the confidence you have in your conclusions and scientific explanations, but it can't prove your explanations are correct.

Tip

Make sure you relate your conclusions to the hypothesis you are investigating. Do the results confirm or reject the hypothesis? Quote some results to back up your statement, for example 'My results at 35 °C and 65 °C show that over a 30 degree change in temperature the time taken to produce 50 cm^3 of carbon dioxide halved'.

Tip

Communicate your points clearly, using the appropriate scientific terms, and checking carefully your use of spelling, punctuation and grammar. Your quality of written communication is important, as well as your science.

Controlled assessment in GCSE 21st Century Separate Sciences

Introduction

The controlled assessment task for each of GCSE Biology, Chemistry and Physics, is a practical investigation. It is worth 25% of the total marks, so it is important to do it well.

Investigations are central to the nature of science as an evidence-based activity, and practical investigations provide an effective assessment method. Your ability to formulate a hypothesis and to explain patterns in results will be related to your knowledge and understanding of the topic.

✳ Controlled assessment

In the controlled assessment you will need to:

✔ develop a hypothesis

✔ plan practical ways to test your hypothesis

✔ do and record a risk assessment for the procedures you plan to use

✔ manage the risks when carrying out the practical work

✔ collect primary data

✔ process, analyse and interpret your primary data and also secondary data

✔ draw evidence-based conclusions

✔ evaluate the reliability of your data and review the effectiveness of your procedures

✔ review your hypothesis in the light of your results.

The task provided will be open-ended and investigative in nature. At the start of a task, you will be given a sheet about the topic of the investigation, putting the task into a wider context. You need to use the information provided to plan how to collect data, including any preliminary work required, and to develop a testable hypothesis before carrying out the investigation.

After you have collected primary data, you will be given a sheet of secondary data for analysis. You need to interpret and evaluate your own data, and also analyse relevant secondary data. As well as the sheet of secondary data provided, you may include experimental results from other students, as well as information from textbooks and websites.

You need to use your results and your comparison of these with secondary data to develop and evaluate your conclusions, and finally review your original hypothesis.

Your written report of the completed work will be presented for assessment.

Tip

Pages 192–204 give guidelines on all these investigative skills.

Tip

Work through the 'Preparing for assessment' tasks in each module of this book to help build your skills for your controlled assessment.

How to be successful in your GCSE 21st Century Separate Sciences exam

Introduction

OCR uses assessments to test your understanding of scientific ideas, how well you can apply your understanding to new situations and how well you can analyse and interpret information you've been given. The assessments are opportunities to show how well you can do these things.

To be successful in exams you need to:

✔ have a good knowledge and understanding of science

✔ be able to apply this knowledge and understanding to familiar and new situations, and

✔ be able to interpret and evaluate evidence that you've just been given.

You need to be able to do these things under exam conditions.

✹ The language of external assessment

When working through an assessment paper, make sure that you:

✔ re-read the question enough times until you understand exactly what the examiner is looking for

✔ highlight key words in the question. In some instances, you will be given key words to include in your answer

✔ look at how many marks are allocated for each part of the question. In general, you need to write at least as many separate points in your answer as there are marks.

✹ What verbs are used in the question?

A good technique is to see which verbs are used in the wording of the question and to use these to gauge the type of response you need to give. The table lists some of the common verbs found in questions, the types of responses expected and then gives an example.

Verb used in question	Response expected in answer	Example question
> write down > state > give > identify	These are usually straightforward types of question in which you're asked to give a definition, make a list of examples, or select the best answer from a series of options	'Write down three types of microorganism that cause disease' 'State one difference and one similarity between radio waves and gamma rays'
calculate	Use maths to solve a numerical problem	'Calculate the percentage of carbon in copper carbonate'

estimate	Use maths to solve a numerical problem, but you do not have to work out the exact answer	'Estimate from the graph the speed of the car after 3 minutes'
describe	Use words (or diagrams) to show the characteristics, properties or features of, or build an image, of something	'Describe how meiosis halves the number of chromosomes in a cell to make egg or sperm cells'
suggest	Come up with an idea to explain information you're given	'Suggest why eating fast foods, rather than wholegrain foods, could increase the risk of obesity'
> demonstrate > show how	Use words to make something evident using reasoning	'Show how enzyme activity changes with temperature'
compare	Look for similarities and differences	'Compare aerobic and anaerobic respiration'
explain	Offer a reason for, or make understandable, information you're given	'Explain why alpha and beta radiations are deflected in opposite directions by a magnetic field'
justify	Give reason(s) for a conclusion, or statement(s) to back up an opinion	'Which person's idea gives the best explanation? Justify your response'
evaluate	Examine and make a judgement about an investigation or information you're given	'Evaluate the evidence for vaccines causing harm to human health'

✺ What is the style of the question?

Try to get used to answering questions that have been written in lots of different styles before you sit the exam. Work through past papers, or specimen papers, to get a feel for these. The types of questions in your assessment fit the three assessment objectives shown in the table.

Assessment objective	Your answer should show that you can...
AO1 Recall the science	Recall, select and communicate your knowledge and understanding of science
AO2 Apply your knowledge	Apply skills, knowledge and understanding of science in practical and other contexts
AO3 Evaluate and analyse the evidence	Analyse and evaluate evidence, make reasoned judgements and draw conclusions based on evidence

Tip

Of course you must revise the subject material adequately. But it's as important that you are familiar with the different question styles used in the exam paper, as well as the question content.

✳ How to answer questions on: AO1 Recall the science

These questions, or parts of questions, test your ability to recall your knowledge of a topic or a process. There are several types of this style of question:

✔ Fill in the spaces (you may be given words to choose from)

✔ Tick the correct statements or use lines to link a term with its definition or correct statement

✔ Add labels to a diagram or complete a table

✔ Describe a process

✔ Explain observations

✔ Write a full account or explanation of a topic or a process

To revise for these types of questions, make sure that you have learnt definitions and scientific terms. Produce a glossary of these, or key facts cards, to make them easier to remember. Make sure your key facts cards also cover important practical techniques.

Tip

Don't forget that concept diagrams – either drawn by you or by using a computer program – are very helpful when revising key points.

Example 1

1 What is meant by the term *exothermic reaction*?
   Tick (✓) **one** box.
   ☐ a reaction that gives out heat energy
   ☐ a reaction that takes in energy from the surroundings
   ☐ a reaction that can go in either direction

2 Describe two factors scientists can change to affect the amount of product produced in an equilibrium reaction, e.g. the Haber process.

✳ How to answer questions on: AO2 Apply skills, knowledge and understanding

Some questions require you to apply basic knowledge and understanding in your answers.

You may be presented with a topic that's familiar to you, but you should also expect questions in your Separate Sciences exam to be set in an unfamiliar context.

Questions may be presented as:

✔ experimental investigations

✔ data for you to interpret and analyse

✔ a short paragraph or article.

The information required for you to answer the question might be in the question itself, but for later stages of the question, you may be asked to draw on your knowledge and understanding of the subject material in the question.

You may be expected to describe patterns in data from graphs you are given or that you have drawn from given data.

Practice will help you to become familiar with some contexts that examiners use and common question styles. But you will not be able to predict all of the contexts used. This is deliberate; being able to apply your knowledge and understanding to different and unfamiliar situations is a skill the examiner tests.

Practise doing questions where you are tested on being able to apply your scientific knowledge and on your ability to understand new and unfamiliar situations. In this way, when this type of question comes up in your exam, you will be able to tackle it successfully.

Example 2

A student measured the pH of two different brands of beer over seven days, to compare how quickly the ethanol in each beer was oxidised to ethanoic acid. His results are shown in the table.

Beer	pH on each day					
	1	2	3	4	5	6
Old Brew	6.6	5.8	4.0	3.0	2.1	2.1
Eagle Lager	6.3	5.9	4.1	3.5	2.2	2.1

a Calculate the total pH decrease for each beer over the six days.

b Plot the results as a line graph.

c Explain how the graph enables you to compare how quickly ethanoic acid is being formed in the two beers.

You will also need to analyse scientific evidence or data given to you in the question. Analysing data may involve drawing graphs and interpreting them, and carrying out calculations. Practise drawing and interpreting graphs from data.

When drawing a graph, make sure you:

✔ choose and label the axes fully and correctly

✔ include units, if this hasn't been done for you already

✔ plot points on the graph carefully – the examiner will check individual points to make sure that they are accurate

✔ join the points correctly; usually this will be by a line of best fit.

When reading values off a graph you have drawn or one given in the question, make sure you:

✔ do it carefully, reading the values as accurately as you can

✔ double-check the values.

When describing patterns and trends in the data, make sure you:

✔ write about a pattern or trend in as much detail as you can

✔ mention anomalies where appropriate

✔ recognise there may be one general trend in the graph, where the variables show positive or negative correlation

✔ recognise the data may show a more complex relationship. The graph may demonstrate different trends in several sections. You should describe what's happening in each

✔ describe fully what the data show.

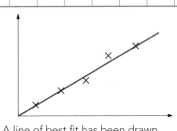

A line of best fit has been drawn through the plotted points

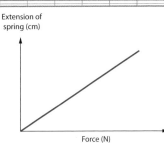

Make sure you know what type of relationship is shown in this graph.

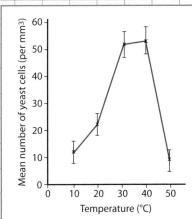

What type of relationship does this graph show?

☀ How to answer questions needing calculations

✔ The calculations you're asked to do may be straightforward, for example the calculation of the mean from a set of practical data.

✔ Or they may be more complex, for example calculating the yield of a chemical reaction.

✔ Other questions will require the use of formulae. These are often given to you on the question paper, but sometimes you will be expected to recall and use them.

Remember, this is the same maths that you learnt in your Maths lessons.

Example 3

A dog runs out in front of the school bus and the driver brakes hard. The bus slows from 20 m/s to rest in 10 seconds. Calculate the acceleration of the bus.

Tip

Check the specification, or with your teacher, to make sure that you know the formulae that you have to learn and remember.

Tip

Remember, when carrying out any calculations, you should include your working at each stage. You may get credit for getting the process correct, even if your final answer is wrong.

Tip

When completing your calculation, make sure you include the correct units.

☀ How to answer questions on: AO3 Analysing and evaluating evidence

For these types of questions, in addition to analysing data, you must also be able to evaluate the information you're given. This is one of the hardest skills. Think about the validity of the scientific data: did the technique(s) used in any practical investigation allow the collection of accurate and precise data?

Your critical evaluation of scientific data in class will help you to develop the evaluation skills required for these types of questions.

Example 4

Three new types of grass have been bred and are being tested for growth rate. The mean height of the seedlings is calculated every two days.

Type	Number of days after germination			
	2	4	6	8
A	4 mm	6 mm	9 mm	13 mm
B	3 mm	7 mm	10 mm	13 mm
C	4 mm	7 mm	9 mm	10 mm

Compare the growth rate patterns of the three types of grass between day 2 and day 8.

You may be expected to compare data with other data, or come to a conclusion about its reliability, its usefulness or its implications. It is possible that you won't be familiar with the context. You may be asked to make a judgement about the evidence or to give an opinion with reasons.

✳ The quality of your written communication

Scientists need good communication skills to present and discuss their findings. You will be expected to demonstrate these skills in the exam. Some questions will end with the sentence: The quality of written communication will be assessed in your answer to this question. It will be worth 6 marks.

✔ You must try to make sure that your writing is legible and your spelling, punctuation and grammar are accurate, so that it's clear what you mean in your answer. Examiners can't award marks for answers where the meaning isn't clear. When describing and explaining science, use correct scientific vocabulary.

✔ You must present your information in a form that suits its purpose: for example, a series of paragraphs, with lists or a table if appropriate, and a conclusion if required. Use subheadings where they will be helpful.

✔ You must use a suitable structure and style of writing: ensure that in continuous text you use complete sentences. Remember the writing skills you've developed in English lessons. For example, make sure that you know how to construct a good sentence using connectives.

Practise answering some 'quality of written communication (QWC)' questions. Look at how marks are awarded in mark schemes. You'll find these in the specimen question papers, and past papers.

> **Tip**
>
> You will be assessed on the way in which you communicate scientific ideas.

Example mark scheme

For 5–6 marks:
Ideas about the topic are correctly described and correctly used to explain it. All information in the answer is relevant, clear, organised and presented in a structured and coherent format. Specialist terms are used appropriately. Few, if any, errors in grammar, punctuation and spelling.

For 3–4 marks:
Some aspects of the topic are correctly described, but only some are made use of in explaining it. For the most part information is relevant and presented in a structured and coherent format. Specialist terms are used for the most part appropriately. There are occasional errors in grammar, punctuation and spelling.

For 1–2 marks:
Some aspects of the topic are correctly described, but not used to explain it. Answer may be simplistic. There may be limited use of specialist terms. Errors of punctuation, grammar and spelling hinder communication of the science.

0 marks:
Insufficient or irrelevant science. Answer not worthy of credit.

✳ Revising for your exam

You should revise in the way that suits you best. But it's important that you plan your revision carefully, and it's best to start well before the date of the exams. Take the time to prepare a revision timetable and try to stick to it. Use this during the lead up to the exams and between each exam.

When revising:

✔ find a quiet and comfortable space in the house where you won't be disturbed. It's best if it's well ventilated and has plenty of light

✔ take regular breaks. Some evidence suggests that revision is most effective when you revise in 30 to 40 minute slots. If you get bogged down at any point, take a break and go back to it later when you're feeling fresh. Try not to revise when you are feeling tired. If you do feel tired, take a break

✔ use your school notes, textbook and possibly a revision guide. But also make sure that you spend some time using past papers to familiarise yourself with the exam format

✔ produce summaries of each module

✔ draw concept diagrams covering the key information in a module

✔ make revision cards containing condensed versions of your notes

✔ ask yourself questions, and try to predict questions, as you're revising modules

✔ test yourself as you're going along. Try to draw important labelled diagrams, and try some questions under timed conditions

✔ prioritise your revision of topics. You might want to allocate more time to revising the topics you find most difficult.

> **Tip**
>
> Try to make your revision timetable as specific as possible – don't just say 'physics on Monday, and Thursday', but list the topics that you'll cover on those days.

> **Tip**
>
> Start your revision well before the date of the exams, produce a revision timetable, and use the revision strategies that suit your style of learning. Above all, revision should be an active process.

✳ How do I use my time effectively in the exam?

Timing is important when you sit an exam. Don't spend so long on some questions that you leave insufficient time to answer others. For example, in a 60-mark question paper, lasting one hour, you will have, on average, one minute per question.

If you're unsure about certain questions, complete the ones you're able to do first, then go back to the ones you're less sure of.

If you have time, go back and check your answers at the end of the exam.

✳ On exam day...

A little bit of nervousness before your exam can be a good thing, but try not to let it affect your performance in the exam. When you turn over the exam paper keep calm. Look at the paper and get it clear in your head exactly what is required from each question. Read each question carefully. Don't rush.

If you read a question and think that you have not covered the topic, keep calm – it could be that the information needed to answer the question is in the question itself or the examiner may be asking you to apply your knowledge to a new situation.

Finally, good luck!

Data sheet

Fundamental physical quantity	Unit(s)
length	metre (m); kilometre (km); centimetre (cm); millimetre (mm); nanometre (nm)
mass	kilogram (kg); gram (g); milligram (mg)
time	second (s); millisecond (ms); year (a); million years (Ma); billion years (Ga)
temperature	degree Celsius (°C); kelvin (K)
current	ampere (A); milliampere (mA)

Derived physical quantity	Unit(s)
area	cm^2; m^2
volume	cm^3; dm^3; m^3; litre (l); millilitre (ml)
density	kg/m^3; g/cm^3
speed, velocity	m/s; km/h
acceleration	m/s^2
momentum	kg m/s
force	newton (N)
energy	joule (J); kilojoule (kJ); megajoule (MJ)
power	watt (W); kilowatt (kW); megawatt (MW)
frequency	hertz (Hz); kilohertz (kHz)
p.d. (voltage)	volt (V)
resistance	ohm (Ω)
radiation dose	sievert (Sv)
power of a lens	dioptre (D)
distance in astronomy	light-year (ly); parsec (pc)

Prefixes for units

nano (n)	one thousand millionth	0.000 000 001	$\times 10^{-9}$
micro (µ)	one millionth	0.000 001	$\times 10^{-6}$
milli (m)	one thousandth	0.001	$\times 10^{-3}$
kilo (k)	× one thousand	1 000	$\times 10^{3}$
mega (M)	× one million	1 000 000	$\times 10^{6}$
giga (G)	× one thousand million	1 000 000 000	$\times 10^{9}$
tera (T)	× one million million	1 000 000 000 000	$\times 10^{12}$

Useful equations

$$speed = \frac{distance\ travelled}{time\ taken}$$

$$acceleration = \frac{change\ in\ velocity}{time\ taken}$$

momentum = mass × velocity

change of momentum = resultant force × time it acts

change in gravitational potential energy = weight × height difference

kinetic energy = ½ × mass × (velocity)²

resistance = voltage × current

energy transferred = power × time

electrical power = voltage × current

$$efficiency = \frac{energy\ usefully\ transferred}{total\ energy\ supplied} \times 100\%$$

$$power\ of\ a\ lens = \frac{1}{focal\ length}$$

$$magnification\ of\ a\ telescope = \frac{focal\ length\ of\ objective}{focal\ length\ of\ eyepiece}$$

$$R_f = \frac{distance\ travelled\ by\ solute}{distance\ travelled\ by\ solvent}$$

$$\%\ yield = \frac{actual\ yield}{theoretical\ yield} \times 100\%$$

$$concentration\ of\ solution\ (g/dm^3) = \frac{mass\ of\ solute\ (g)}{volume\ of\ solution\ (dm^3)}$$

continued

Organic molecules

	Name	Molecular formula	Structural formula
Alkanes*	methane	CH_4	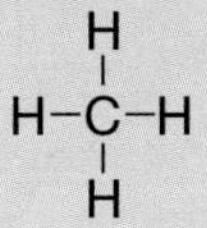 (structure shown)
	ethane	C_2H_6	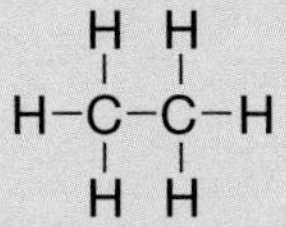 (structure shown)
	propane	C_3H_8	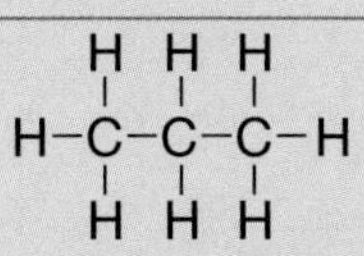 (structure shown)
	butane	C_4H_{10}	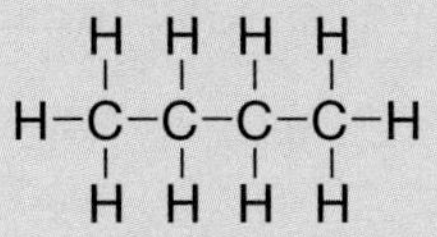 (structure shown)
Alcohols*	methanol	CH_3OH	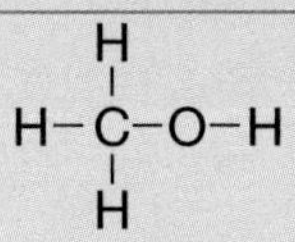 (structure shown)
	ethanol	C_2H_5OH	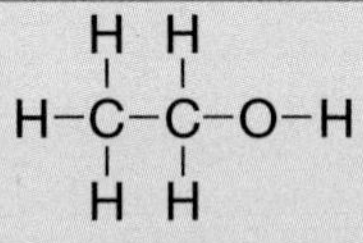 (structure shown)
Carboxylic acids*	methanoic acid	$HCOOH$	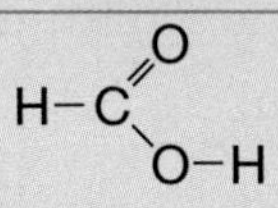 (structure shown)
	ethanoic acid	CH_3COOH	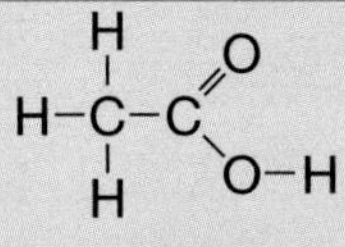 (structure shown)
Esters	methyl methanoate	$HCOOCH_3$	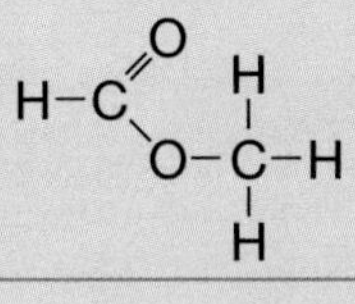 (structure shown)
	ethyl ethanoate	$CH_3COOC_2H_5$	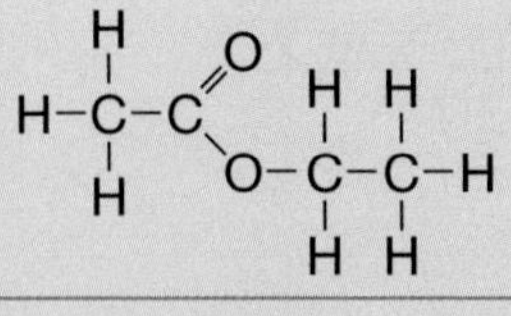 (structure shown)
Fats and oils		$(C_xH_yCOO)_3C_3H_5$	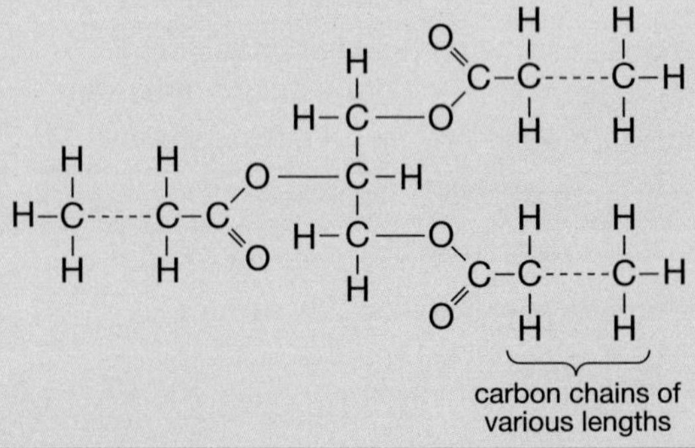 (structure shown) carbon chains of various lengths

* These will not be provided in your exam. You need to learn them.

Periodic Table

Key

relative atomic mass
atomic symbol
name
atomic (proton) number

1																	0
	2											**3**	**4**	**5**	**6**	**7**	4 **He** helium 2
						1 **H** hydrogen 1											
7 **Li** lithium 3	9 **Be** beryllium 4											11 **B** boron 5	12 **C** carbon 6	14 **N** nitrogen 7	16 **O** oxygen 8	19 **F** fluorine 9	20 **Ne** neon 10
23 **Na** sodium 11	24 **Mg** magnesium 12											27 **Al** aluminium 13	28 **Si** silicon 14	31 **P** phosphorus 15	32 **S** sulfur 16	35.5 **Cl** chlorine 17	40 **Ar** argon 18
39 **K** potassium 19	40 **Ca** calcium 20	45 **Sc** scandium 21	48 **Ti** titanium 22	51 **V** vanadium 23	52 **Cr** chromium 24	55 **Mn** manganese 25	56 **Fe** iron 26	59 **Co** cobalt 27	59 **Ni** nickel 28	63.5 **Cu** copper 29	65 **Zn** zinc 30	70 **Ga** gallium 31	73 **Ge** germanium 32	75 **As** arsenic 33	79 **Se** selenium 34	80 **Br** bromine 35	84 **Kr** krypton 36
85 **Rb** rubidium 37	88 **Sr** strontium 38	89 **Y** yttrium 39	91 **Zr** zirconium 40	93 **Nb** niobium 41	96 **Mo** molybdenum 42	[98] **Tc** technetium 43	101 **Ru** ruthenium 44	103 **Rh** rhodium 45	106 **Pd** palladium 46	108 **Ag** silver 47	112 **Cd** cadmium 48	115 **In** indium 49	119 **Sn** tin 50	122 **Sb** antimony 51	128 **Te** tellurium 52	127 **I** iodine 53	131 **Xe** xenon 54
133 **Cs** caesium 55	137 **Ba** barium 56	139 **La*** lanthanum 57	178 **Hf** hafnium 72	181 **Ta** tantalum 73	184 **W** tungsten 74	186 **Re** rhenium 75	190 **Os** osmium 76	192 **Ir** iridium 77	195 **Pt** platinum 78	197 **Au** gold 79	201 **Hg** mercury 80	204 **Tl** thallium 81	207 **Pb** lead 82	209 **Bi** bismuth 83	[209] **Po** polonium 84	[210] **At** astatine 85	[222] **Rn** radon 86
[223] **Fr** francium 87	[226] **Ra** radium 88	[227] **Ac*** actinium 89	[261] **Rf** rutherfordium 104	[262] **Db** dubnium 105	[266] **Sg** seaborgium 106	[264] **Bh** bohrium 107	[277] **Hs** hassium 108	[268] **Mt** meitnerium 109	[271] **Ds** darmstadtium 110	[272] **Rg** roentgenium 111							

Elements with atomic numbers 112–116 have been reported but not fully authenticated

* The lanthanoids (atomic numbers 58–71) and the actinoids (atomic numbers 90–103) have been omitted.

Glossary

absolute temperature   Temperature measured in kelvin; numerically equal to the temperature in Celsius (centigrade) +273.

absolute zero   The temperature at which all molecular movement stops; equivalent to −273 °C.

absorption spectrum   A series of dark lines on a continuous spectrum, caused by the absorption of photons of specific wavelengths; can be caused by the cooler gases surrounding a star.

accuracy   A measurement result is considered accurate if it is judged to be close to the true value.

activation energy   The minimum amount of energy needed by the reactants for a reaction to take place.

alcohol   A family of organic compounds containing an OH group, for example, methanol (CH_3OH); the common name for ethanol (C_2H_5OH).

algal blooms   A thick mat of algae near the surface of water that stops sunlight getting through

alkanes   A family of hydrocarbons found in crude oil with single covalent bonds, for example, methane.

antagonistic pair   Two muscles that work in opposite directions.

antagonistically   Acting in opposite directions.

anti-matter   Particles with the same mass but opposite charge to particles of matter, for example, the positron is the anti-matter equivalent of the electron.

aorta   Main blood vessel that carries blood from the heart to other parts of the body.

aperture   Opening at the front of a telescope (or the eye) through which light can enter.

aqueous   Dissolved in water.

atom economy   The efficiency of a chemical process in terms of the fraction of the reactant atoms that end up in the useful product.

atomic number   The total number of protons in a nucleus.

average   A typical value, used to summarise complicated data sets. For example, the arithmetic mean is produced by finding the total of all the results and then dividing by the number of results to produce a representative figure.

best estimate   The closest you can get to the true value of a quantity from a set of data: it is usually the mean of a set of data.

biceps   A muscle running up the inside of the upper arms; it causes the arm to bend at the elbow when it contracts.

binary star   A pair of stars that orbit a common centre of mass; an optical binary is just two stars that look as if they are close together simply because they are in the same direction.

bioaccumulation   The accumulation of a substance, such as a toxic chemical, in various tissues of a living organism.

biodiversity   The variety in terms of number and range of different life forms in an ecosystem.

biomass   The amount of organic material present in an ecosystem, such as a pond; also, the amount of organic material in an organism (usually measured as dry mass). Also, plant material (often waste from other uses) that is used as a source of energy, for example, through burning in an electricity generator.

black hole   A region of enormous gravitational force, sometimes due to the collapse of a supergiant star.

body mass index (BMI)   A measure of someone's weight in relation to their height, used as a guide to thinness or fatness; values over 30 indicate obesity.

Boyle's law   The pressure of a fixed mass of an ideal gas is inversely proportional to its volume, at a constant temperature.

bulk chemical   A chemical that is manufactured and used in large amounts, in excess of 1 million tonnes a year, for example, sulfuric acid.

by-product   A product of a reaction that is not the main useful product. By-products may be useful or not.

carboxylic acids   A family of organic compounds with the −COOH functional group.

catalyst   A substance added to a chemical reaction to alter the speed of the reaction but that is not itself used up.

celestial sphere   An imaginary sphere of large radius centred on the Earth; all the objects in the sky are thought of as being on the sphere. The celestial sphere rotates with the Earth.

Cepheid variable stars   A type of star with luminosity that varies in a regular way; the period of the variation depends on the size of the star.

charge conservation   A physical law governing nuclear reactions, which says that the total charge before a reaction must be the same as the total charge after a reaction.

chromatic aberration   Coloured fringes seen on an image due to different refraction of different wavelengths of light.

chromatography   A method of separating a mixture of substances, using a stationary and mobile phase.

closed loop process   A loop in which the output from one part becomes the input for another with the whole system feeding back on itself.

coma   A very deep sleep.

concave mirror   A mirror that converges light.

constellation   A named group of stars that form a pattern in the sky as seen from Earth, although the stars themselves usually have no connection with each other.

contract   To get shorter.

convection   Mechanism of heat transfer, where hot gases or liquids rise and cooler gases or liquids fall.

converge   Bring together; a converging lens refracts light rays so as to bring them to a focus.

convex lens   A lens that is thicker in the middle than at the edges.

correlation   Two quantities that are linked are said to be correlated; a scatter graph of the two quantities would give a straight line. The closer the points are to the line, the stronger the correlation.

declination   One of two angles that describe a star's location on the celestial sphere. Declination is similar to latitude and gives the star's position in degrees north or south of the celestial equator.

dehydrated   The result of a body losing too much water.

denature   An enzyme is denatured if its shape changes so that it is no longer able to act as a catalyst.

deuterium   A heavier isotope of hydrogen with one neutron in the nucleus.

diffraction   The spreading out of waves round an obstacle or through a gap.

diffraction gratings   Set of ruled lines through which light is transmitted, or reflected; used for creating spectra.

dioptres   Unit of refractive power, abbreviated to D; a lens of power 1 D has a focal length of 1 m.

directly proportional   Two variables are directly proportional if their ratio is constant, for example, if one quantity doubles, the other one also doubles. A graph of the two variables would be a straight line through the origin.

dislocation   A dislocation occurs when the head of one bone is pulled out of its normal position in the socket of another bone at a joint.

distilled   Liquids are separated (distilled) by boiling them, then condensing the vapours.

distribute   Spread (of a solute) between two immiscible solvents.

DNA probe   A segment of DNA that can link with a particular gene; the probe is usually labelled with a dye or radioactive marker.

double circulation system   A circulatory system in which blood travels twice through the heart for each single trip around the body.

dynamic equilibrium   An equilibrium in which the forwards and backwards reactions are taking place at the same rate.

ecliptic   A line on the celestial sphere that shows the apparent path of the Sun relative to the stars.

ecological services   Services provided by an ecosystem that do not necessarily depend on a single organism, for example, pollination, decay of materials.

ecosystem   The collection of different organisms in an area together with the important non-living factors such as water supply and temperature.

effector   A part of the body that produces a response, for example, a muscle or a gland.

emission spectrum   A line spectrum from a hot vapour.

endothermic   A reaction that takes in energy from the surroundings; the temperature falls in endothermic reactions.

energy level diagram   A visual way of showing the change in energy level during a chemical reaction.

energy levels   The allowed orbits for an electron in an atom.

enzyme   A substance (usually protein) produced in cells that act as catalysts in reactions. Enzymes control many of the processes in cells but can also be used as catalysts outside cells.

equilibrium   The state of a reversible reaction when the amount of reactants and products remains constant.

ester   A family of organic compounds formed when an alcohol reacts with a carboxylic acid; esters contain the –COO functional group.

ethanoic acid   A carboxylic acid (CH_3COOH) found in vinegar; also known as acetic acid.

eutrophication   The processes that occur when water is enriched with nutrients (from fertilisers) which allow algae to grow and use up all the oxygen; when waterways become too rich with nutrients (from fertilisers) which allows algae to grow wildly and use up all the oxygen.

exothermic   A reaction that gives out energy to the surroundings, causing a rise in temperature.

extended objects   Astronomical objects that are not merely a point, such as the Moon or a galaxy.

eyepiece   The (smaller diameter) lens through which the observer looks when using a telescope.

faeces   Waste material passed out of the gut of animals.

fatty acids   Carboxylic acids with a long hydrocarbon chain; the chain may be saturated or unsaturated.

feedstock   The chemicals used in a manufacturing process.

fermentation   A process in which sugar is converted into ethanol (alcohol) by the action of enzymes, such as in yeast.

fermenters   Equipment that produces the highest rate of fermentation in a microorganism.

fine chemical   A chemical that is manufactured and used in small amounts, up to a few tonnes a year, for example, drugs and flavourings.

fitness   A measure of a person's general health with particular reference to their ability to carry out sustained physical activity.

fixing (nitrogen)   A process in which nitrogen gas in the air is converted into soluble compounds in the soil that can be used by plants.

focal length   The distance from the centre of the lens to the focal point.

focal point   Rays of light that strike a convex lens, parallel to the principal axis, converge to a focus at the focal point.

focus   The point where rays of light are brought together.

fringes   Pattern of light and dark regions around an image, caused by diffraction.

functional group   The part of a molecule that is responsible for the reactions of the molecule, for example, the OH group in alcohols.

gas laws   The three laws that link the pressure, volume and temperature of an ideal gas.

genetically engineered   Occurs when the genes in an organism are altered by bringing in genes from other species, using recombinant DNA techniques.

giant star   Stars that are 10–100 times larger and brighter than the Sun.

globular clusters   Groups of older stars that surround a galaxy.

glucose   A simple sugar.

glycerol   An organic compound with three carbon atoms, each with the alcohol functional group (–OH); glycerol combines with fatty acids to make esters that are fats and oils.

Goldilocks zone   The range of orbits in a solar system where the temperature allows liquid water to form. This region is 'just right' for life to begin.

Haber process   An industrial process for making ammonia.

haemoglobin   A chemical found in red blood cells that carries oxygen.

Hertzsprung–Russell diagram   A chart that plots the luminosity of a star (vertical axis) against its surface temperature (horizontal axis).

Hubble constant   The ratio of the recessional velocity of a distant galaxy to its distance from Earth; measured in km/s/Mpc.

hypothalamus   Part of the brain that has several functions, the most important being to link the nervous system to the endocrine system; detects temperature of blood.

hypothermia   A condition caused by the body getting too cold, which can lead to death if untreated.

ideal gas   A theoretical model of a gas whose molecules take up no space and do not interact with each other. A gas that is well above its boiling point and at low pressure is a good approximation of an ideal gas.

immiscible   Liquids that do not mix, but form separate layers, are immiscible.

input   Something put into a system, for example, food and oxygen for animals, mineral nutrients for plants.

insulin   A hormone, produced by the pancreas, that increases the rate of uptake of sugar by body cells and encourages storage of sugar in the liver as glycogen.

inverse proportionality   Two variables are inversely proportional if their product is constant. for example, if one quantity doubles, the other halves.

ion   An atom that has lost or gained an electron.

ionisation   The loss or gain of an electron from an atom.

isotopes   Atoms with identical numbers of protons but different number of neutrons. Isotopes of the same element are chemically identical.

kelvin   Unit of absolute temperature.

leukaemia   A cancer of the blood-producing cells that causes a massive increase in the number of white blood cells.

lever   A rigid object that moves about a pivot and multiplies the mechanical force that can be applied to another object.

ligament   A flexible, slightly elastic tissue connecting bone to bone at joints.

light-year (ly)   Distance travelled by light in one year.

line spectrum   A series of coloured lines emitted by a vapour. The line spectrum from each element is unique.

linear relationship   When a graph of two quantities is a straight line, not necessarily passing through the origin.

locating agent   A chemical used to show up the position of colourless materials in paper or thin layer chromatography.

luminosity   Total power emitted by a star in all directions, across all wavelengths.

lunar eclipse   When the Moon passes into the Earth's shadow.

lunar month   The time between two successive new (or full) moons, equal to 29 days, 12 hours, 44 minutes, 2.8 seconds.

magnification   The ratio of image size to object size.

main sequence   The stage in a star's life where the fusion of hydrogen into helium takes place in the core.

mass number   The total number of protons and neutrons in a nucleus.

mass spectrometer   An instrument that can be used to identify compounds by a comparison of the abundance and mass of fragments of the molecules.

mean   An average of a set of data, found by adding up all the data values and dividing the sum by the number of data values.

methanoic acid   A carboxylic acid (HCOOH), found in ant and nettle stings; also known as formic acid.

mobile phase   The moving part of a chromatography system, consisting of a liquid or gas, which carries the components of the mixture at varying speeds.

nanometre   The unit used to measure very small things (one-billionth of a metre, or 10^{-9} m).

nanotechnology   Technology making use of nanoparticles.

nebulae   Extended, cloud-like, objects in space, for example galaxies or gas clouds.

negative feedback   Information that causes a reversal in a control system, for example, when we get too hot our body responds to bring our temperature back to normal through sweating and vasodilation.

neutrino   A neutral particle of very low mass.

neutron stars   Very dense remnants of a giant star, following a supernova.

non-aqueous   A liquid consisting of a compound that is not water-soluble.

normal   A line drawn at right angles to an interface between two materials, such as air and glass; used to assist in drawing ray diagrams.

nuclear fusion   The formation of heavier nuclei from two lighter nuclei. The reaction releases large amounts of energy (until the product nucleus is iron).

objective lens   The (larger diameter) lens at the front of a refracting telescope.

open loop process   A loop that does not feed back on itself and so is not stable.

organic matter   Material produced by living organisms, typically containing carbon in complex chemicals.

outlier   A measurement that does not follow the trend of other measurements.

output   Something produced by a system, often as a waste product, for example, oxygen from a plant in the light.

overfishing   Removing more fish in a season than can be replaced in the same time by reproduction of the fish population.

oxyhaemoglobin   The chemical formed when oxygen combines with haemoglobin.

p–p cycle   A sequence of nuclear fusion reactions that takes place in small to average sized stars.

pacemaker   An electronic device used to regulate the beating of the heart.

pancreas   The organ that produces the hormones insulin and glucagon (from endocrine tissue) and digestive enzymes (from exocrine tissue).

parallax   The apparent motion of nearby stars against the background of distant stars due to the orbital motion of the Earth.

parsec   Astronomical unit of distance, equal to 3.26 light years.

period   Time taken for one complete cycle, for example, of brightness changes by a variable star.

pesticide   A chemical designed to kill pests.

pH   A scale, running from 0 to 14, that shows how acidic or alkaline a substance is; a measure of the acidity or alkalinity of a substance.

phases of the Moon   The different appearances of the Moon, depending on its position relative to the Earth.

photosphere   The region of a star from which light is emitted.

physiotherapist   A physiotherapist treats illnesses, usually muscle and bone damage, with exercises and massage rather than drugs.

planetary nebula   A shell of gas ejected from a star towards the end of its life. Nothing to do with planets!

plasma   A gas of electrons and ions.

positron   A positively charged particle. The anti-matter equivalent of the electron.

power (of a convex lens)   A measure of how much the lens converges light; power (D) = $\dfrac{1}{\text{focal length (m)}}$

principal axis   A line drawn through the centre of the lens and perpendicular to it; used to assist in drawing ray diagrams.

protostar   A star in the early stages of its formation, before nuclear fusion has started.

pulsars   Rapidly rotating neutron stars that emit pulses of radio waves.

qualitative data   Data that describes or depends on a property or characteristic, such as colour, not expressed using numbers.

quantitative data   Numerical data.

quantum physics   The laws that govern the behaviour of atoms, electrons, photons and other sub-atomic particles; 'quantum' refers to the discrete nature of some physical quantities, for example, energy.

quasar   Quasi-stellar object: distant object that emits immense power from a relatively small region of space.

quotas   The amount of fish that can be legally removed from a system in a given time.

radiation zone   The region of a star where most of the energy is transported by photons.

range   In a series of data, the spread from the highest number to the lowest number.

ray   A light ray is a line drawn at right angles to the wave-front; a ray shows the direction in which the wave is travelling.

ray diagram   Drawn to show the path of light through an optical system, such as a telescope; often used to show image formation by a lens.

recombinant DNA   A form of DNA produced by combining genetic material from two or more different sources by means of genetic engineering.

recovery period   The time taken after exercise for breathing and heart rate to return to normal.

red giant   An enormous star with a relatively low surface temperature. A phase in a star's life when hydrogen fusion in the core has ceased.

redshift   The stretching of light to longer wavelengths caused by the expansion of space, or by the recessional velocity of the source.

reference materials   Known substances used for comparison in analysis, particularly in chromatography.

reflux   A process in which reactants can be kept at boiling point by condensing gases that are formed and returning them to the reaction vessel.

refraction   The change in direction of a wave as it travels from one medium to another, due to the change in wave speed.

relative atomic mass (RAM) The mass of an atom compared to the mass of an atom of carbon (which has a value of 12).

relative formula mass (RFM) The mass of a molecule or formula unit of an element or compound compared to the mass of an atom of carbon (which has the value 12). The sum of the RAMs of all the atoms or ions in the formula of a compound.

reliable Data that is accurate and relevant enough to draw conclusions from it.

repeatability Data shows repeatability if similar data collected by another researcher, to check the results, is consistent. This indicates that the results collected were not a fluke.

reproductive structures Parts of a living organism concerned with producing offspring.

resolution Ability to distinguish detail in an image or to recognise two nearby objects as distinct.

retention time The time taken for a chemical to pass through a gas chromatography column.

retrograde motion The backward motion of a planet over a number of days, as seen against the background of stars.

reversible A reaction that can go both forwards and backwards.

R_f value The ratio of the distance moved by a chemical to the distance moved by the solvent in paper or thin layer chromatography.

right ascension One of two angles that describe a star's location on the celestial sphere. Right ascension is similar to longitude and gives the star's position relative to a point on the celestial equator. Usually measured in units of time: hours, minutes and seconds.

risk The likelihood of an event, usually used to describe the chance of harm occurring.

saturated A molecule that contains only single carbon-to-carbon covalent bonds.

selective herbicide A herbicide that only kills certain types of plants, leaving others unharmed.

sewage Liquid and solid wastes carried in sewers.

shell The outer parts of the body, for example, arms and legs, which can tolerate lower temperatures than the core (heart and brain).

sidereal day The time taken for a specific star to be in the same position in the sky on two successive nights.

slash-and-burn A form of agriculture in which an area of forest is cleared by cutting and burning and is then planted, usually for several seasons, before being left to return to forest.

solar day The time taken for the Sun to reach the highest point in the sky on two successive occasions.

solar eclipse When the Moon passes between the Sun and the Earth, casting a shadow onto the Earth and obscuring the Sun.

solvent A liquid in which solutes dissolve to form a solution.

sprain A sprain occurs when the ligaments around a joint are stretched too much and the joint becomes less stable.

stable system A system that tends to remain the same over time.

standard candle An astronomical object of known brightness; used to measure distance.

standard solution A solution with a known concentration of solute.

stationary phase The part of a chromatography set up which does not move, consisting of a solid or liquid to which components of a mixture can stick to a greater or lesser extent.

stem cells Unspecialised body cells that can develop into other, specialised cells.

stock biomass The total mass of living organisms in a given area.

strong nuclear force Force that acts between protons and neutrons to hold the nucleus together.

supergiants Massive stars that can fuse heavier elements and emit enormous power. When they run out of fuel they explode in a supernova, eventually forming a black hole.

supernova An enormous explosion at the end of a giant star's life.

sustainable A resource or process that will still be available to future generations.

synovial joint A type of joint that allows a good degree of movement.

synthesis The building up of larger molecules through chemical reactions.

tap funnel Apparatus for separating liquids that do not mix together, consisting of a container with a tap at the bottom.

temperate The climate of regions between the tropical regions and the polar regions, marked by well-defined cool and warm seasons.

tendon A flexible, not-elastic tissue connecting bones to muscles.

tissue fluid Fluid bathing all cells in the body; it is formed by blood plasma leaking out of capillaries.

transpiration Loss of water from the leaves and stems of plants by evaporation.

triceps A muscle running along the outside of the upper arm; it causes the arm to straighten at the elbow when it contracts.

tritium An isotope of hydrogen with two neutrons in the nucleus.

tropics The part of the globe between the tropic of Cancer and the tropic of Capricorn. The tropics have hot climatic conditions, usually with a dry season and a wet season.

true value A theoretically accurate value that could be found if measurements could be made without errors.

uncertainty The interval within which the true value can be expected to lie, with a given level of confidence or probability.

unsaturated A molecule that contains one or more carbon-to-carbon double covalent bonds.

valve A flap of tissue that allows fluid to pass one way but not the other.

variable stars Stars whose brightness changes significantly over a period of time.

vasoconstriction The narrowing of the lumen (internal space) of blood vessels; in cold conditions, the diameter of small blood vessels near the surface of the body decreases, reducing the flow of blood.

vasodilation The widening of the lumen (internal space) of blood vessels; in hot conditions, the diameter of small blood vessels near the surface of the body increases, increasing the flow of blood.

vector An organism that transmits pathogens from host to host – insects are common disease vectors; an animal that carries a pathogen without suffering from it.

virus Very small infectious organisms that reproduce within the cells of living organisms and often cause disease; they consist of a protein layer surrounding a strand of nucleic acid.

volumetric flask A glass vessel with a long neck that has a gradation marked on it; when the volumetric flask is filled to the mark it contains a known volume of liquid to considerable accuracy.

weak acid An acid that reacts more slowly and has a higher pH than a strong acid with the same concentration; only partly split up into ions.

white dwarf A small dense star of high surface temperature where fusion has stopped. The remnant of an average star at the end of its life.

yield The amount of useful material produced by a system.

Index

Acknowledgements

The publishers wish to thank the following for permission to reproduce photographs. Every effort has been made to trace copyright holders and to obtain their permission for the use of copyright material. The publishers will gladly receive any information enabling them to rectify any error or omission at the first opportunity.

Cover & p1 GustoImages/Science Photo Library, p8t Suzanne Tucker/Shutterstock, p8u Roca/Shutterstock, p8l Gareth Price, p8b geopaul/iStockphoto, p9t Eoghan McNally/Shutterstock, p9u BestPhoto1/Shutterstock, p9l Timothy Epp/Shutterstock, p9b Juergen Berger/Science Photo Library, p10 AlamyCelebrity/Alamy, p12 AlamyCelebrity/Alamy, p13 Caroline Green, p14t Dmitriy Shironosov/Shutterstock, p14b Dimitri Messinis/AFP/Getty Images , p16 crazychris84/Shutterstock, p17t Fotokostic/Shutterstock, p17b Jeannot Olivet/iStockphoto, p18 jeff gynane/Shutterstock, p20 Reflekta/Shutterstock, p21 Audie/Shutterstock, p22t Nyvlt-art/Shutterstock, p22b National Cancer Institute/Science Photo Library, p23 Eye of Science/Science Photo Library, p24 phanlop88/Shutterstock, p25t Science Photo Library, p25b Sebastian Kaulitzki/Shutterstock, p26 sébastien Baussais/Alamy, p27 Rido/Shutterstock, p28 Reuter TV, p29 louise murray/Alamy, p30 Dmitry Lobanov/Shutterstock, p32t Ulrich Mueller/Shutterstock, p32b Leah-Anne Thompson/Shutterstock, p34t Jiang Hongyan/Shutterstock, p34b Monkey Business Images/Shutterstock, p35 EC Photography/Alamy, p36 Joerg Beuge/Shutterstock, p38t Jim Reed/Science Photo Library, p38b ClassicStock/Alamy, p39t Photoshot Holdings Ltd/Alamy, p39b Timothy Large/Shutterstock, p40 Jan Krutisch, p41 Gareth Price, p42 Kokhanchikov/Shutterstock, p43 Gareth Price, p44t Gareth Price, p44b Gareth Price, p45 Lee Torrens/Shutterstock, p46 Stephen Ausmus/US Department of Agriculture/Science Photo Library, p47 John Li/Getty Images, p48 Fotokostic/Shutterstock, p50 Monkey Business Images/Shutterstock , p51 Gareth Price, p52 Massimo Brega/Look at Sciences/Science Photo Library, p53t University of Strathclyde, p53b Caroline Green, p54t Peter Menzel/Science Photo Library, p54b skyhawk/Shutterstock, p64t Juburg/Shutterstock, p64u Charles D. Winters/Science Photo Library, p64l teekid/iStockphoto, p64b Martyn F. Chillmaid/Science Photo Library, p65t Againstar/Shutterstock, p65u Cordelia Molloy/Science Photo Library, p65c Sofia/Shutterstock, p65l US Department of Agriculture/Science Photo Library, p65b VILevi/Shutterstock, p66t johnnyscriv/iStockphoto, p66r Colin Cuthbert/Science Photo Library, p66l Khram/Shutterstock, p67t Patrick Wallet/Eurelios/Science Photo Library, p67b Park Dale/Alamy, p68t Robert Brook/Science Photo Library, p68l Elena Elisseeva/Shutterstock, p68r Rudchenko Liliia/Shutterstock, p69 EIGHTFISH/Alamy, p70 Charles D. Winters/Science Photo Library, p72t Victor De Schwanberg/Science Photo Library, p72b catlook/Shutterstock, p73l Clive Freeman, The Royal Institution/Science Photo Library, p73r James King-Holmes/Science Photo Library, p74t NASA/Tony Gray & Robert Murray, p74b Charles D. Winters/Science Photo Library, p76 Martin Bond/Science Photo Library, p78 JeffreyRasmussen/Shutterstock, p79 Ria Novosti/Science Photo Library, p80t Art Directors & TRIP/Alamy, p80b inga spence/Alamy, p81 Charles D. Winters/Science Photo Library, p82 Tom Mc Nemar/Shutterstock, p84t George Bernard/Science Photo Library, p84c Martyn F. Chillmaid/Science Photo Library, p84b Jaime Pharr/Shutterstock, p85r Rosenfeld Images Ltd/Science Photo Library, p85l Power and Syred/Science Photo Library, p86t charobnica/Shutterstock, p86b bepsy/Shutterstock, p87 Steve Gschmeissner/Science Photo Library, p88t Pongsiri/Shutterstock, p88b Chris Andrews, p89l Diane Labombarbe/iStockphoto, p89r Patrycja Mueller/Shutterstock, p90t alexnika/Shutterstock, p90r Trevor Clifford Photography/Science Photo Library, p90l Andrew Lambert Photography/Science Photo Library, p91l Andrew Lambert Photography/Science Photo Library, p91r Charles D. Winters/Science Photo Library, p92t Paul Cowan/Shutterstock, p92c Sofia/Shutterstock, p92b sheff/Shutterstock, p93l Li Wa/Shutterstock, p93r studiomode/Alamy, p94t olly/Shutterstock, p94b Martyn F. Chillmaid/Science Photo Library, p95t Martyn F. Chillmaid/Science Photo Library, p95b Andrew Lambert Photography/Science Photo Library, p96t Ed Walsh, p96c Catherine Lall/Shutterstock, p96b Gertan/Shutterstock, p97 Andrew Lambert Photography/Science Photo Library, p98t Khorkova Olga (aka Mamontenok)/Shutterstock, p98b Martyn F. Chillmaid/Science Photo Library, p Martyn F. Chillmaid/Science Photo Library, p99 Dr. Arthur Winfree/Science Photo Library, p100t Meryll/Shutterstock, p100b Science Photo Library, p102t Elenamiv/Shutterstock, p102c hjschneider/Shutterstock, p102b Dr Jeremy Burgess/Science Photo Library, p103t Dr Kari Lounatmaa/Science Photo Library, p103b EuToch/Shutterstock, p104t ChameleonsEye/Shutterstock, p104c Jerry Mason/Science Photo Library, p104b Terry Williams/Rex Features , p105t Jody/Shutterstock, p105b Capifrutta/Shutterstock, p106l 501room/Shutterstock, p106r Sinclair Stammers/Science Photo Library, p106b Martyn F. Chillmaid/Science Photo Library, p107 Andrew Lambert Photography/Science Photo Library, p108t Charles D. Winters/Science Photo Library, p108b Andrew Lambert Photography/Science Photo Library, p109 ORNL/Science Photo Library, p110t NASA, p110b Massimo Brega, The Lighthouse/Science Photo Library, p112t Jim Varney/Science Photo Library, p112b originalpunkt/Shutterstock, p113 Andrew Lambert Photography/Science Photo Library, p114 John McLaird/Shutterstock, p116 Laurence Gough/Shutterstock, p126t PRIMA/Shutterstock, p126u MilanB/Shutterstock, p126l violetkaipa/Shutterstock, p126b cbpix/Shutterstock, p127t zhanna ocheret/Shutterstock, p127u Yuri Arcurs/Shutterstock, p127c NASA/JPL-Caltech/UCLA, p127l NASA, p127b NASA/JPL-Caltech/R. Hurt (SSC), p128t Bartlomiej K. Kwieciszewski/Shutterstock, p128b elena moiseeva/Shutterstock, p129 Markus Gann/Shutterstock, p130 NASA/Roger Arno, p131t Stefan Seip/Shutterstock, p131b SuriyaPhoto/Shutterstock, p133t Tunc Tezel, p133b Wikimedia Commons, p134t gregg williams/Shutterstock, p134b Larry Landolfi/Science Photo Library, p136 NASA , p138 Center for Vision in the Developing World, p140t NASA/Johns Hopkins University Applied Physics Laboratory/Southwest Research Institute/Goddard Space Flight Center, p140b Jan Sandberg, p141t Steve Cole/iStockphoto, p141b Richard Wainscoat/Alamy, p142 GIPhotostock/Science Photo Library, p144t NASA , p144b Paul Hickson, University of British Columbia/NASA, p146t SKA Project Development Office and Swinburne Astronomy Productions, p146c Tom Leigh, p146b PHOTOTAKE Inc./Alamy, p147 sciencephotos/Alamy, p148t NASA, p148l voylodyon/Shutterstock, p148r Theo Gottwald/Alamy, p149t Paul Cowan/Shutterstock, p149b Lynette Cook/Science Photo Library, p150 Andrzej Mirecki, p151 ESA, p152t NASA/Science Photo Library, p152b NASA, p153 John Sanford/Science Photo Library, p154t NASA, p154b Mark Garlick/Science Photo Library, p155t Science Photo Library, p155b Maroš Markovic/Shutterstock, p156t S. Beckwith (STScI) and the HUDF Team/NASA, p156c Allan Morton/Dennis Milon/Science Photo Library, p156b Robert Gendler/Science Photo Library, p157 John Chumack/Science Photo Library, p158t A.A.O., p158c NASA, p158b Physics Dept., Imperial College/Science Photo Library, p159t Huntington Library, p159b NASA/Science Photo Library, p160t Tony McConnell/Science Photo Library, p160b Jozef Sedmak/Shutterstock, p161 David Hardy/Science Photo Library, p162 Physics Dept., Imperial College/Science Photo Library, p163 N.A.Sharp, NOAO/NSO/Kitt Peak FTS/Aura/NSF/Science Photo Library, p164 Volodymyr Goinyk/Shutterstock, p166 Alfred Leitner, p167 Joanna Zopoth-Lipiejko/Shutterstock, p168 Andrew Lambert Photography/Science Photo Library, p170t John Chumack/Science Photo Library, p170b Hubble Space Telescope Center, p171 Daniel Price/Science Photo Library, p172 Philippe Plailly/Eurelios/Science Photo Library, p174t NASA/SDO/AIA, p174b David Hardy/Science Photo Library, p175 Mark Garlick/Science Photo Library, p176t Robin Scagell/Science Photo Library, p176b NASA/JPL-Caltech/University of Arizona, p177 NASA, p178 Pictorial Press Ltd/Alamy, p179t B. Murton/Southampton Oceanography Centre/Science Photo Library, p179b NASA, p180t NASA, p180b ESA/Van Der Geest/Eurelios/Science Photo Library, p181t dave jepson/Alamy, p181b Adam-Hart Davis/Science Photo Library, p182t Kamioka Observatory, ICRR, University of Tokyo, p182b European Southern Observatory/Science Photo Library, p183t NASA/GSFC-SVS/Science Photo Library, p183b NASA, ESA, and Q.D. Wang (University of Massachusetts, Amherst); Spitzer: NASA, Jet Propulsion Laboratory, and S. Stolovy (Spitzer Science Center/Caltech), p196t Andrew Lambert Photography/Science Photo Library, p196c Pedro Salaverría/Shutterstock, p196b Shawn Hempel/Shutterstock, p202 Martyn F. Chillmaid/Science Photo Library.